I0824834

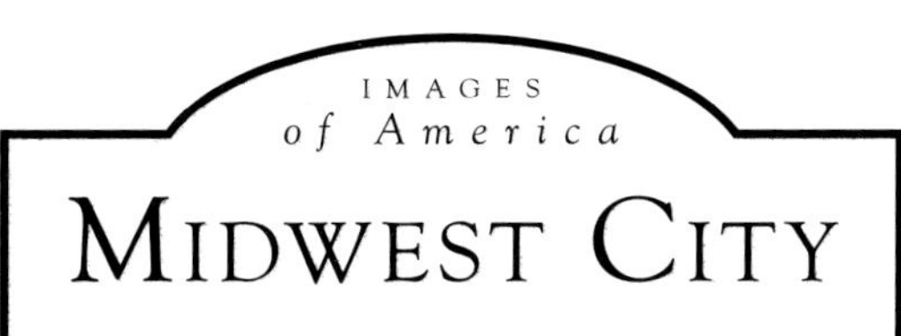
IMAGES
of America
MIDWEST CITY

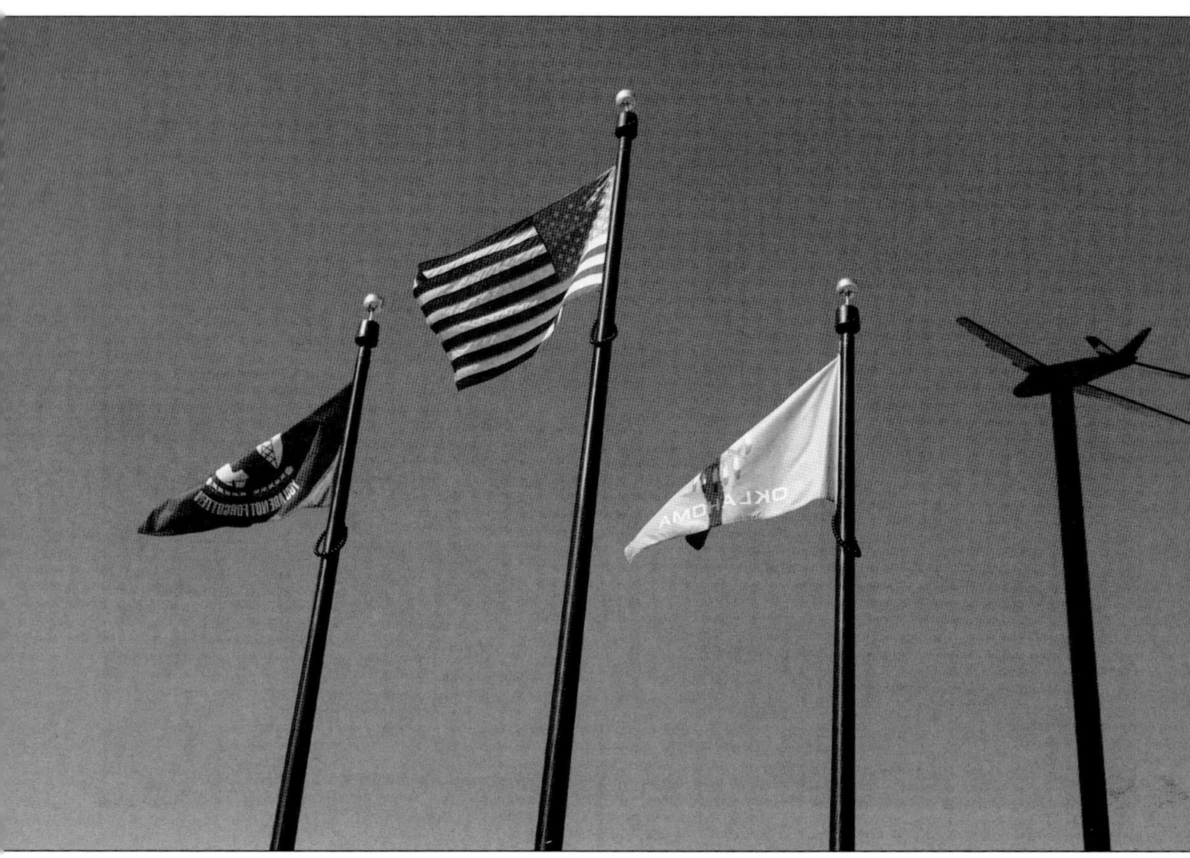

Midwest City will forever be, first and foremost, a patriotic city, ready to support the nation's military service men and women. Positioned across the road from Tinker Air Force Base, Midwest City's foundations cultivate family life and American values and inspire a pioneering spirit. Midwest City is the city where the spirit flies high in hope and purpose, raising a standard of excellence for the surrounding region. The photograph here is of the Prisoner of War flag, the American flag, the Oklahoma flag, and a replica of the metal planes displayed outside of the original Midwest City High School. These flags can be found at the entrance of the Midwest City High School History Center and Vietnam War Memorial, also called Bomber Plaza. (Courtesy of American Corporate Photography.)

On the Cover: Children play on a playground—an ode to the simpler times in life. Midwest City found pride in its parks and their close proximity to homes and schools. Pictured here is a playground in the Original Mile of Midwest City on Mid-America Boulevard and East Douglas Drive. The white building behind the playground is the original First Baptist Church of Midwest City in the 1940s. (Courtesy of the Midwest City High School History Center.)

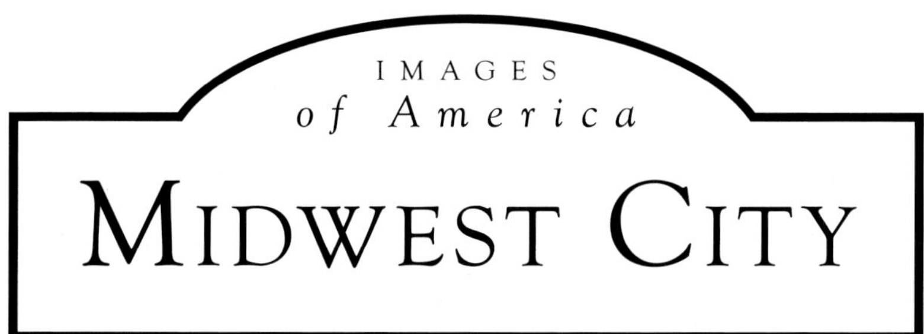

Malana Bracht
Foreword by Cindy Mikeman

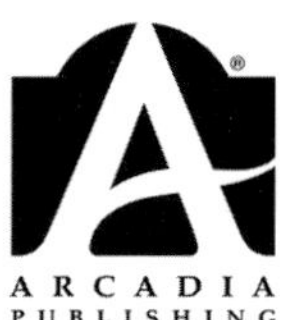

ISBN 978-1-4671-6232-6

Published by Arcadia Publishing
Charleston, South Carolina

Printed in the United States of America

Library of Congress Control Number: 2024951601

For all general information, please contact Arcadia Publishing:
Telephone 843-853-2070
Fax 843-853-0044
E-mail sales@arcadiapublishing.com

Visit us on the Internet at www.arcadiapublishing.com

This book is dedicated to the faithful leaders and community members of Midwest City who have loved and sacrificed to build a city for families like mine to have a better future. And to my husband and children, who love Midwest City as I do.

Also to my grandfather, Michael Furley, a 20-year Air Force retiree from Tinker Air Force Base and former employee of the Midwest City Water Company. I hope you can see this from Heaven.

CONTENTS

FOREWORD

W.P. "Bill" Atkinson was more than a visionary, developer, builder, politician—he was my Granddaddy. It fills me with immense pride to honor his many accomplishments and reflect on the incredible impact he had on our community. As the "Father of Midwest City," his legacy is etched in the very fabric of the community he helped to create. In a time when the world was engulfed in the turmoil of World War II, he recognized an unprecedented opportunity to shape the future of a new community.

When the announcement came that the Midwest Air Depot would be established just outside Oklahoma City, Granddaddy's instinct and determination set him on a path that would forever alter the course of the area. With a keen understanding of the requirements for the new military installation, he tirelessly studied maps, ultimately discovering the perfect site. His audacity to purchase land before anyone realized its value demonstrated not just foresight but an innate entrepreneurial spirit.

Granddaddy's interactions with military officials in Washington, DC, reveal much about his character. He approached them not with greed but with a genuine desire to support the new depot and the community it would foster. His commitment to creating a model city—complete with parks, schools, and vibrant neighborhoods—reflects his belief that a community thrives when it is designed for families and connectedness.

His innovative ideas did not stop with the planning phase. From naming streets after aircraft manufacturers to gifting trees and shrubs to new homeowners, Granddaddy infused his developments with a sense of identity and community. The inclusion of Shetland ponies in his Ridgecrest addition was a testament to his understanding of what families truly valued: joy, connection, and a bit of whimsy.

Granddaddy had a love of Shetland ponies and provided rolling pastures for them to roam nearby his and my grandmother Rubye's beautiful Georgian Colonial home. My grandparents built their home to be a welcoming space for family gatherings, business meetings, and memorable parties. It was a home that reflected their values, where hospitality and warmth were always at the forefront.

Granddaddy's vision extended beyond mere real estate developments; he sought to build a community that would support the local military base and provide a fulfilling life for its residents. His leadership within the home-building industry paved the way for future developments, and his influence can still be felt today.

As I reflect on Granddaddy's remarkable contributions, it is essential to recognize not just the buildings and streets he created but the enduring spirit of community he fostered. Midwest City stands as a testament to his vision—a vibrant place where families continue to thrive, rooted in the ideals he championed.

In the pages that follow, his story, along with many individuals whose contributions made a profound impact on the developing community, serve as a reminder that vision, determination, and a genuine commitment to community can indeed change the world.

—Cindy Mikeman, granddaughter of W.P. "Bill" Atkinson

Acknowledgments

This book exists because of the generous souls of this great city. To the granddaughter of founder W.P. "Bill" Atkinson, Cindy Mikeman, thank you for allowing me to document and bring to life the story of the early years of Midwest City. Thank you for your tireless work of promoting your grandfather's legacy and for supporting the younger generation. A big thank you goes to Midwest City's economic development director, Robert Coleman, for welcoming me on my first call after moving back from out of state and listening patiently to any ambitious idea I brought your way. Thank you to leaders of the Midwest City Chamber of Commerce, director Shaina Bennett, and the team made up of Kim Ley, Dylan Marone, and Jason Chartrand. A special thank you to FNB Community Bank, the Croak family, and Julie Waddle for your support and for allowing us a glimpse of your legacy in Midwest City. I am so grateful to two of my biggest supporters, Bob Osmond and Marty Thompson, and the board of the Midwest City High School History Center, who have provided most of the historical photographs in this book. Words cannot express how grateful I am for all you do behind the scenes to protect this history of Midwest City. Your love and passion show clearly, and the Good Book says when you serve in private, your heavenly Father will reward you openly. So, Bob and Marty and board, thank you! I want to express gratitude to my editor, Caroline Vickerson, for being understanding of my juggling four children and all of my community roles. Thank you for taking a chance on me! I must thank my parents for moving me to Midwest City as a preteen and fighting for me to attend Midwest City High School. That one decision changed the course of my entire life, and I credit that to you and the providence of my ultimate Savior, Jesus Christ. And last but not least, the biggest thank you to my husband and children, who have supported me as I donated my time to this project for months and months. You knew this was important to me, even if you did not understand it completely. Thank you for letting me do this.

All images used in this book come from the Midwest City High School History Center unless otherwise noted. The royalties from this book will help continue the work of sharing the history of Midwest City through the Rose State College Foundation and the Midwest City High School History Center.

INTRODUCTION

On a brisk morning in 1941, a man named W.P. "Bill" Atkinson drove south on Midwest Boulevard in a rural area east of Oklahoma City, Oklahoma. With wheat fields on each side, he remembered the words he read from an article from E.K. Gaylord's newspaper, the *Oklahoman*. Word on the street was that the military was going to build an air depot, and Oklahoma was on their list of potential sites. The Oklahoma City Chamber of Commerce had created incentives for the military to "Build it Here" in Oklahoma, but where in Oklahoma? The location was a secret, but the military had four characteristics they were looking for in the areas around the Oklahoma City metro area: located within 10 miles of a major city, near a railroad, four miles from any oil field, and contain several thousand acres of level ground.

By 1941, Oklahoma was scarred by hardship. Beginning with World War I, Oklahoma lost over 1,000 soldiers to combat and survived the war at home against the 1918 Spanish flu, which killed over 7,500 people. Like most of the world, Oklahomans were hopeful that the "War That Would End All Wars" would finally bring peace. Just as families began to rebuild their lives, they took another step back on October 29, 1929, as the stock market crashed and ushered in the Great Depression in what would later be known as Black Tuesday. Oklahoma was then rocked again as dust storms began to wipe away the agricultural livelihoods of so many farmers, causing a mass exodus of over 440,000 people out of Oklahoma through 1941. Apart from Jesus himself, where could Oklahoma look for hope for the future of their state? These hardworking communities were ready for a new beginning.

As Atkinson's peer, C.B. Warr, looked west to purchase land on the northwest side of Oklahoma City (later known as Warr Acres); Atkinson looked to the east. As Atkinson drove south on Midwest Boulevard toward Twenty-Ninth Street, he noticed that about 10 miles away were oil rigs. He looked west and saw railways. He looked to the south and saw flat land. And he was about five miles from downtown Oklahoma City.

"I've got to be close," he thought.

Most of the area was owned and cultivated by wheat farmers. Atkinson began going door-to-door, inquiring if they would be willing to sell their land. He turned on what is now Twenty-Ninth Street, and on the south side of the street, he approached the farmers. Curiously, they refused to talk to him. The salesman that he was, he offered them a competitive amount for their land. No one was interested. He then went across the street to approach the farmers on the north side of Twenty-Ninth Street. The farmers there were more than happy to sell their land.

Testing a hunch, Atkinson pressed. What if the farmers on the south side of Twenty-Ninth Street did not want to sell their farms because they had already been approached by the US military? Atkinson knocked on another door on the south side of Twenty-Ninth Street where the owners had previously not wanted to share any information.

A timid woman came out, ready to shut the young developer down. He quickly reassured her that she did not have to talk. He just asked if he could ask her questions, and all she would have to do is wink once for yes and two for no.

"Ma'am, has someone already approached you to sell your farm?"

She winked once. Yes.

"Was it the US military?"

She winked once more. Yes, again.

At that moment, Bill Atkinson realized the treasure that he had stumbled upon. It was the treasure of opportunity. Though he would reap not sharing in this good fortune with his fellow connections in Oklahoma City, Atkinson seized the opportunity to build a name for himself that would not only bless his future generations but also thousands and thousands of families and the whole world, as this future city would support the war effort in World War II. Four years later, World War II was won by the Allies, and Midwest City went on to grow into an award-winning city in only 10 short years. It was documented that Midwest City's vast and intricate city planning was unprecedented since Oklahoma's founding, making it the first massive community development project in the region in the 20th century.

Just like the parable of the man who found treasure in a field and sold all he had to buy that field to keep the treasure, Bill Atkinson took one of the largest risks of his entire life to purchase all of the land he could north of Twenty-Ninth Street. He believed, and it would later be confirmed as true, that this land surrounded the future heartland Air Force Depot of the United States. Now, he had the chance to build a community for every civilian who would travel to work at this new depot.

That day, the vision of Midwest City was born, all from a hunch and a wink.

Much like individual men have a story to tell about their lives, so do cities. Just as every human is born, so is a city. Like people, cities have highs and lows in their histories, other cities they were in relationships and conflict with, milestones in their development and maturity, offenses and conflict that impose wounds that need healing, and a great spirit that sets them apart as a unique identity with a specific purpose only that very city can fulfill.

Midwest City, Oklahoma, and its people are subject to great purpose and contain great spirit.

Midwest City has been known by many names, including "City of Tomorrow," "the Model City of the Midwest," and "Mudwest City" when the roads were not paved during a long rainy season, causing everything to be muddy during development. We will explore these names within this work.

This book shares the origin story of Midwest City and does its best to give an understanding of the intent of its design from historical quantitative research from documents, interviews, and data. As we look back at the photographs, news articles, and daily experiences of local business owners and families, a picture begins to develop. An understanding that may even lead to a love. This book is not a comprehensive history from the womb to the present of Midwest City, but it does its best to capture the milestones and heart of the original intent and foundations from which it was raised. You may find some areas of Midwest City's history not included in this specific title. There were some parts of the history, such as the civil rights history, where there were not any primary sources to work from. I encourage you that if you feel inspired by this work, continue the work of research that I as well as many other authors and academics have recovered and documented. Let us be the foundation that you can build on.

Readers may wonder how I, the author, am qualified to tell this story and share Midwest City with the world. The truth is, there are many more people qualified to do this project. So many more leaders have gone before me, sacrificed for this city, and have a deep understanding of the intricacies of the development of this city. I was not alive, nor were my parents or even my grandparents, at the founding of this city. But what I can share with you is that I am good at asking questions, and I love this city.

From the time I was 13, I wandered the halls of the Midwest City Library as a volunteer for the summer reading program. I walked the safe streets without fear of harassment as I traveled from work and school. Coming from much adversity, my family purchased their first home in Midwest City, and just like so many others, Midwest City became a city of new beginnings for us. I was fortunate enough to attend all four years of high school and graduate from Midwest City High School and the Mid-Del Technology Center. I was married one year later to a wonderful man from

Choctaw who graduated from Rose State College and worked at Tinker Air Force Base. We bought our first home one year later in Midwest City and had our first child at what was then Renaissance Women's Center, formally Midwest City Memorial Hospital.

I graduated from the University of Central Oklahoma with a bachelor's degree in family life education with a minor in human environmental sciences and sociology. Understanding the macro level of systems, problems, and cultures and creating solutions makes me feel alive. As places are just like people, I recognized that the state of a location can be traced back to its historical wounds, milestones, victories, and the intention of the founders for that area in its design. I began to understand why Midwest City was such a helpful place for my family: Midwest City was designed to support and cultivate family life and be a resting place for the air base and those who visit it. It is much more nuanced than that, but it impacted my family in that way and many others I have met with.

At the time of the publishing of this book, Midwest City has grown and flourished but also has quite a transient population. From military families stationed temporarily to annual renters, the area could be subject to instability if it were not for the strong local foundation of permanent residents and retirees. These retirees could have chosen any base to spend their final days, and they chose us. How do we convince newcomers that Midwest City is worth planting a life into? We make sure they and the people currently living in Midwest City understand its identity. Its heart. Its vision and goals. That is one of the reasons this book was necessary. Many of the newer generations that reside in Midwest City are unaware of its rich history. They may not realize it is a leader in the area and how much we provide for the neighboring cities and counties east of Oklahoma City. In order for us to move forward into tomorrow, we must understand where we have been.

When my husband and I were called out of state for three years, I grieved. I had unfinished business in Oklahoma. My heart was to serve the people of Oklahoma and Midwest City. I would joke with my husband that I would be content if I lived in Midwest City for the rest of my life. When we were released to move back, we chose Midwest City again to become planted in our personal lives and in business.

This precocious community did not just happen. At the right moment in time, one man (Bill Atkinson) used his expertise and keen sense of intuition to take an opportunity when he saw it. He built a team and would not take no for an answer.

Midwest City received the blessing of an original land-run participant in 1889, Frank Trosper, who sold Atkinson the first 160 acres of what would later be known as Midwest City's Original Mile. Trosper gave Atkinson the crocodile-skin saddle he rode on his mule during the land run, and Atkinson kept it in his pony barn throughout the years. Trosper also recommended Atkinson gain the support of the US government: Atkinson needed to build a community around the air depot that included schools, churches, and stores to keep it successful since it was so far from downtown Oklahoma City. As Washington, DC, recommended, Atkinson also promised to build parks for the children. Strategically, he gathered a team, made a plan, and carried it out without concern for consequence.

And it grew. Despite weather interruptions and supply shortages due to the war, Midwest City flourished. Atkinson's ability to make deals and use a team helped attract others to this new city of hope. More local leaders planted their families and influence in Midwest City. It received national recognition as the "Model City of the Midwest" only 10 years after its founding. Families moved into the newly built houses, and the new public school system became one of the largest school systems in the state—all the while supporting the nation's military.

Over the decades that followed, Midwest City asserted its place at the table of influence in the region and continued to cultivate its relationship with Tinker Air Force Base and the surrounding Oklahoma City metropolitan area. Midwest City experienced triumph in award-winning city planning, tragedy of loss through plane crashes and tornadoes, and a resilient spirit to bring meaning to the highs and lows of its lifetime.

Midwest City brings so much value and offers a bright future for many families and businesses. From its founding to today, many businesses and families still choose Midwest City as their home and base of operations because of its culture and values. A common phrase used to describe Midwest City is that it is one of the "biggest small towns" a family will ever live in. Its role as a support city for Tinker Air Force Base has not changed and is continuing to progress and grow in innovation and leadership.

Midwest City is proof that having a vision can determine not just a person's future but a whole region.

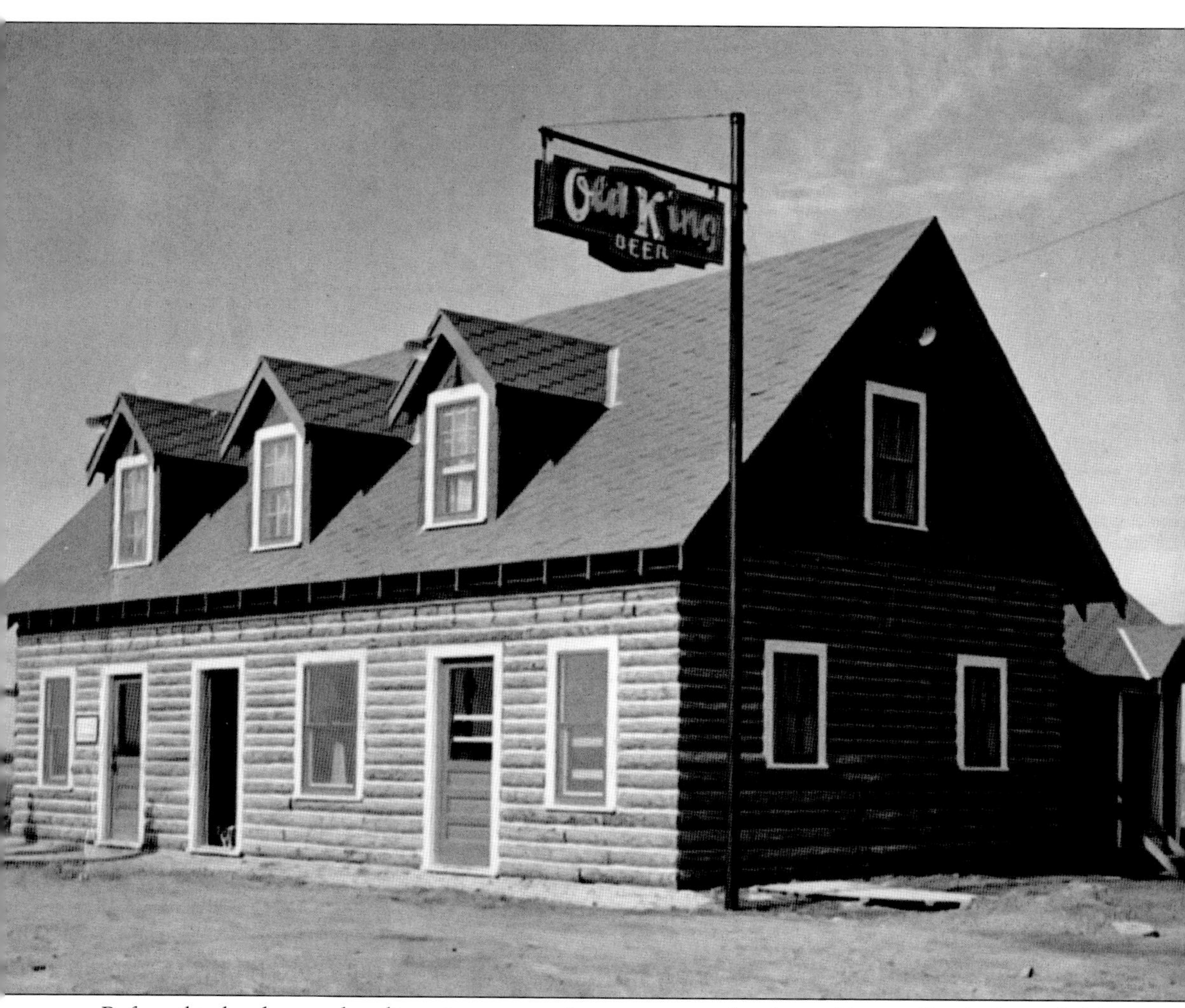

Before this land was a bustling city center of commerce and culture, Twenty-Ninth Street held a lone Log Cabin Grill in 1939 in the midst of miles of farmland. Weary travelers or local residents could come and enjoy a warm meal and drink beer like Old King Beer, a local Oklahoma-born brewery company that opened right after the end of Prohibition until 1948. It also held a truck stop. (Courtesy of the Rose State College Foundation.)

One

From Wheat Fields to City of Tomorrow

Once a prehistoric residence of mammoth hunters to then where buffalo roamed thousands of years later, a segment of the Osage Plains became what is now known as Midwest City. Previously owned by the Seminole tribe from the agreement from the Trail of Tears in 1845, the Seminoles were forced to sell their land to the government as part of a reconstruction treaty following the Civil War. The land then became known as the Unassigned Territory. This same area gained its first railroad in 1882, which was completed in the early 1900s. A depot was built called Marion Station after a local man named Marion Cunningham. The land became open to settlers from the 1889 land run, and European immigrants took their chance and settled these lands known as the Mishak Community. In the years following, according to the *Final Report: Reconnaissance Level Architectural/Historical Survey of the Original Mile*, the area was used for agriculture with abundant wildlife and abandoned Native American teepees.

In 1941, after discovering where the air depot was to be built, W.P. "Bill" Atkinson seized the opportunity and purchased 160-plus acres north of Twenty-Ninth Street in 1941 from one of those original settlers from the land run. Knowing he would need additional backing and favor, Atkinson visited the Pentagon and enrolled the services of a well-known city planner named Seward Mott, director of the Federal Housing Administration (FHA) Land and Planning Division. By this time, the US War Department formed the Midwest Air Depot and broke ground. By April 1942, the first home was built by Atkinson's team in Midwest City on the corner of East Turnbull Street and East Boeing Drive, later to be known as the "Original Mile." From the cul-de-sacs to curvilinear streets to encourage vehicles to be more aware of pedestrians as they walked to the local schools, churches, shopping, and parks, design elements of this city encouraged families to move to the area and support the air depot as civilian workers and city support workers. The homes held a variety of designs, sizes, textures, and color palettes from the early 1940s, as the reader will discover within this chapter. Despite a rainy season, Atkinson secured 700 building permits to construct this city and began developing the land. In his entrepreneurial spirit, he founded his own lumberyard, Bill Atkinson Lumber and Manufacturing Co., and planted his own nursery to self-fulfill much of his developments and also turn a profit. On March 11, 1943, Midwest City was officially incorporated as a city of Oklahoma.

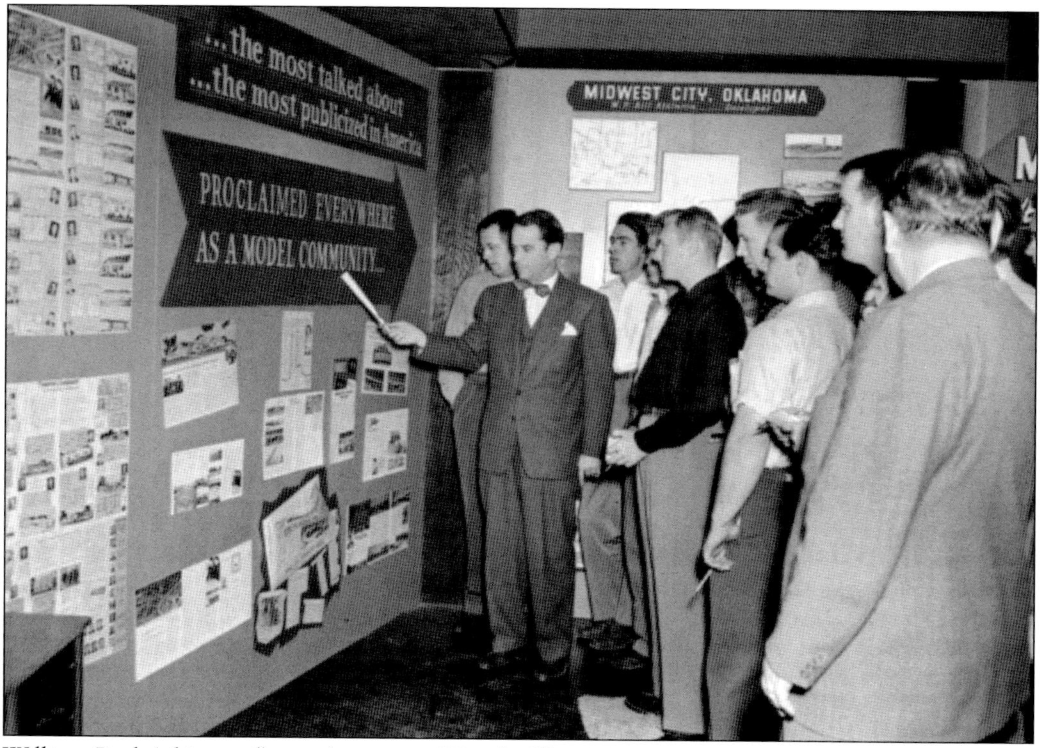

William Paul Atkinson (better known as W.P. "Bill" Atkinson) was the founder of Midwest City, Oklahoma, and a publicist/civic leader. An intelligent and cunning entrepreneur, he cast a vision of an innovative city that promoted family life unlike any other. His faithful wife, Rubye, supported him and helped raise three children and 15 grandchildren. Beginning his career as a journalist, he then used his media giftings to gain relationships and connections that led him into housing development. Midwest City was born and paved the way for other advancements in Atkinson's professional life, such as running for public office, opening a newspaper, and urban development across Oklahoma City and across the nation. He was inducted into the Oklahoma Hall of Fame in 1963. In the photograph above, Atkinson presents the vision of Midwest City during one of his open houses. (Both, courtesy of the Oklahoma Historical Society.)

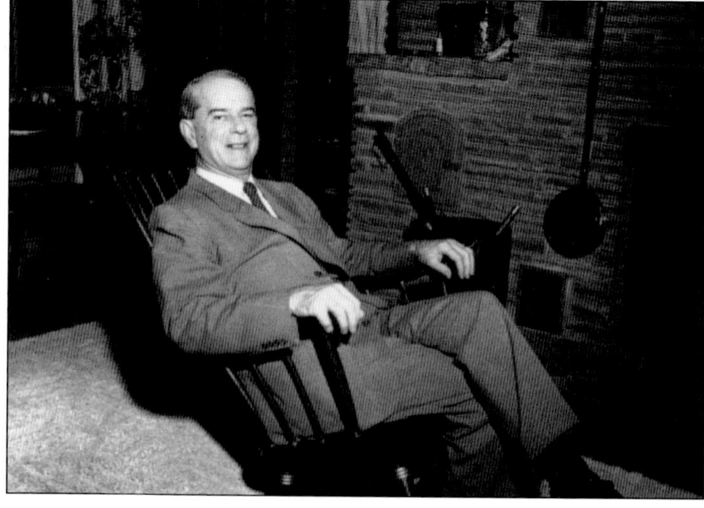

This is the portion of land Bill Atkinson purchased and developed to become Midwest City alongside the growing Midwest Air Field. During World War II, food ration stamps were issued for tires, meat, gasoline, sugar, coffee, shoes, and more. Businesses were not allowed to inflate prices. Citizens had to have a special permit to purchase a vehicle. This also affected the supplies available to build Midwest City, though Atkinson seemed to have favor. Before the first boom houses were built in early 1942, the Original Mile on Twenty-Ninth Street (in between Midwest Boulevard and Air Depot Boulevard) was unincorporated wheat fields owned by local farmers. This aerial view shows the already constructed Tinker Air Field, later called Tinker Air Force Base. (Courtesy of Midwest City High School History Center.)

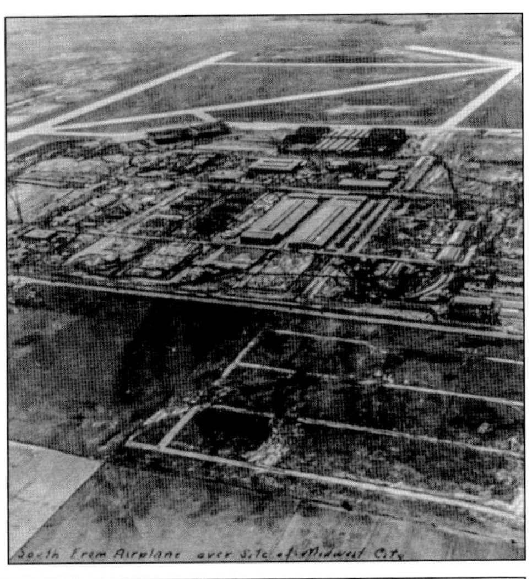

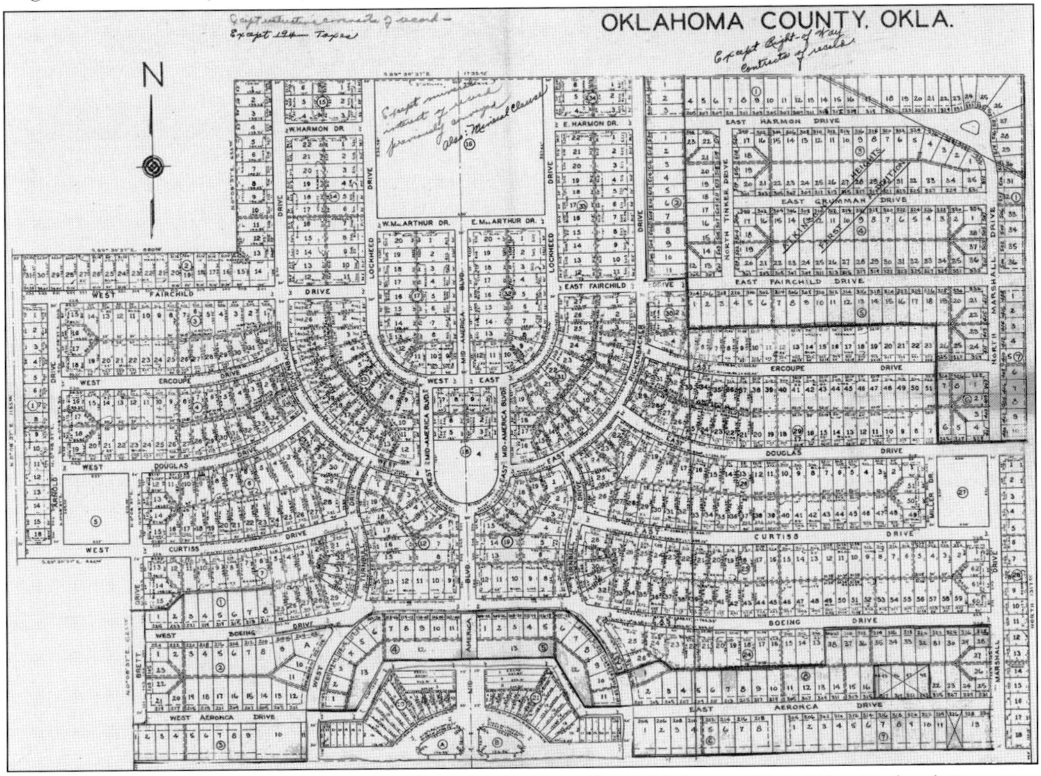

This is the blueprint for the Original Mile developed in Midwest City. The Federal Housing Administration's Land Planning Division director Seward Mott helped Atkinson and 15 home builders plan the design of what is now known as Midwest City. These builders included John W. Lyon, Sylvanus G. Felix, Steve Pennington, W.P. "Bill" Atkinson, Amos Bouse, H.B. Atkinson, Manly M. Moore, Russel Showalter, C.E. Duffner, N.D. Woods, Ed Jensen, Curtis I. Smith, Ben C. Wileman, Cord Wilson, and Roger Givens. These men split each part of the city, and each did their own style of architecture for residential and commercial areas. Midwest City was one of the first cities in America to be completely blueprinted before construction was begun. (Courtesy of the Rose State College Foundation.)

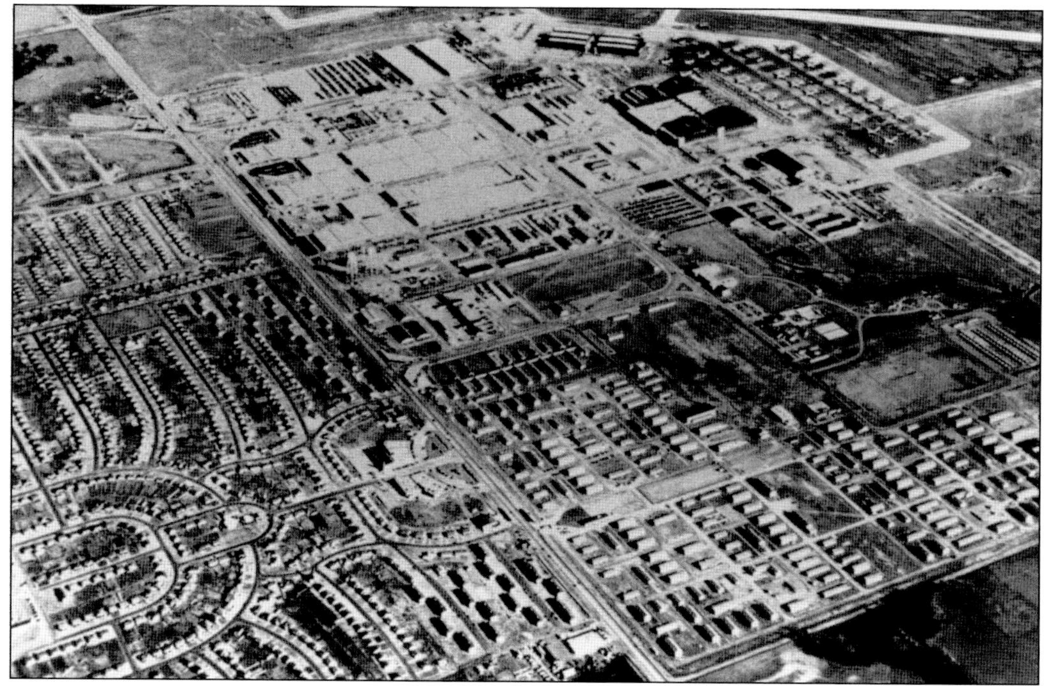

The aerial shot above of Midwest City's Original Mile (left) and Midwest Air Depot (right) shows the immense development of the area in the mid-1940s. The iconic curved residential roads of the Original Mile show the intentionality and vision of city planner Seward Mott and founder Bill Atkinson to create a family-friendly and aesthetically pleasing community, many of the streets being named after a prominent military leader or aerospace company. They were also listed in alphabetical order for ease of location. The city's theme was aviation. Looking to the bottom left of the photograph, readers can see the street layout, which resembles that of an airplane with wings. (Courtesy of Midwest City High School History Center.)

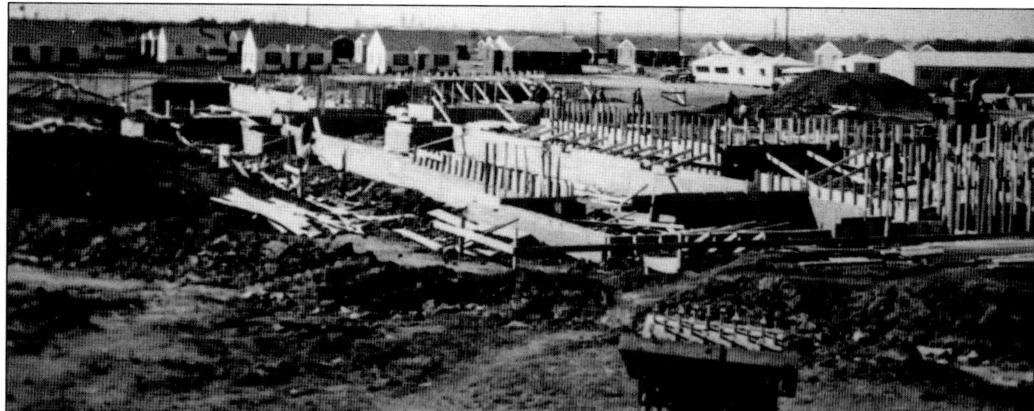

Pictured here is Midwest City School under construction in the Original Mile in 1943. The iconic boom houses are pictured to the left in the background, and to the right are the hutments (temporary facilities) and barracks used by local students for seven months as they wait for the permanent brick school to be completed. During the rainy season, this area was nothing but a muddy mess. As most of the city's main roadways were also dirt due to the road-building material shortage from the war effort, Midwest City earned the temporary nickname "Mudwest City." (Courtesy of Midwest City High School History Center.)

Pictured here at right is a gas line being installed in Midwest City. Integral utility systems were laid, including water, gas, sewage, and electricity. Atkinson personally owned and installed the water system in Midwest City, making it independent from other cities' water, such as Oklahoma City. This established what would later be the Midwest City Water Company. He sold the water company to the City of Midwest City for $188,000 on May 1, 1944. He also owned the sewer system. Oklahoma City provided the electric, gas, and telephone services. In 1961, the Midwest City Municipal Authority established the Midwest City Utilities Authority to increase efficiency and convenience. (Both, courtesy of Midwest City High School History Center.)

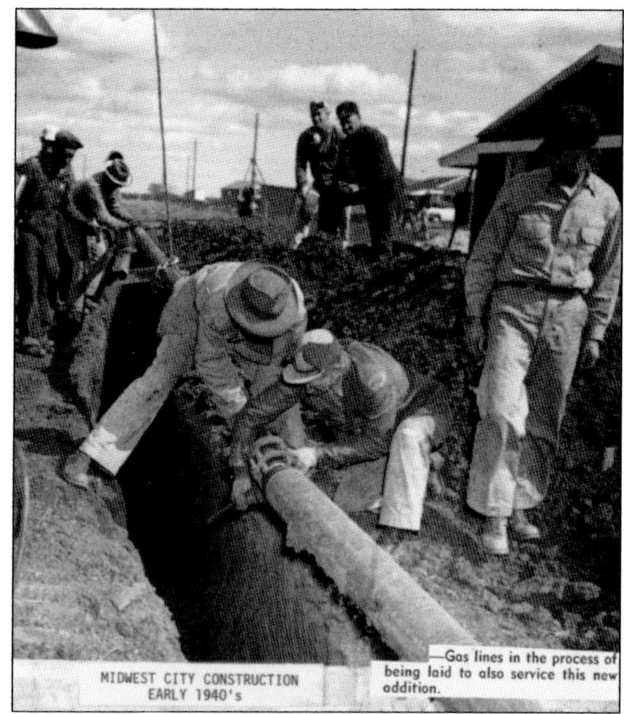

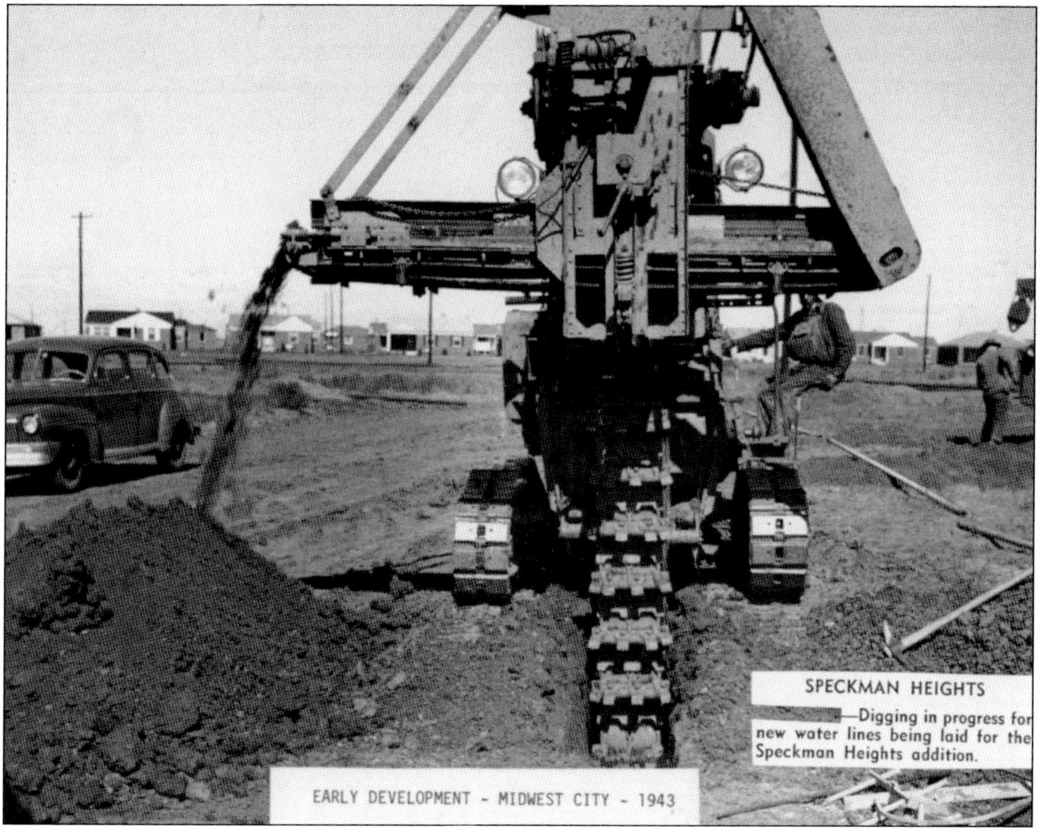

SPECKMAN HEIGHTS

—Digging in progress for new water lines being laid for the Speckman Heights addition.

EARLY DEVELOPMENT - MIDWEST CITY - 1943

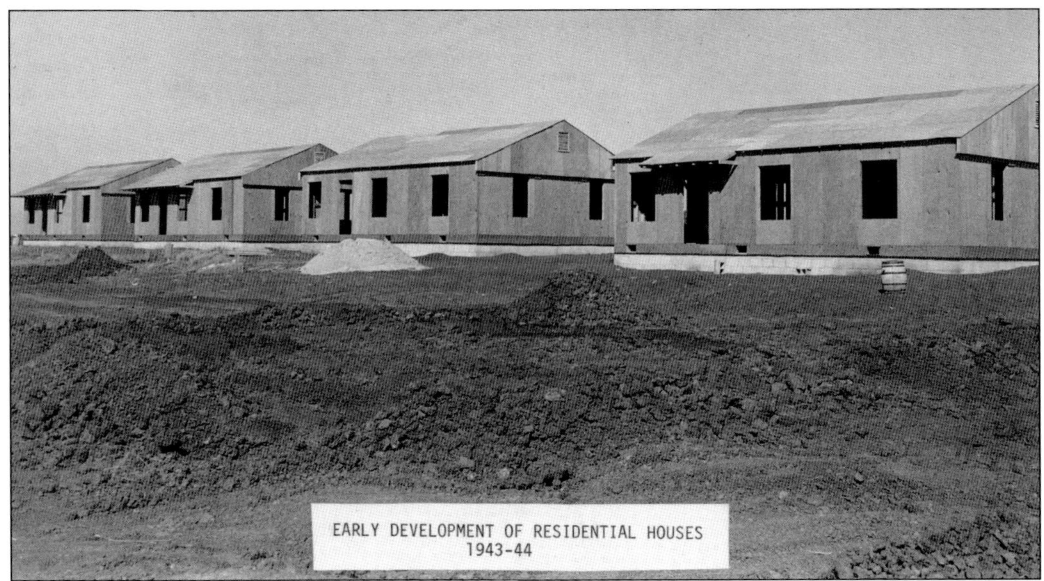

"Minimal Traditional Homes" was a house style coined by Virginia and Lee McAlester in their book *A Field Guide to American Houses*. These homes were built in the 1940s with key identifiers like a low-stooped roof, a single door in the middle or to the side of the front of the home with a window on each side, and painted clapboard siding. For the first neighborhood in Midwest City, these postwar homes were the perfect fit for families moving to work at the air depot. Each had a small front and backyard, held about two bedrooms and one bath, and were under 850 square feet. Some were adorned with additional woodwork, brick, landscaping, and even a garage. Later on, founder Bill Atkinson's granddaughter Cindy Mikeman recalled her grandfather would sometimes choose the color scheme of each home by looking at the color palette of the tie he was wearing that day. (Both, courtesy of Midwest City High School History Center.)

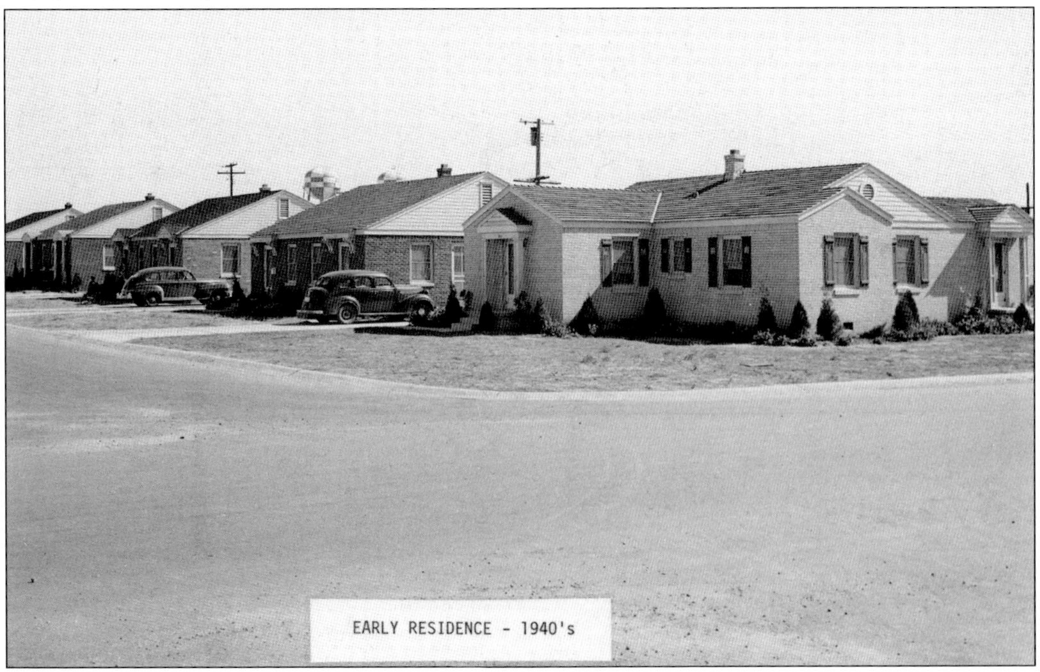

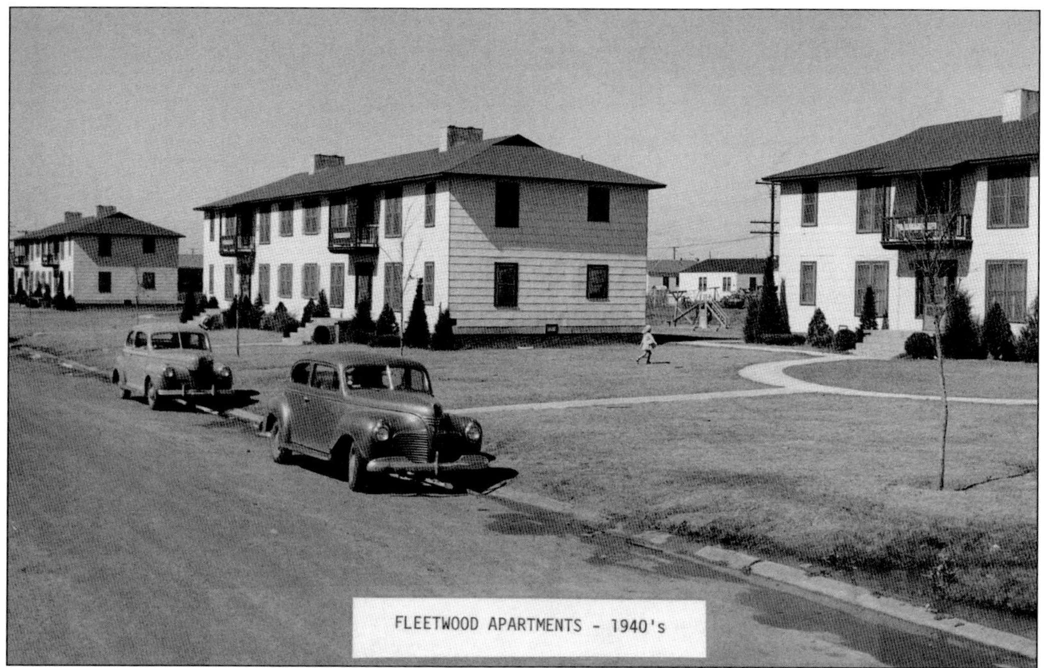

Located in Midwest City's Original Mile on the streets of Aeronca and Boeing Drive, north of Twenty-Ninth Street, Fleetwood Apartments were a housing staple for families working on the airfield. These apartments were later demolished after decades of use to make way for a new flagship shopping center for the city in the early 1990s. (Courtesy of Midwest City High School History Center.)

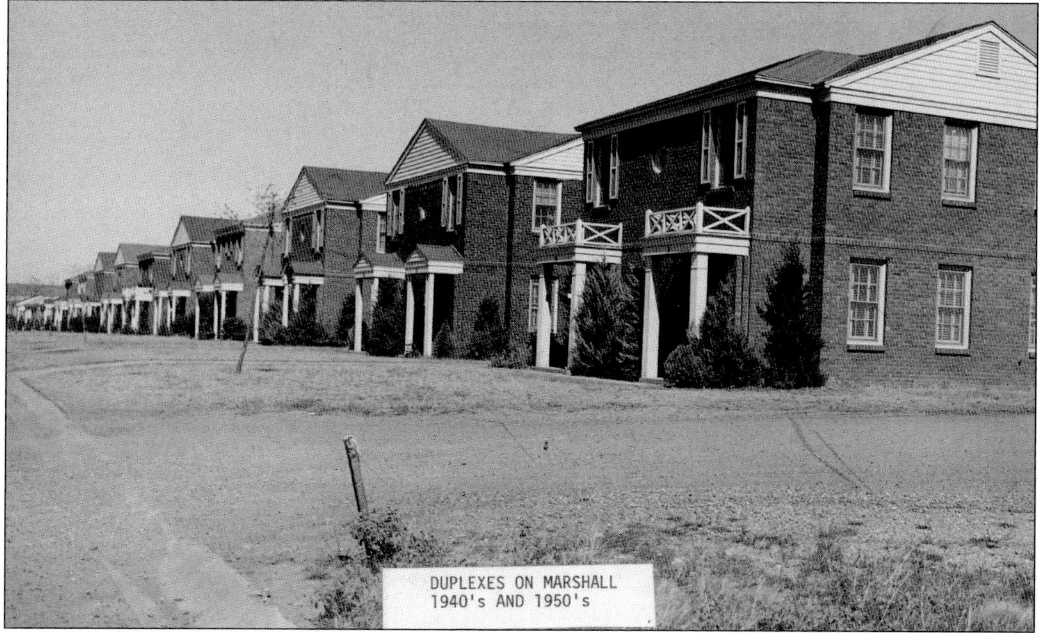

In addition to building the variation of style of minimal traditional houses and apartment complexes, Midwest City's founder Bill Atkinson ensured that the area also included duplexes. All forms of housing were considered to attract and accommodate a variety of life stages to work at the air depot. (Courtesy of Midwest City High School History Center.)

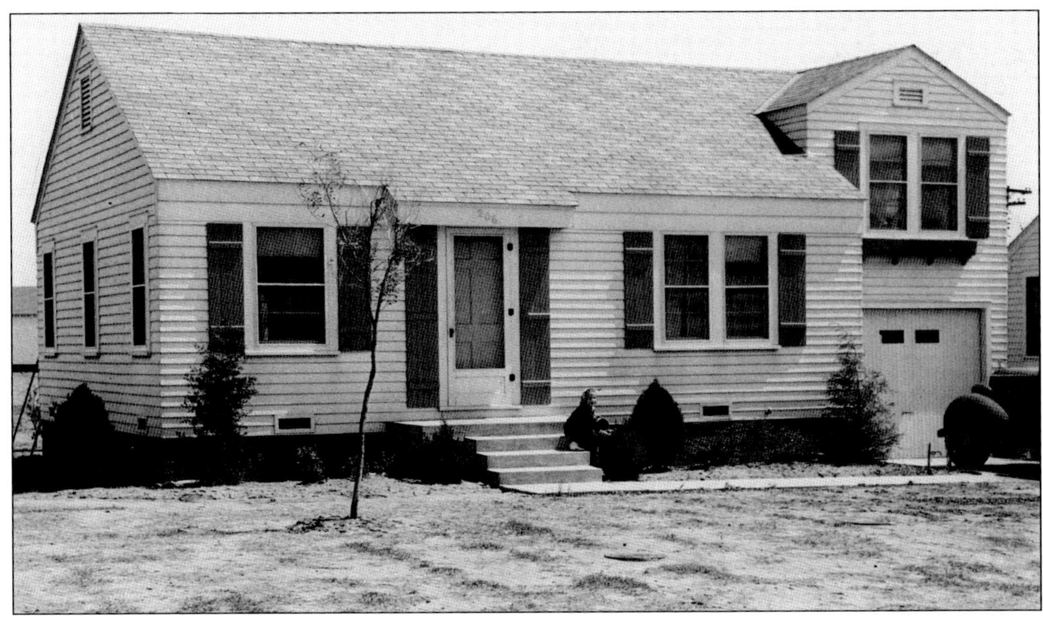

Houses in the Original Mile sold for around $2,750 to $3,350. Monthly rent payments were between $21.50 and $33.50 per month. Here are two examples of variations of Original Mile homes. Some minimal traditional houses were one-and-a-half stories tall in contrast to the traditional single-story. The house above is located at 206 Mid-America Boulevard in the Original Mile and was the former home of Tom and Marie Pulliam and daughter Jonell in 1956. The home below was built in 1942 and showcases the use of clapboard siding and brick at 207 West Fairchild Drive. The Wilcox family resided here during the late 1940s and early 1950s. The child pictured is believed to be Bob Wilcox. (Both, courtesy of Midwest City High School History Center.)

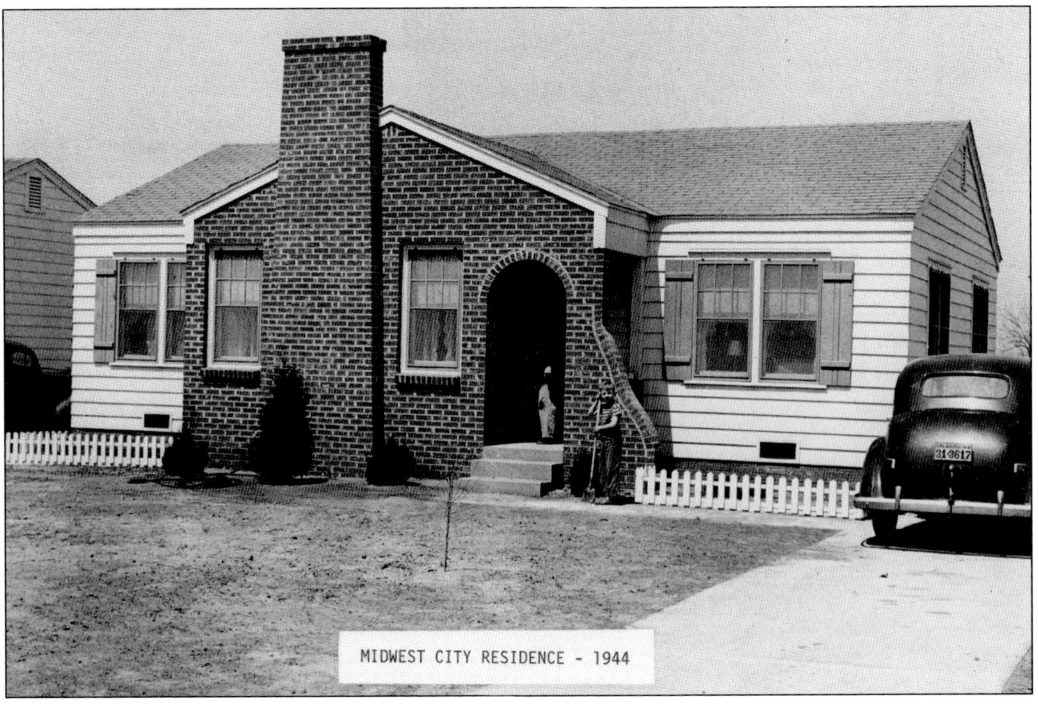

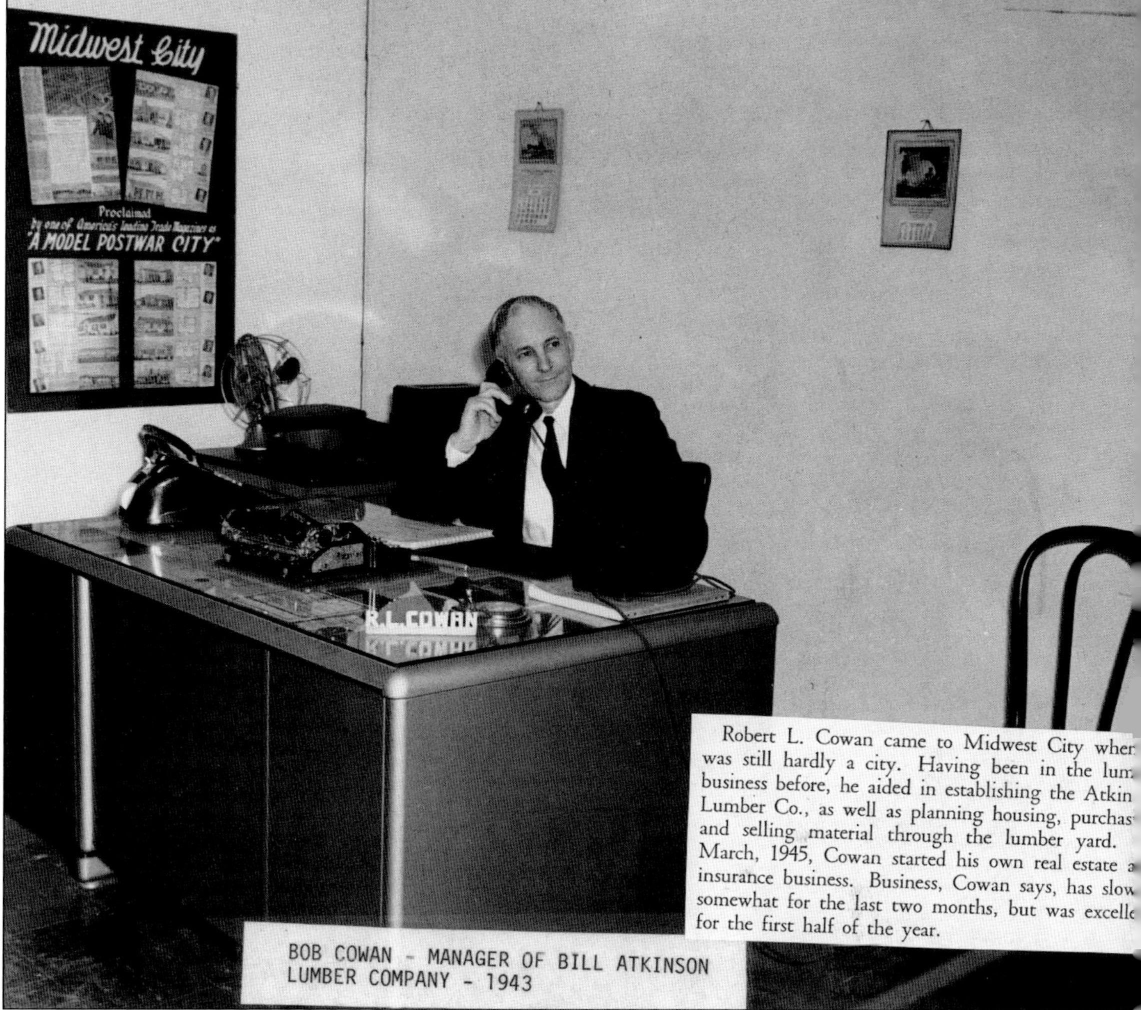

Entrepreneur Bill Atkinson not only figured out where the new airfield would be placed, bought the surrounding land around it, worked with leaders to plan, and developed the homes of the new township, he also supplied himself with his own materials through his own lumber company. Pictured here is the manager of the Bill Atkinson Lumber and Manufacturing Co., Bob Cowan, in 1943. The description within the picture reads as follows: "Robert L. Cowan came to Midwest City when it was still hardly a city. Having been in the lumber business before, he aided in establishing the Atkinson Lumber Co., as well as planning housing, purchasing and selling material through the lumber yard." In March 1945, Cowan started his own real estate and insurance business." (Courtesy of the Midwest City High School History Center.)

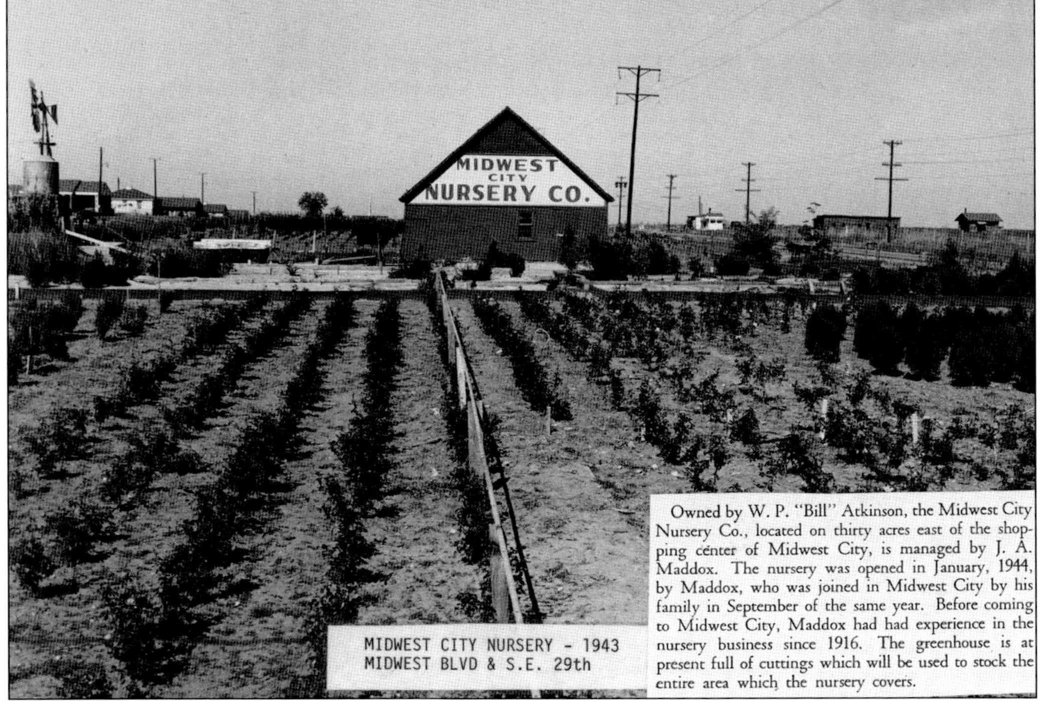

Owned by W. P. "Bill" Atkinson, the Midwest City Nursery Co., located on thirty acres east of the shopping center of Midwest City, is managed by J. A. Maddox. The nursery was opened in January, 1944, by Maddox, who was joined in Midwest City by his family in September of the same year. Before coming to Midwest City, Maddox had had experience in the nursery business since 1916. The greenhouse is at present full of cuttings which will be used to stock the entire area which the nursery covers.

Bill Atkinson saw an opportunity to grow and supply his own landscaping foliage for the house developments in Midwest City. The Midwest City Nursery Co. opened in January 1944 and was on 30 acres of land on the east side of downtown Midwest City. It is said that since Atkinson's wife, Rubye, was an avid gardener, Atkinson named different streets in the Original Mile by names like "Lilac" and "Peach." In accordance with each name, Atkinson would plant that specific plant on the property, such as lilac bushes at houses on Lilac Lane. (Both, courtesy of the Midwest City High School History Center.)

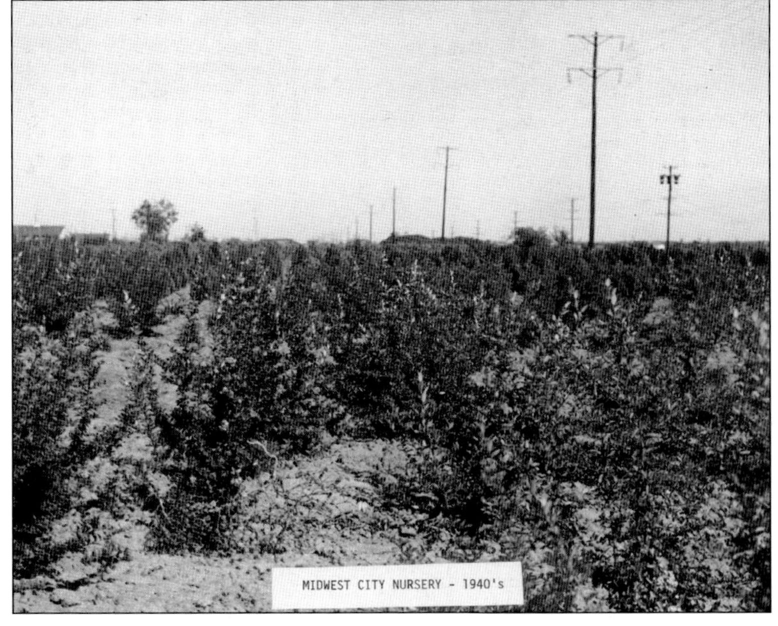

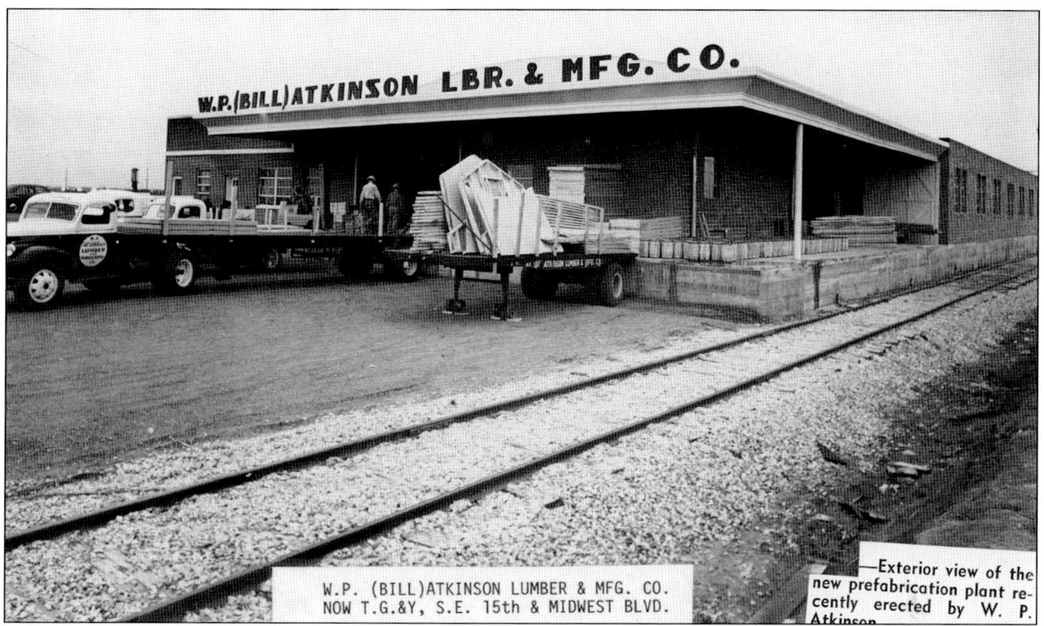

The above photograph shows the exterior of the Bill Atkinson Lumber and Manufacturing Co. prefabricated plant located on Fifteenth Street and Midwest Boulevard. The picture below is of the inside of the plant in the 1940s. This area would later become a Uptown TG&Y in the mid-1970s. (Both, courtesy of the Midwest City High School History Center.)

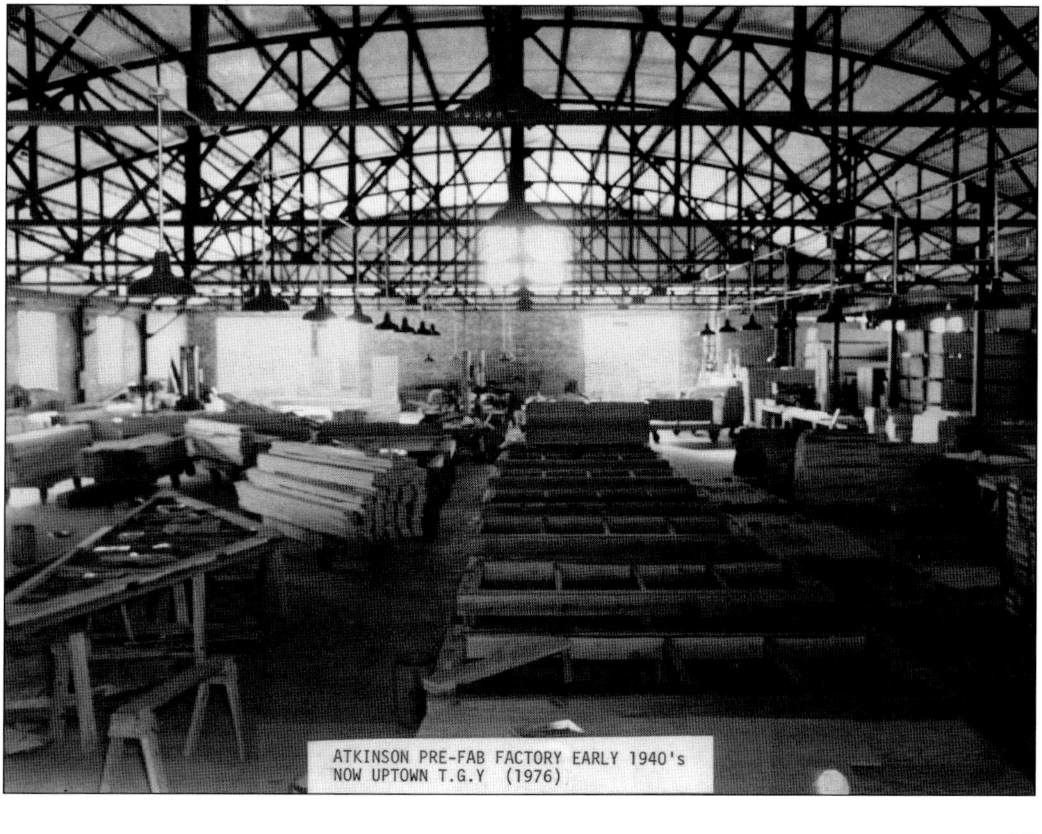

ATKINSON PRE-FAB FACTORY EARLY 1940's
NOW UPTOWN T.G.Y (1976)

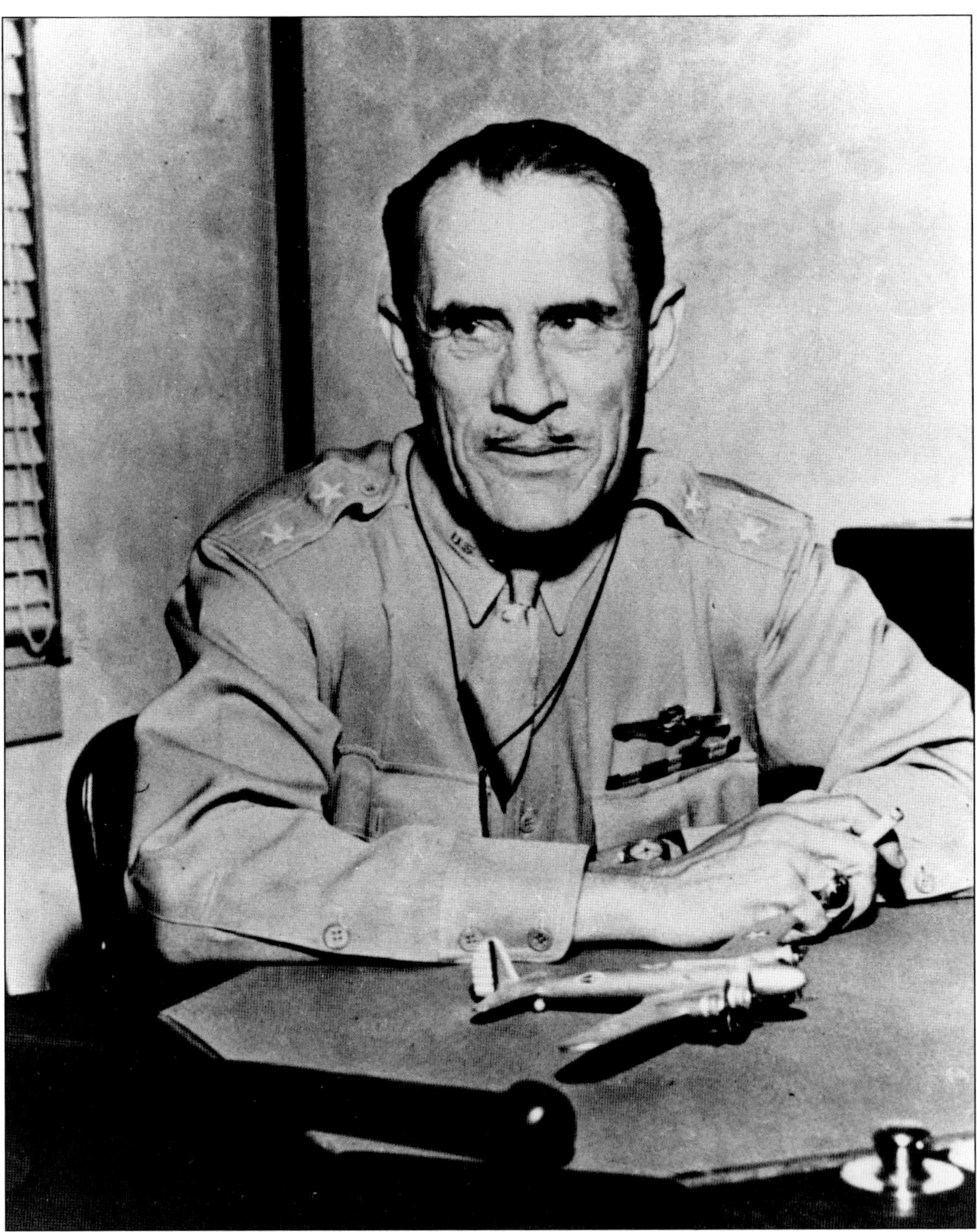

The local airfield that the City of Midwest City supported had many name changes. Initially, it was Midwest Air Depot, which inspired the name of Midwest City. Then it was changed to the Oklahoma City Air Depot. On June 7, 1942, Maj. Gen. Clarence L. Tinker of Pawhuska, Oklahoma, was the first major general to die in World War II, and the site was then named Tinker Field in his honor five months later, on October 14, 1942. This would not be the last name change, as after the US Air Force was formed in 1947, the site was then given the name Tinker Air Force Base. (Courtesy of the Midwest City High School History Center.)

Two

The Fight for Liberty and Supporting the War Effort

W.P. "Bill" Atkinson and his team broke ground on Midwest City as the Midwest Air Field began building its facilities. Before the site was chosen, the air depot was born out of the US Army Air Forces' (USAFF; later to be named the US Air Force) desire to build an air base in the Midwest region of the United States. Through a public trust called the Oklahoma Industries Foundation, Stanley Draper and other leaders like E.K. Gaylord competed for the base with other areas of the country and prepared a 960-acre site for the government. Draper understood exactly what the department was looking for and where it desired to place the base. He did so with the intention to help Oklahoma City and the state as a whole, motivated by the increase in jobs and government contracts. Oklahoma was chosen, and Midwest Air Field officially opened in 1942. During the years 1941–1945, the base was not only repairing planes but also building and storing them through an additional plant, the Douglas Aircraft Company. During the war, 38,000 Oklahomans worked at the Douglas Aircraft Company plant, and 13,500 people worked at the adjacent air base. Once the war was won, the Douglas Aircraft Company closed, but the air depot took over its facilities and expanded its services. Later named Tinker Air Force Base, it went on to be the single greatest employer in the whole state of Oklahoma and the largest maintenance and supply depot in the US Air Force and the world.

The first 75 percent of the base was built within the first year. In 1943, the depot employed over 15,000 employees supporting the war effort. The benefit of the location of the Tinker Air Field was that it was no more than 30 hours away from anywhere in the world. After World War II, Tinker became a permanent entity in Oklahoma and continued to be the largest employer in the state of Oklahoma, servicing planes such as the A-7D Corsair II (1968–1988), B-47 Stratojet (1947–1969), C-47 Skytrain (1943–present), C-135 Stratolifter/Air Force One (1950s–present), F-4D Phantom II (1970–1998), B-29 Superfortress (1943–1953), B-1B Lancer (1980s–present), B-52 Stratofortress (1955–present), and E-3 Sentry/AWAC (Airborne Warning and Control System; 1977–present).

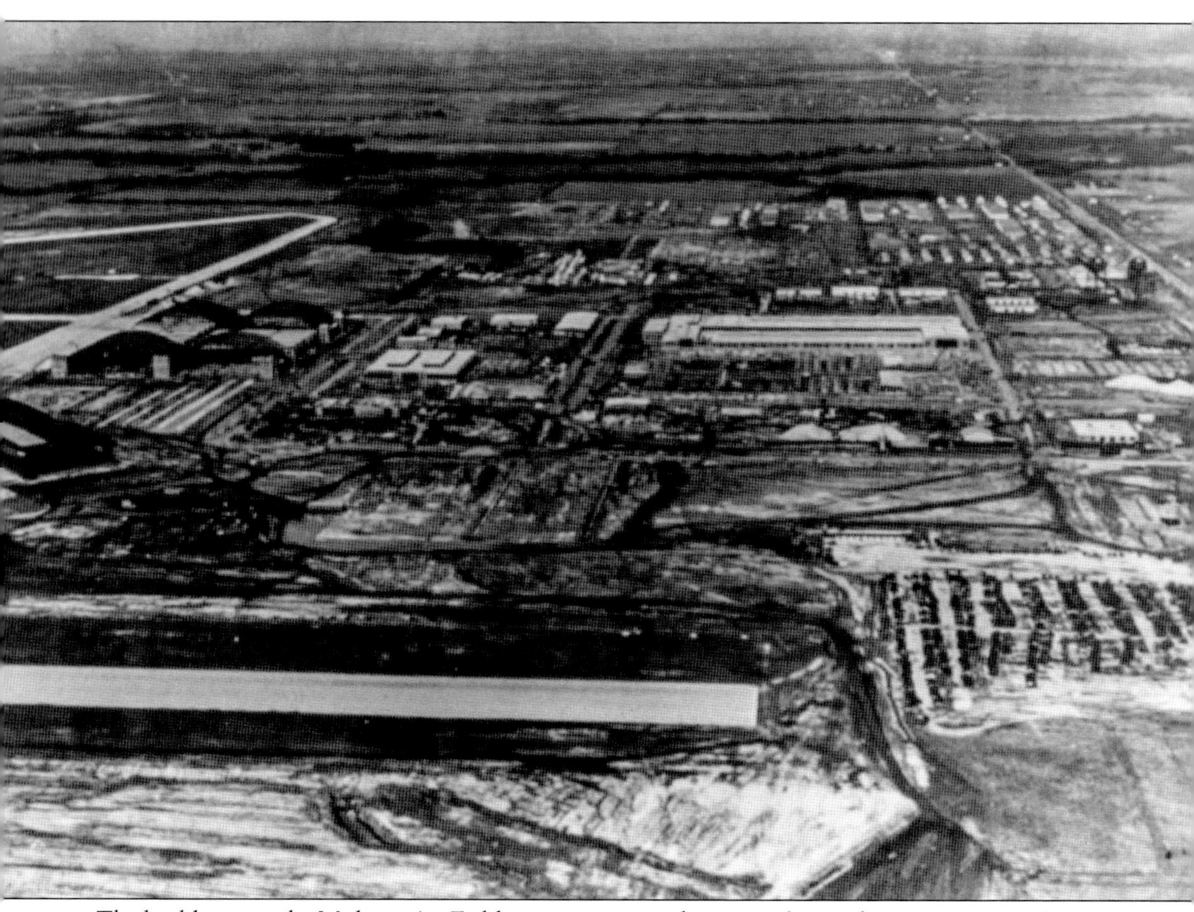

The buildings on the Midwest Air Field were constructed to manufacture large quantities of aircraft and support aircraft repair and maintenance. During World War II, it maintained, repaired, and adjusted the B-17, B-29, and B-29 Bombers. Seven buildings were significant during the foundation stages of Tinker. The Steam Plant (208) was the first building constructed on the base as a heating source for the depot in Area A, as it provided forced steam for cleaning tools located inside the maintenance and repair division. The Depot Supply Building (1) received raw materials for the repair and maintenance of aircraft and later as a supply warehouse. Originally, it received supplies by railroad. The Airplane Repair Building (230) is where large aircraft could be fixed. Workers assembled and disassembled planes, later used for the E-3A aircraft and 552 AWAC wing. Building 240 was one of the original hangars for the repair and maintenance of large aircraft and serving important military and government officials. The Combat Control Center (4209) directed military air traffic for the southwestern United States. It also housed the 32nd Air Division, a division independent of Tinker Air Force Base (AFB) Command that received its orders directly from the Pentagon. (Courtesy of the Midwest City High School History Center.)

Col. William Turnbull of the San Antonio Air Depot in Texas became the first commander of the Midwest Air Depot. Because the base was not built yet, the operations of the base began in downtown Oklahoma City in the Commerce Exchange Building and then the Bass Building. By the time he left the base, it had grown to have over 22,000 military and civilian workers. (Courtesy of the Oklahoma Historical Society.)

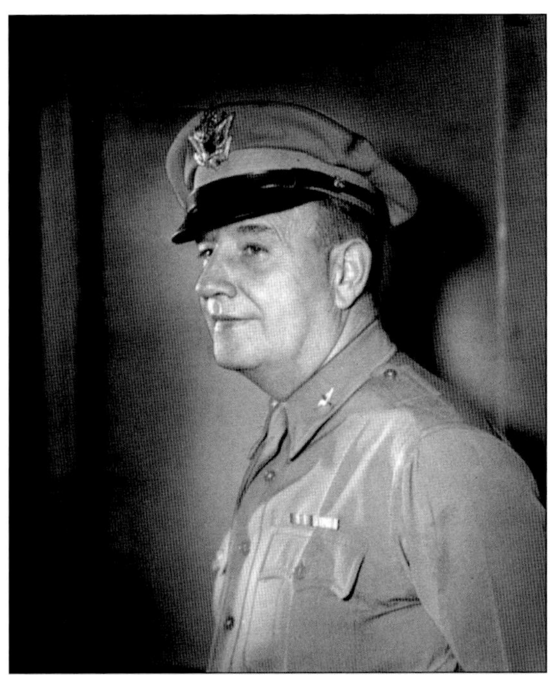

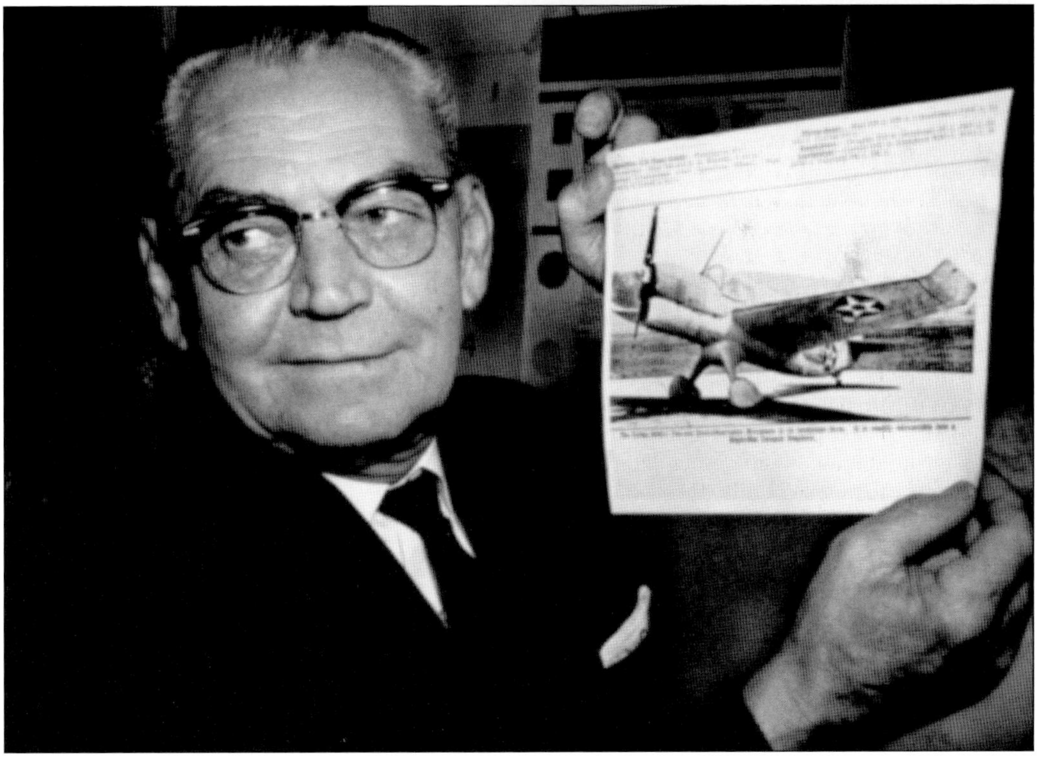

The first aircraft repair to ever be done at Midwest Air Field, later to be known as Tinker Air Force Base, occurred in September 1942 as a Navy SOC3-1 Aircraft made a forced landing on a partially completed runway. Pictured here is Floyd G. Close, chief of the engineering services section, sharing the story in 1962. (Courtesy of the Oklahoma Historical Society.)

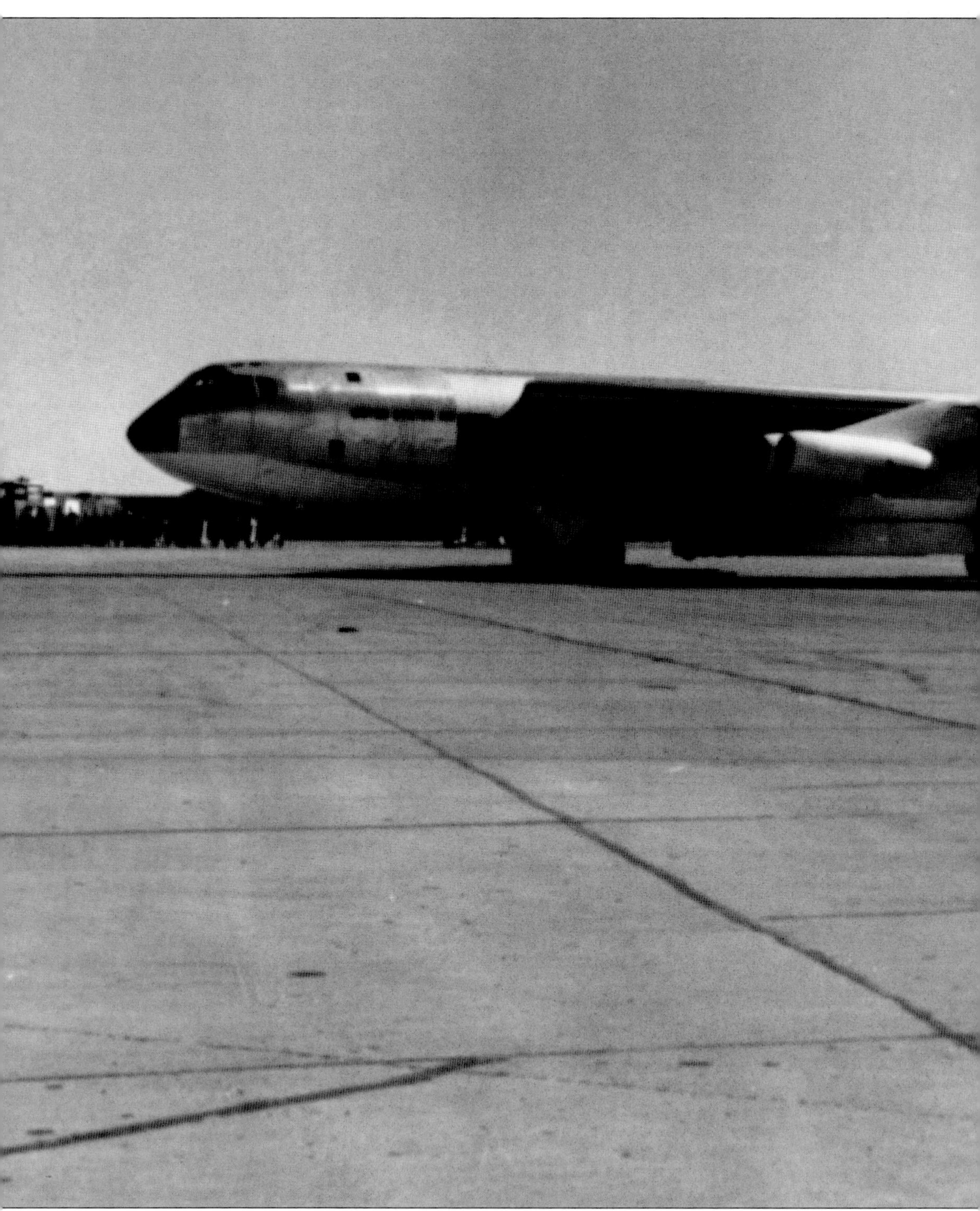

The first B-52 Bomber arrived at Tinker Air Field in November 1955. A total of 744 B-52s were built and still advancing in technology to the present day. The B-52 is seen as the backbone of the bomber force and has the capacity to have the widest array of weapons of any aircraft.

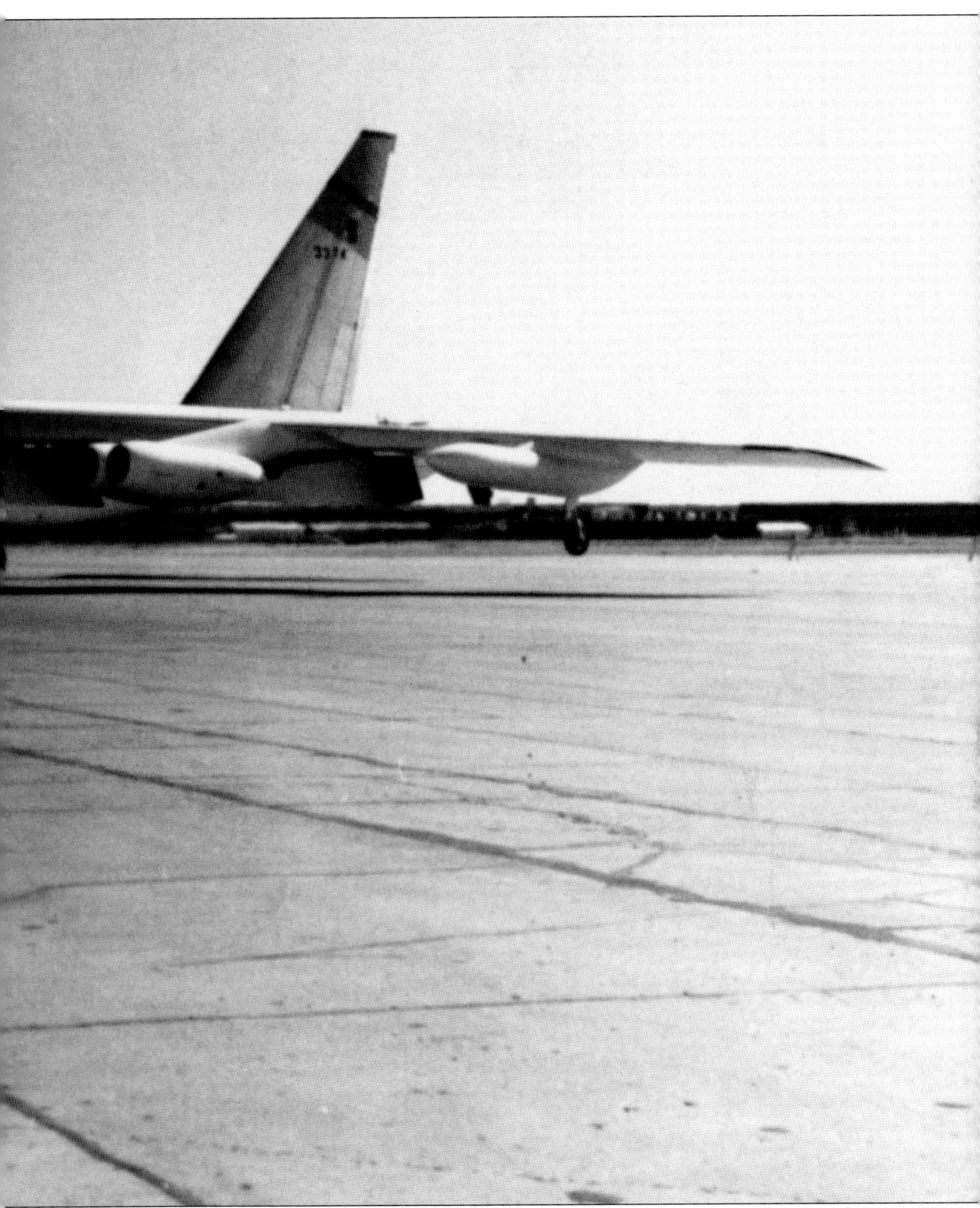

The B-52 Bomber is also the mascot of Midwest City High School. As a tradition at football games, students will carry and run a bomb shell down the football field. (Courtesy of the Rose State College Foundation.)

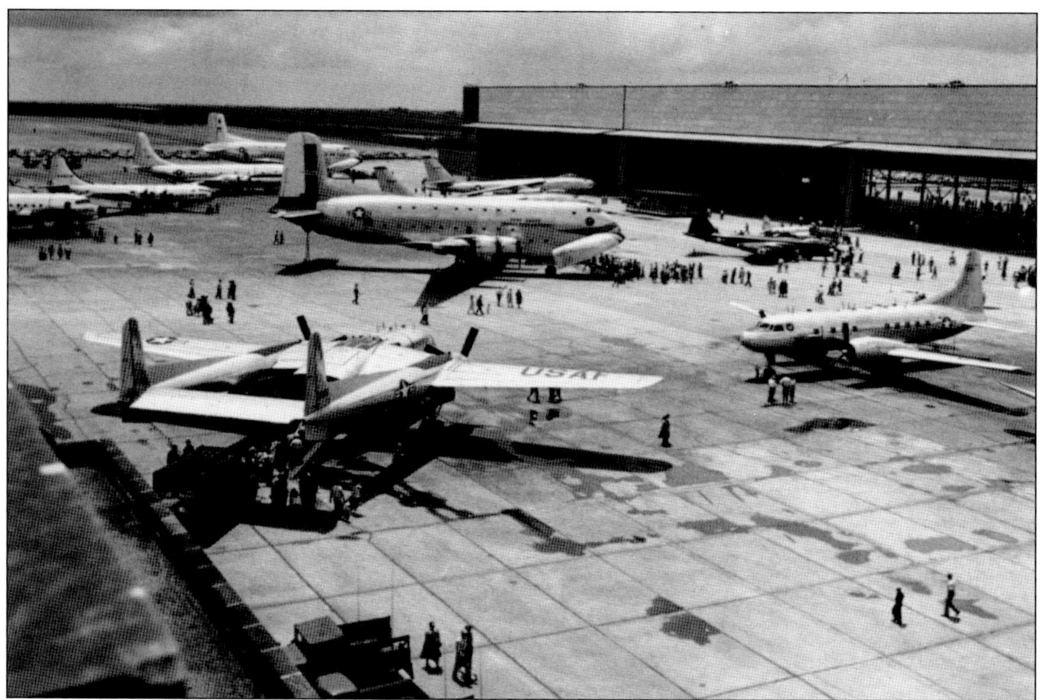
The base would go on and partner with the temporary Douglas Aircraft Company plant, producing more than half of the 10,000 C-47 Skytrain US Army cargo planes (nicknamed "Gooney Birds") built during World War II. The Douglas Aircraft Company also repaired and built a number of planes, especially the C-54 transports and A-26 attack bombers. Gen. Dwight D. Eisenhower remarked that the C-47 was one of four weapons that helped win World War II, including taking part in the D-Day invasion in June 1944 and the Market Garden Assault in September 1944. Tinker Field also prepared the plane that dropped the atomic bomb on Hiroshima and Nagasaki. Pictured is an open house of the air base for the community to see all of the different types of planes serviced at Tinker Field in 1955. (Courtesy of Rose State College Foundation.)

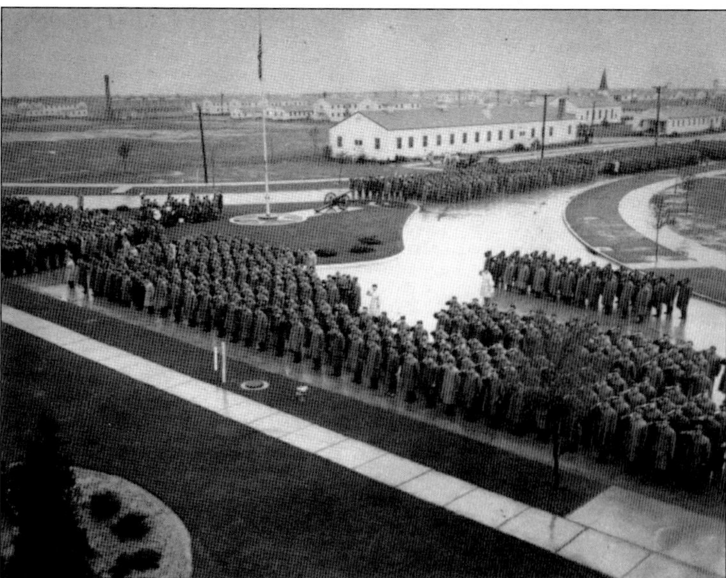
Pictured here is a salute at the Midwest Air Depot in 1945 in response to Pres. Franklin D. Roosevelt's death on April 15, less than a month before the end of World War II. Roosevelt, who had struggled with post-polio syndrome, helped see the nation recover from the Great Depression and led the nation to defeat the Germans, Japanese, and their allies. (Courtesy of Rose State College Foundation.)

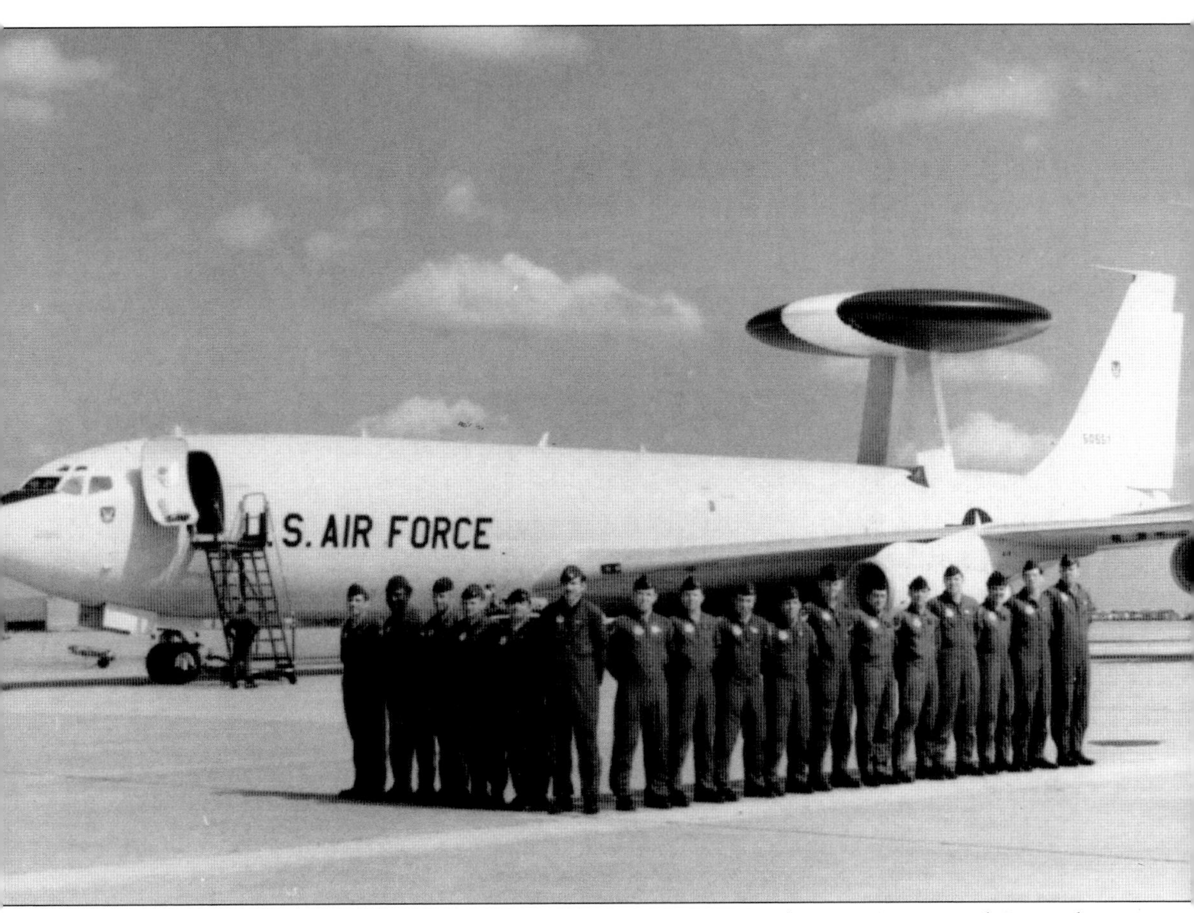

According to the US Air Force, Tinker began using the E-3 Sentry Airborne Warning and Control Wing (AWAC) to provide surveillance, command, control, and communications needed by the commanders of the United States and NATO air defense forces in March 1977. These planes held a large rotating radar dome that could scan, analyze, and track enemy and friendly low-flying aircraft in terrain that typically confuses other surveillance aircraft types. Seeing these in the sky was a staple of Midwest City living through the 2020s. (Courtesy of the Rose State College Foundation.)

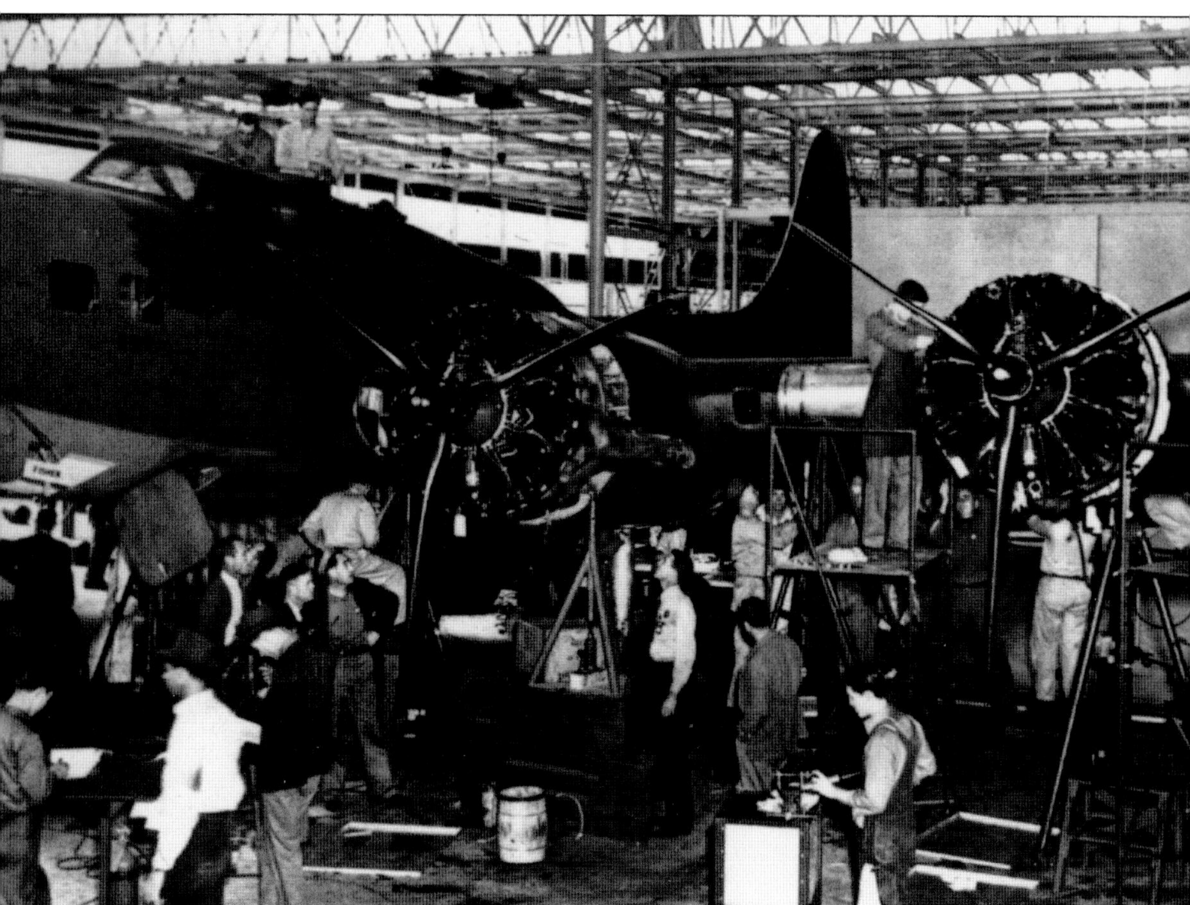

Pictured here, workers are providing maintenance to a B-17 Flying Fortress. Once the war was over, Tinker demobilized and converted thousands of C-47s to civilian DC-3s and sold them as surplus and corporate aircraft. Though the Douglas Aircraft Company plant closed, the Fire Pump Station (3202) continuously pumped water as protection against fire. Building 3001 was formerly known as the Douglas Assembly Building and was three-quarters of a mile long and nearly 1,000 feet wide. The building had no windows to protect it from bombers that would spotlight from the sky. This was the main location where the C-47 was produced during World War II but was later altered for aircraft modification once Tinker took it over. It then specialized in engine overhaul, aircraft overhaul, and repairing aircraft parts. Building 3001 was the largest structure in Oklahoma. The Fire Protection Water Storage Tank held 475,000 gallons of water and has continued that function since World War II. The Woodworking Mill (3313) was later turned into housing for the Precision Measurement Equipment Laboratory. (Courtesy of the Rose State College Foundation.)

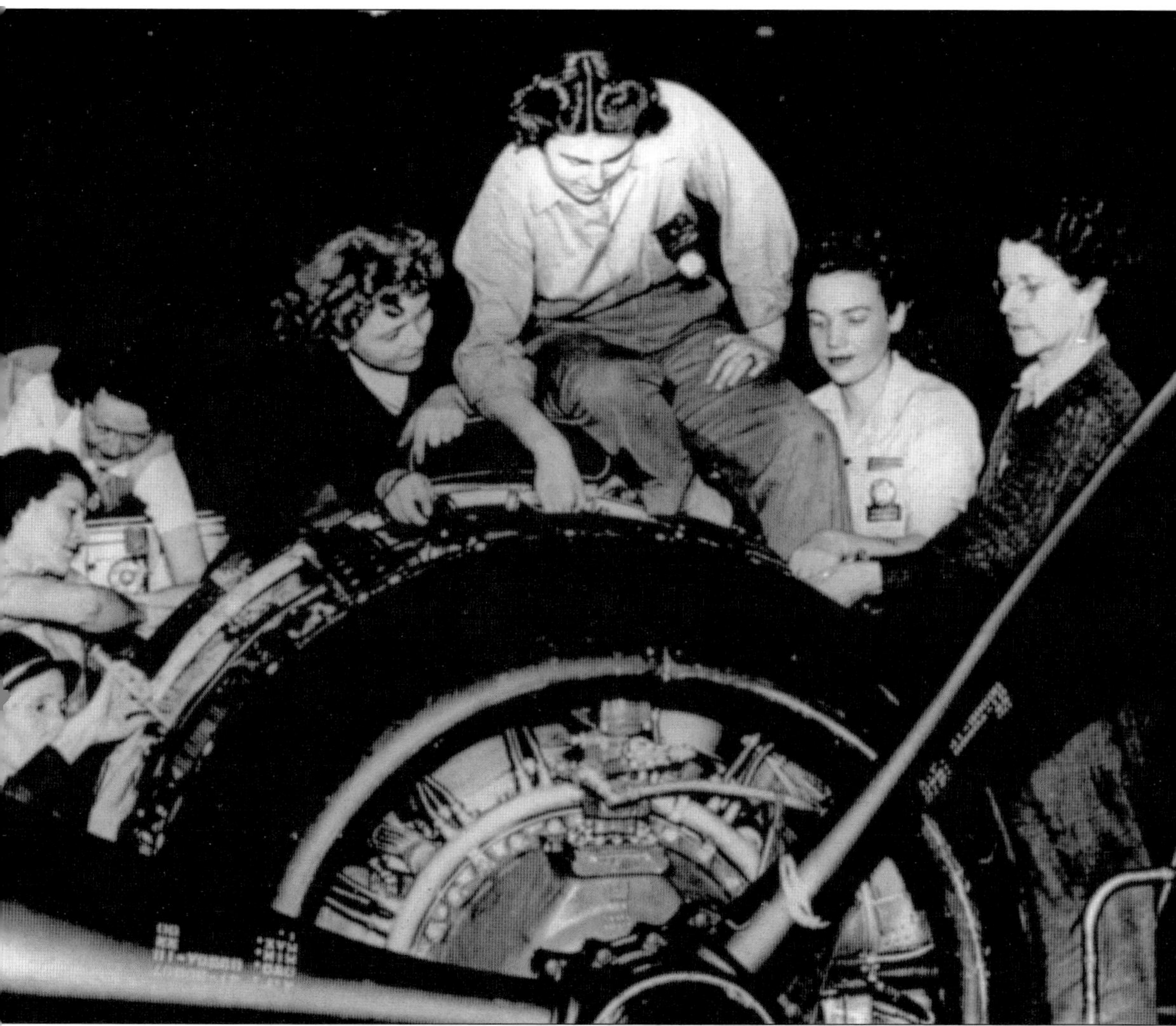

During World War II, Tinker employed over 13,500 people, with nearly half of them being women. As most men were away serving during World War II, women were needed to join the workforce to support infrastructure at home as well as building and repairing weapons and aircraft to use on the front lines. The archetype of Rosie the Riveter was exemplified at Tinker Air Force Base as "Riveters" repaired planes, manufactured parts, and temporarily fulfilled the roles of men in early-1940s society. (Courtesy of the Oklahoma Historical Society.)

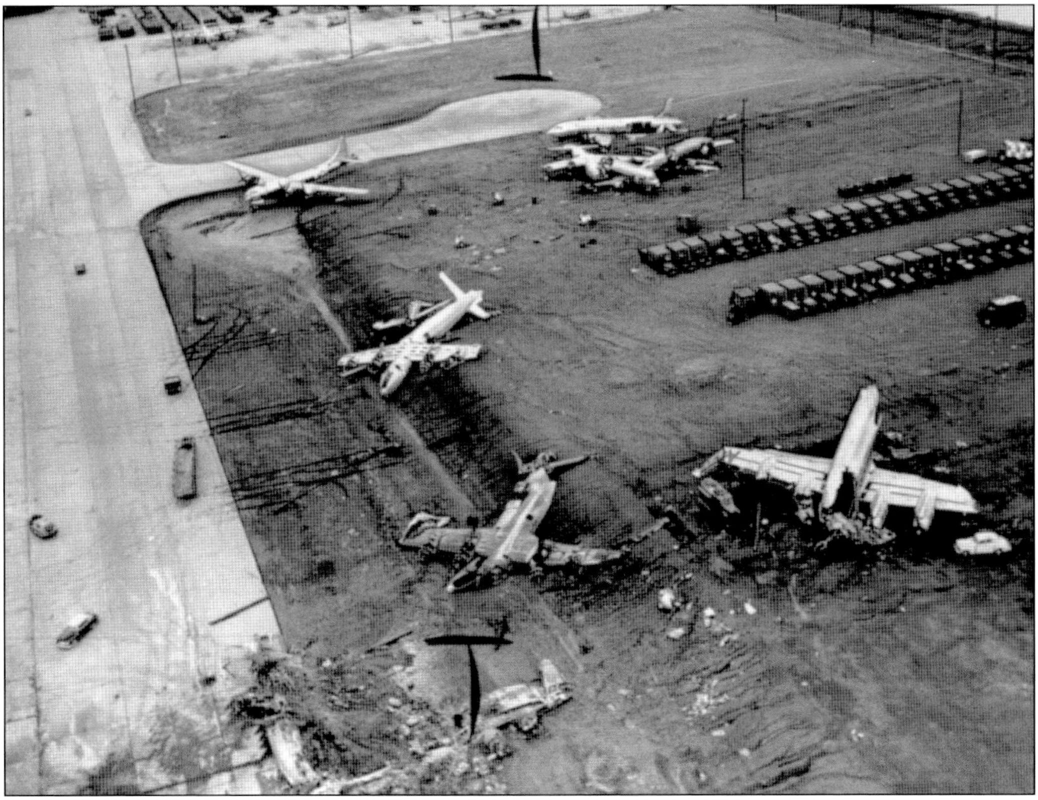

In 1948, a string of tornadoes hit Oklahoma City, including Tinker Air Force Base. This particular storm occurred on March 20, damaging 17 C-54 Skymasters and demolishing two B-29 Superfortresses. In addition, fifteen P-47s, five L-4s, three C-47s, one B-25, three C-47s, one B-25, three AT-11s, a PQ-14, and 100 special purpose military vehicles were also damaged, totaling over $10.25 million. (Courtesy of Oklahoma Historical Society)

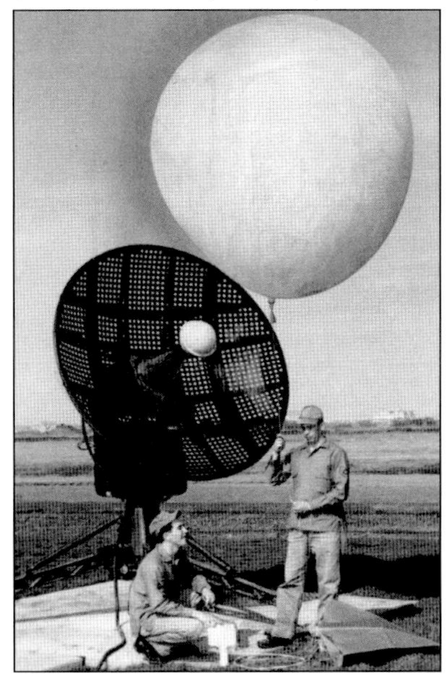

If they could predict rain, could they predict a tornado and prevent further damage to government property and human life? After the first tornado on March 20, 1948, another storm approached Midwest City that looked identical to the storm that produced the previous tornado. Maj. Ernest J. Fawbush and Capt. Robert C. Miller, 1059th Weather Wing meteorologists, contacted the base commanding general, and they issued an alert for Tinker to prepare for another tornado. This became the first official tornado warning in the United States. They were able to formulate a model profile of a thunderstorm able to produce a tornado. They were able to do so by analyzing the data and similarities on the moisture distribution and the flow of surface winds compared to the wind patterns in the lower atmosphere, according to James L. Crowder in the article "Tinker's Twin Sisters of 1948 and the Birth of Tornado Forecasting." Fawbush and Miller received national recognition for their model and continued to grow as authorities in meteorology. (Courtesy of the Oklahoma Historical Society.)

Three

Model City Living

Atkinson's vision of being the model city, the City of Tomorrow, was exemplified in its concept of city planning, civic beauty, and amenities. In 1953, only 10 years after its founding, Midwest City was awarded the "Model City of the Midwest" by the National Society of Home Builders over 100 other cities in the competition. In the early days of Midwest City, there were no televisions, only home record players and radio wire recorders. Life was much simpler than in the decades that followed. Midwest City had areas to go shopping, drive-in movie theaters and cinemas for entertainment, local parks to enjoy the outdoors, churches for worship, and a community swimming pool for families. Residents had opportunities to attend local civic associations and veteran support associations. Some included the Midwest City Rotary Club, Kiwanis International, Lions Club, Wranglers Club, and Elks Lodge. An annual rodeo was held for decades to celebrate the pioneering spirit of the Old West. Locally owned restaurants and city events also cultivated a greater community. Later on, 9- and 18-hole golf courses, sidewalks, and walking trails were added. By the early 2020s, Midwest City would be home to 31 parks and recreation trails in only a 25-square-mile area. The Tinker Air Show would bring families from all over Oklahoma and beyond to see the Navy Blue Angels and Air Force Thunderbirds perform. Midwest City was seen as a Rockwellian picture in the early days of its life as a creatively planned, self-contained city. As the years continued, Midwest City added many community-building events, such as the annual Midwest City Holiday Lights Spectacular, Veterans Day Parade, Tribute to Liberty fireworks show, and more.

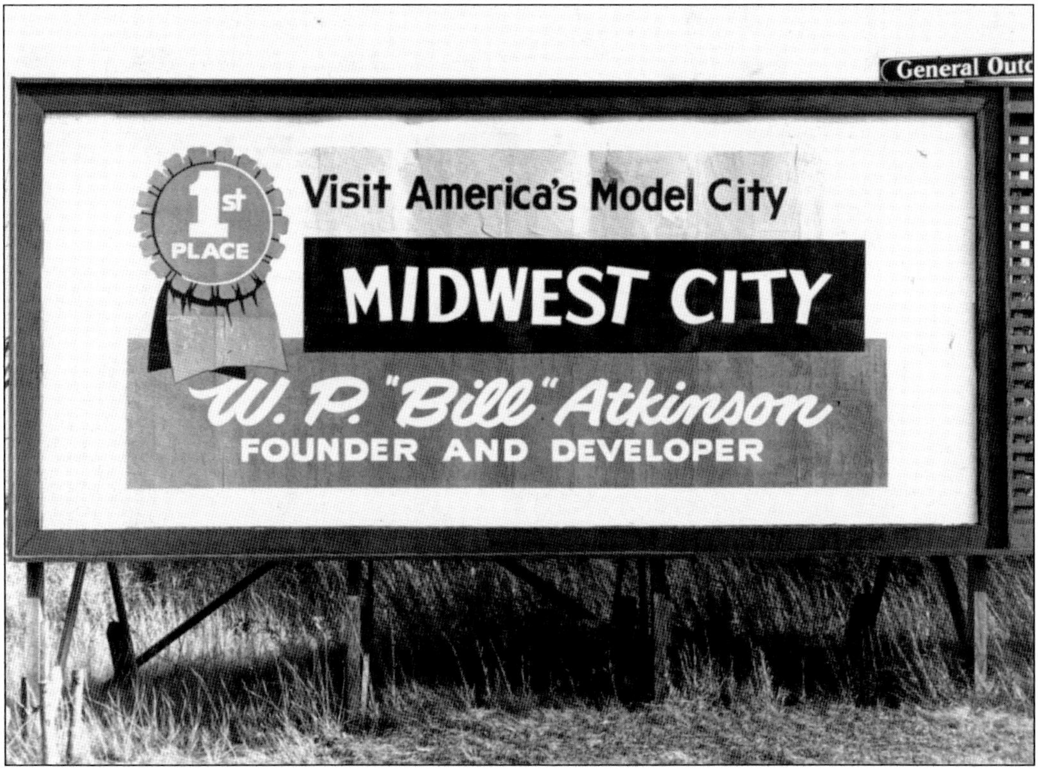

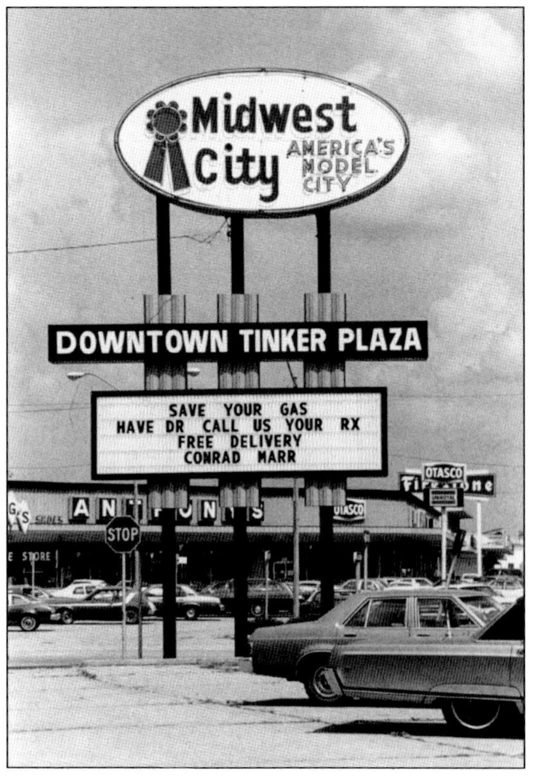

This was just one loud and proud sign put in place by Atkinson. Around Midwest City, visitors would find signs that said, "Midwest City, Founded & Developed by W.P. "Bill" Atkinson." Atkinson was very proud of this city and was not afraid to share about it. Atkinson used his history in media and understanding of marketing to promote Midwest City to the area, and it proved to be a successful tactic. The sign at left was located at the entrance of the city in front of the Downtown Tinker Plaza. (Both, courtesy of Rose State College Foundation.)

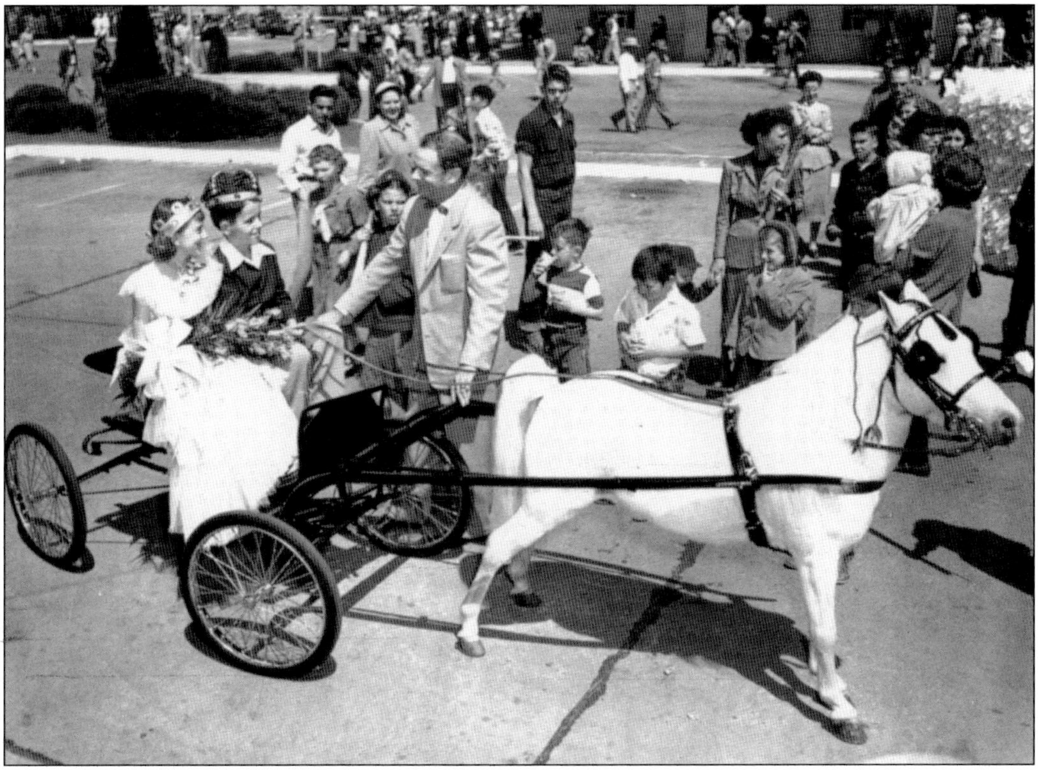

Midwest City celebrated 10 years of impressive growth in 1953 with a parade. Pictured above are two children, Roger M. and Virginia M., elected as the king and queen of a designated event at the parade, with W.P. "Bill" Atkinson. At the parade, Oklahoma governor Johnson Murray spoke, as did Speaker of the House Tim Holt, who was also in attendance. (Both, courtesy of the Rose State College Foundation.)

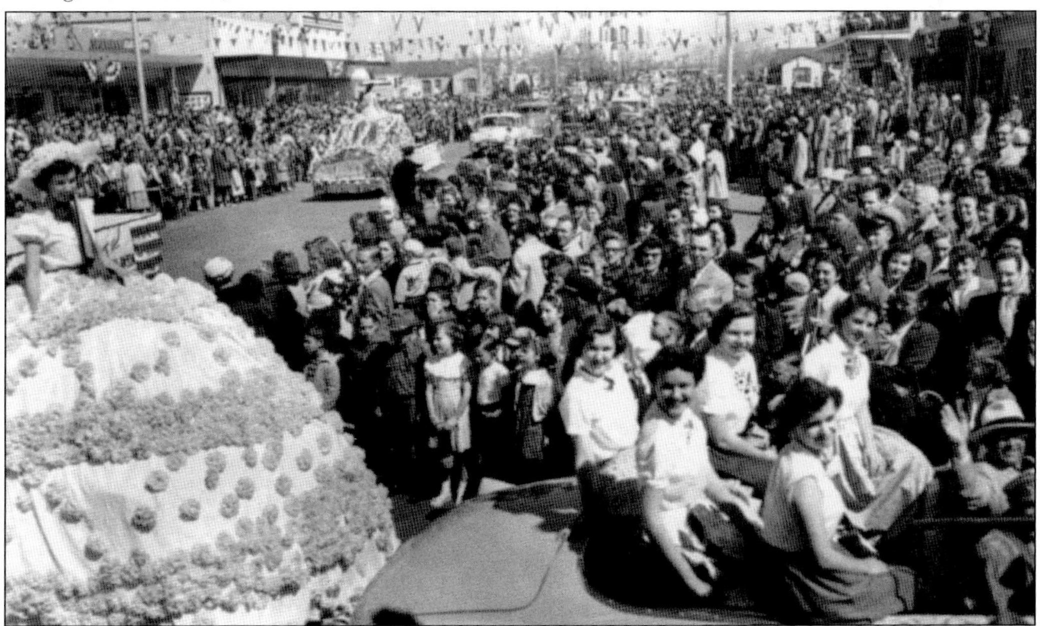

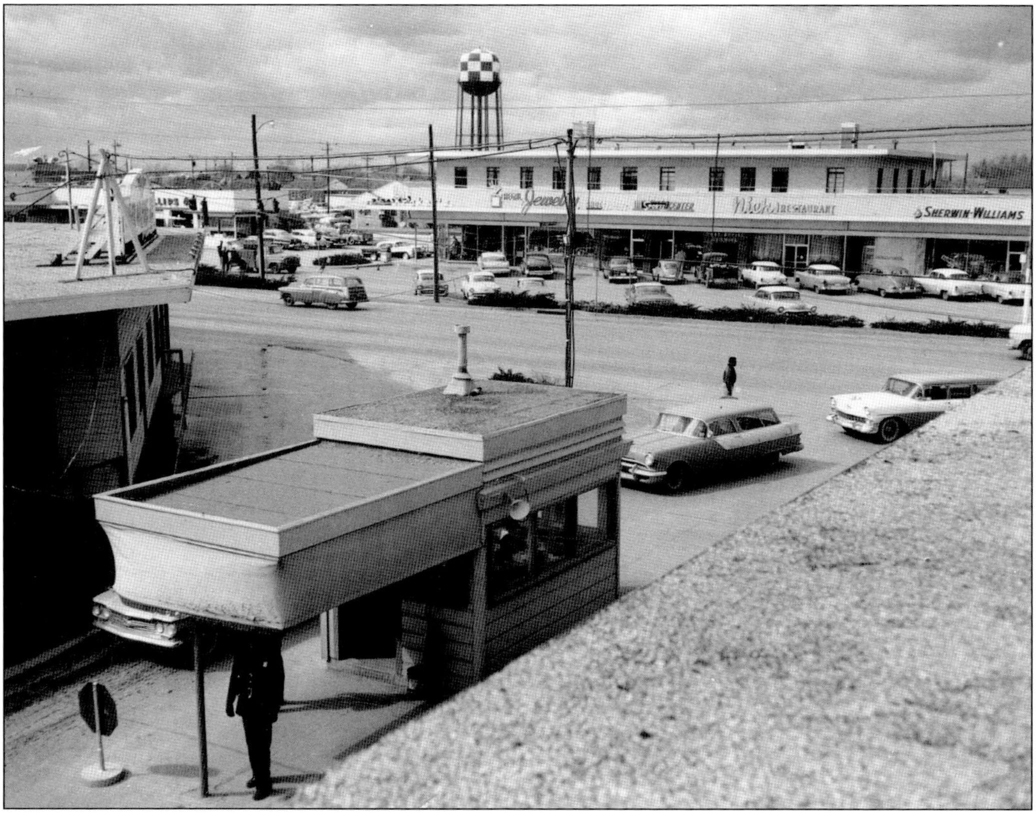

This is the Tinker Air Force Base gate located off Twenty-Ninth Street across from the Original Mile in the 1960s. The red-and-white checkered water tower overlooked the thousands of employees and service members going to and from this gate each morning and afternoon. Emerging from the Cold War and soon to enter the Southeast Asian Conflict of the Vietnam War, Tinker became a place for weary airmen and aircraft in a time of uncertainty. The photograph below shows the gateway to the "City of Tomorrow." (Above, courtesy of Midwest City High School History Center; below, courtesy of Rose State College Foundation.)

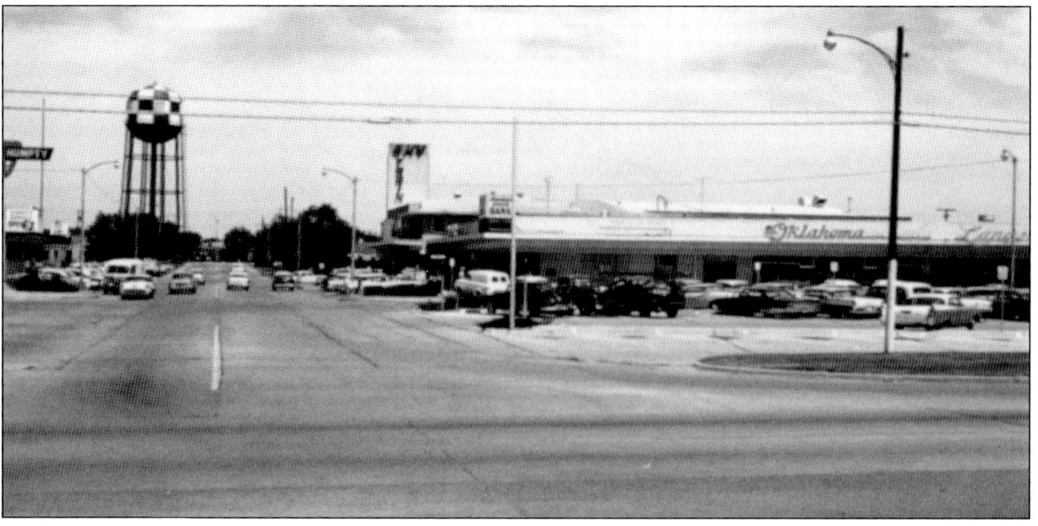

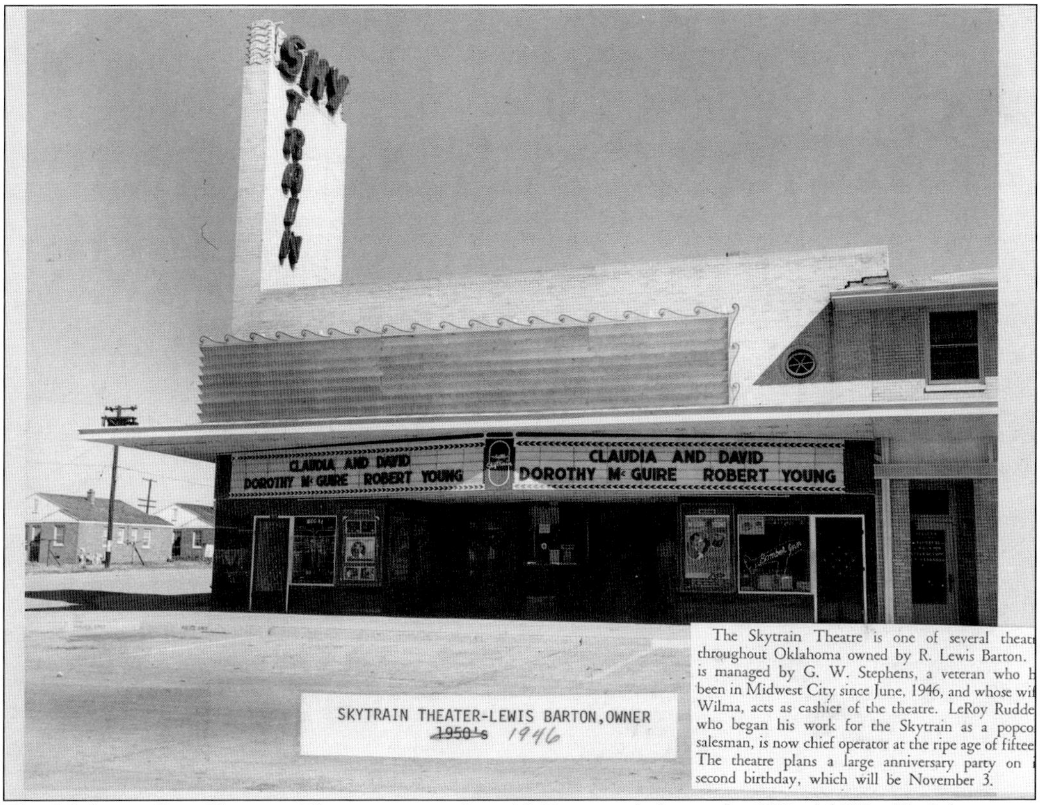

SKYTRAIN THEATER-LEWIS BARTON,OWNER
~~1950's~~ 1946

The Skytrain Theatre is one of several theat
throughout Oklahoma owned by R. Lewis Barton.
is managed by G. W. Stephens, a veteran who h
been in Midwest City since June, 1946, and whose wi
Wilma, acts as cashier of the theatre. LeRoy Rudde
who began his work for the Skytrain as a popco
salesman, is now chief operator at the ripe age of fiftee
The theatre plans a large anniversary party on
second birthday, which will be November 3.

The Midwest City Skytrain Theater opened in 1943 toward the end of World War II. Like many other cities in America, people young and old visited the theater to get away from the stressors of the time. A local recalls how teenagers would "walk through those doors carefully avoiding Ms. Coxy and her flashlight, grasping at the hope that [they] wouldn't get yelled at or lit up by her during or after the news headline, cartoon, or movies" and that they "sat clutching [their] popcorn, Coke, and candy bar, trying to desperately to eat it all at once while awaiting [their] cinema journey." Skytrain was one of the most memorable amenities for those who grew up in Midwest City. A local landmark until its demise in the early 1980s, the Skytrain theater (named after the C-47 World War II plane that was produced at Tinker Air Force Base) was a staple in Midwest City living. Residents young and old remarked on many memories of seeing films at Skytrain. Next door to the Skytrain were the Regal Jewelry Gift Shop and the Bomber Inn, where many would grab lunch. (Both, courtesy of Midwest City High School History Center.)

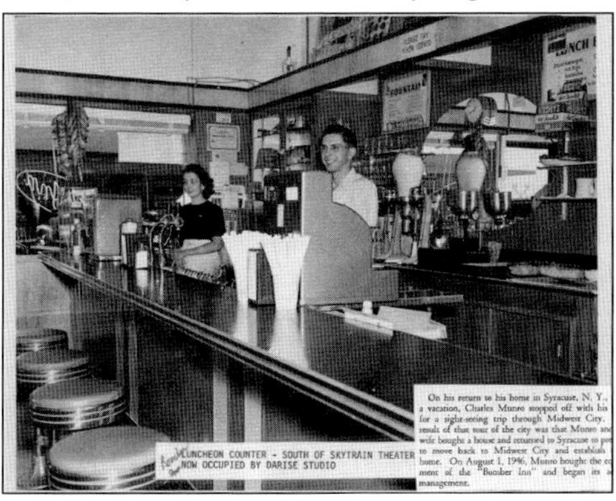

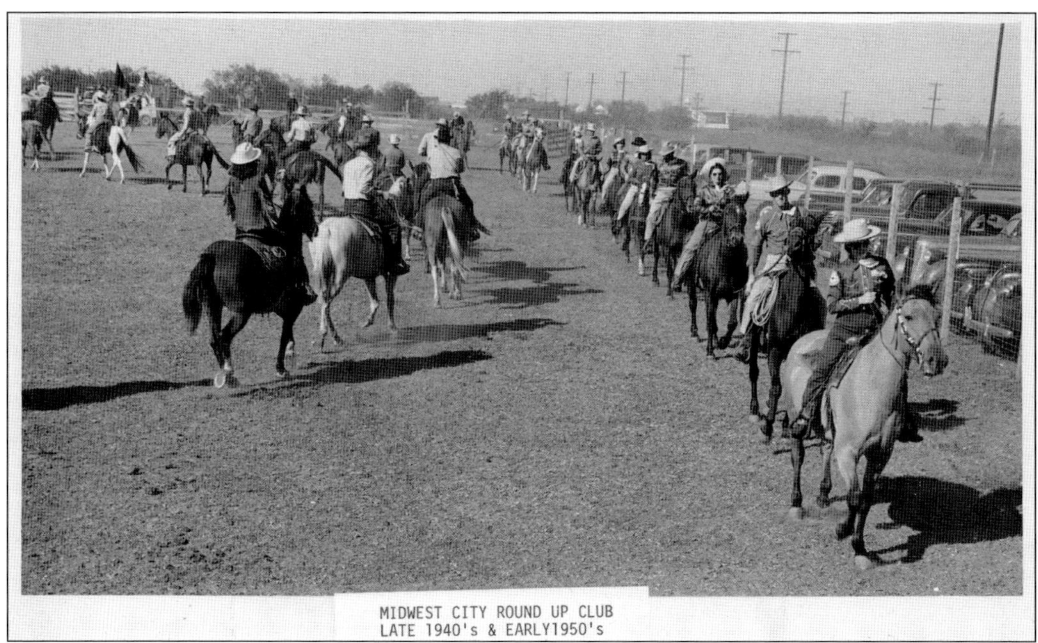

Displaying Western heritage, the Midwest City Round Up Club offered rodeos, barrel racing, and other equestrian events yearly during the 1940s and early 1950s. It would be cosponsored by the Lions Club and Wranglers Club and reminiscent of the Old West. Children would dress up in pioneer clothing and decorate wagons. The pioneering spirit that led many Americans west was said to be alive and well in Midwest City. Each year, a parade would go through Midwest City with trick riding and local school marching bands. (Above, courtesy of Midwest City High School History Center; below, courtesy of the Rose State College Foundation.)

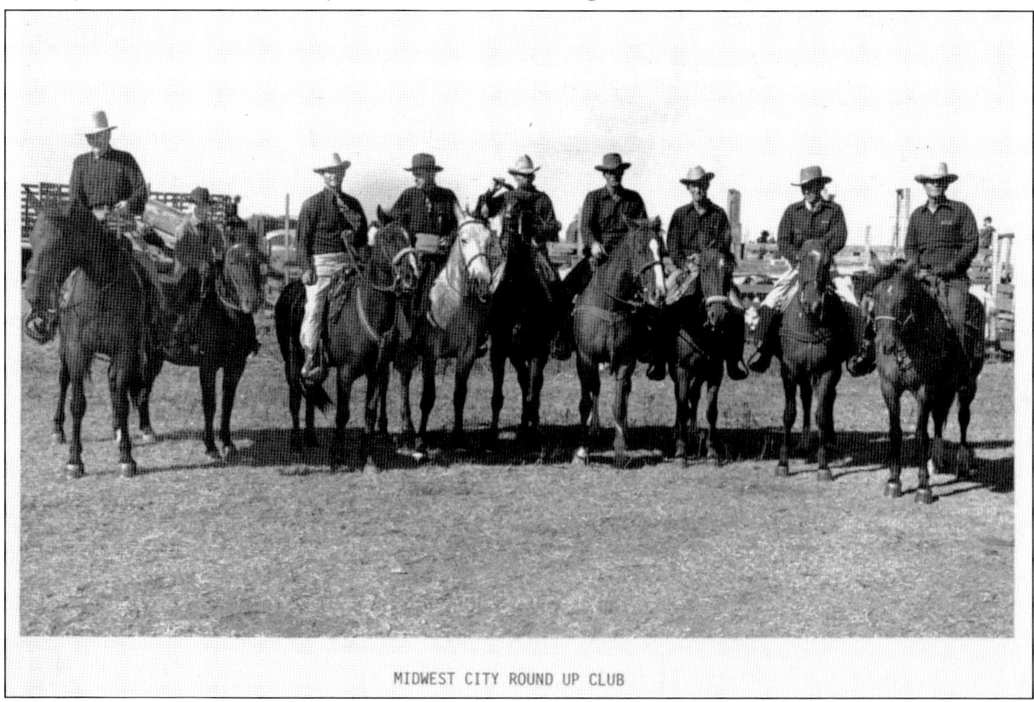

Pictured here is one of the many shops in downtown Midwest City located off Twenty-Ninth Street in the 1940s. It was called the Olive Dyer Dress Shop. Shirtwaist dresses were all the rage during this time period of women's fashion. (Courtesy of the Midwest City High School History Center.)

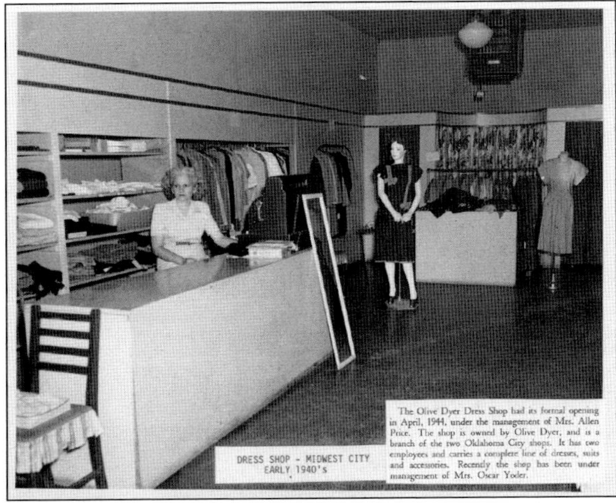

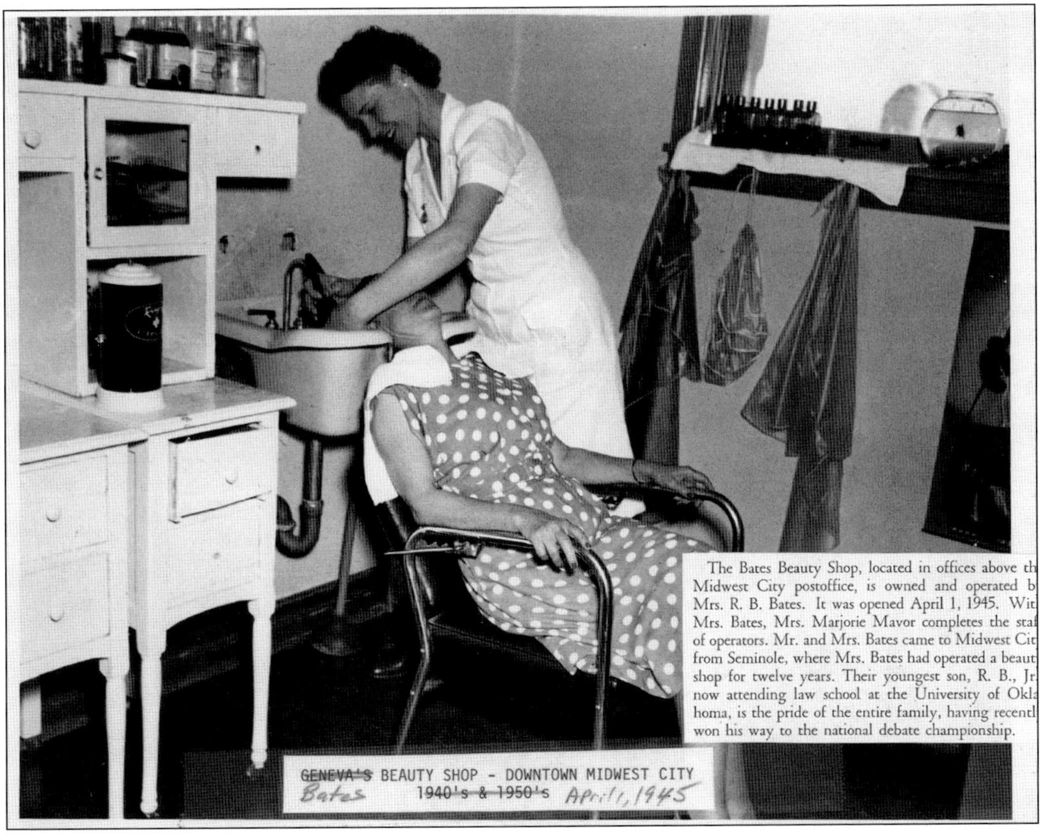

Barbers and beauty shops were very popular in the 1940s, and Midwest City was no exception. This photograph was taken in April 1945 at the Bates Beauty Shop, located in an office above the Midwest City Post Office. The shop was owned and operated by a Mrs. R.B. Bates. It opened on April 1, 1945. With Mrs. Bates, Marjorie Mavor completed the staff of operators. According to the inset, "Mr. and Mrs. Bates came to Midwest City from Seminole [Oklahoma], where Mrs. Bates operated a beauty shop for 12 years. The youngest son, R.B. Jr., now attending law school at the University of Oklahoma, is the pride of their entire family, having recently won his way to the national debate championship." (Courtesy of the Midwest City High School History Center.)

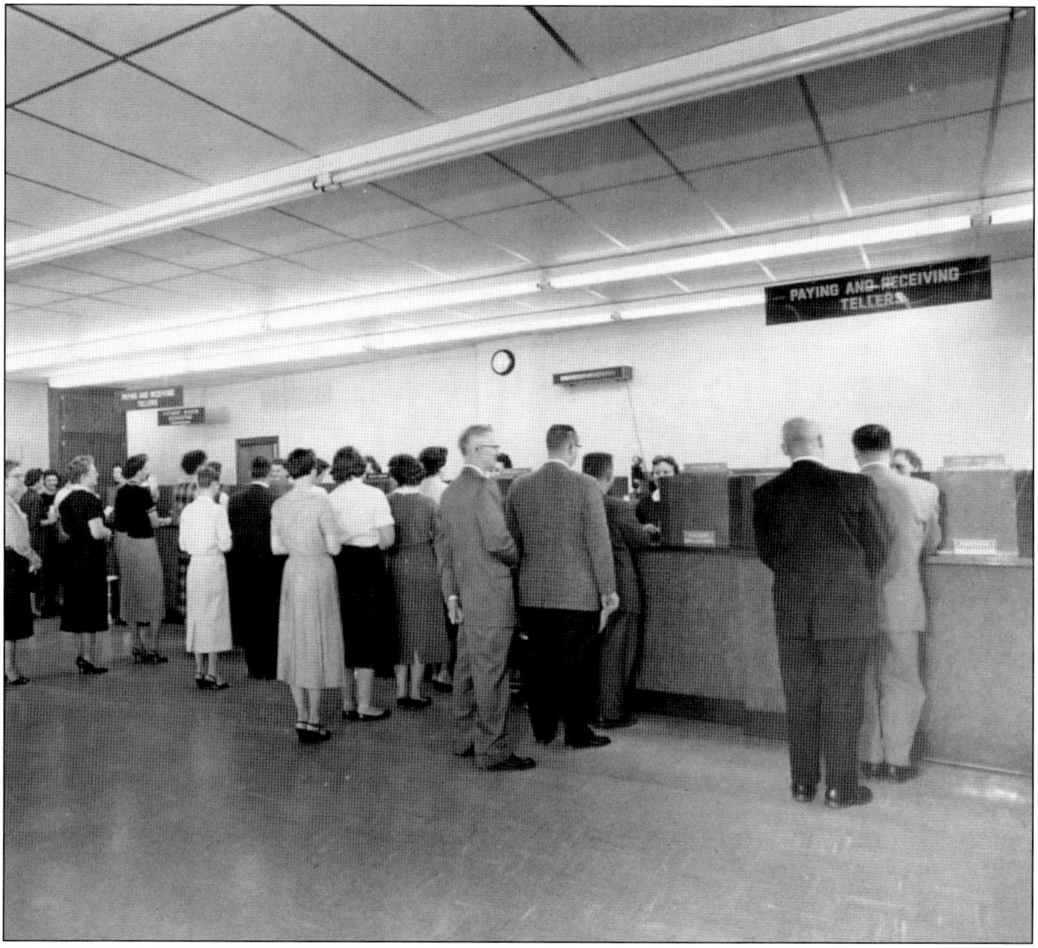

Going to the bank was a typical part of a Midwest Citians' routine. Men and women are working with the tellers at First National Bank of Midwest City in the 1950s. First National Bank of Midwest City, previously known as American State Bank, was one of the first banks in Midwest City. Below is a copy of one of the original checks of American State Bank from the 1940s. (Both, courtesy of FNB Community Bank.)

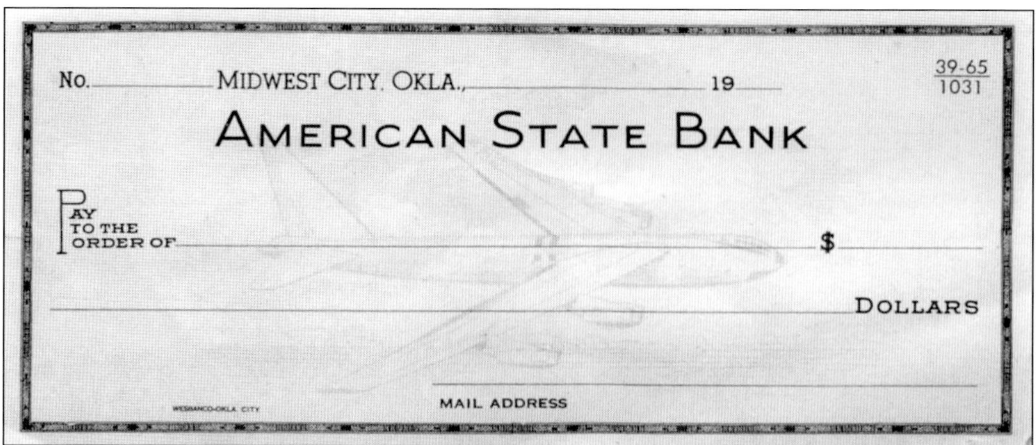

No. ______ MIDWEST CITY, OKLA., ______ 19 ___ 39-65/1031

AMERICAN STATE BANK

PAY TO THE ORDER OF ______ $ ______

______ DOLLARS

MAIL ADDRESS

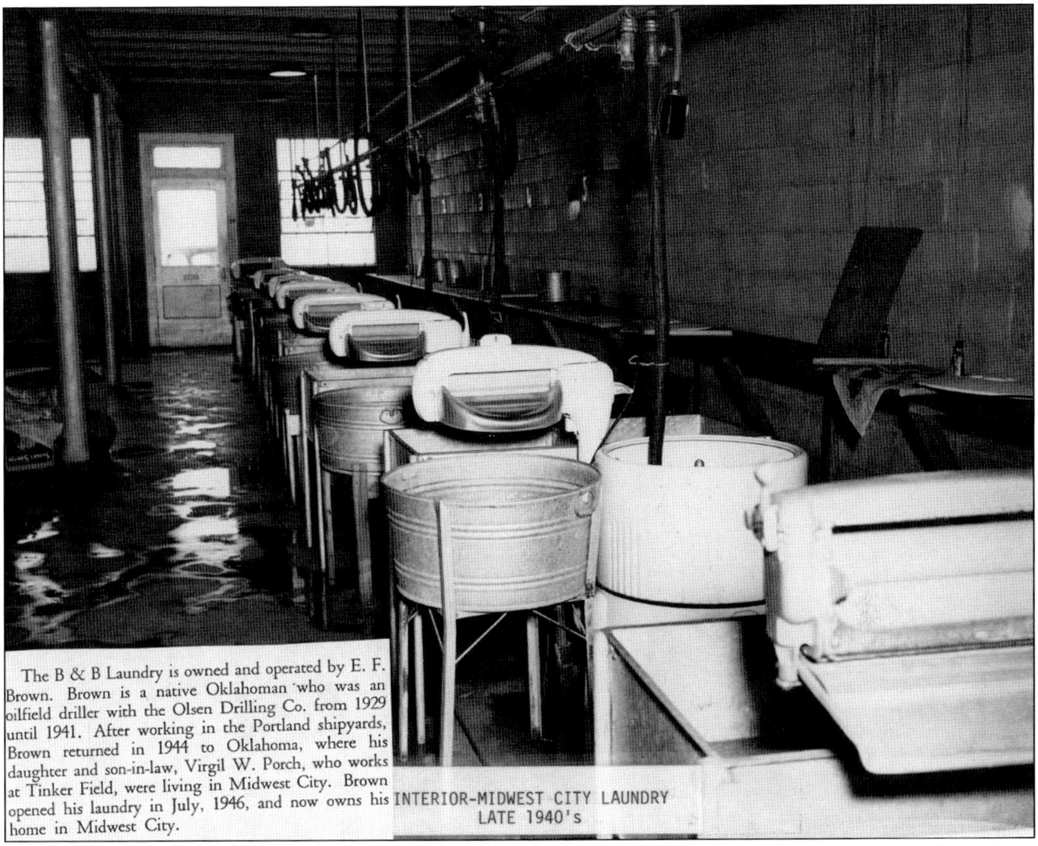

The B & B Laundry is owned and operated by E. F. Brown. Brown is a native Oklahoman who was an oilfield driller with the Olsen Drilling Co. from 1929 until 1941. After working in the Portland shipyards, Brown returned in 1944 to Oklahoma, where his daughter and son-in-law, Virgil W. Porch, who works at Tinker Field, were living in Midwest City. Brown opened his laundry in July, 1946, and now owns his home in Midwest City.

INTERIOR-MIDWEST CITY LAUNDRY
LATE 1940's

Laundry in the 1940s consisted of hand washing on a washboard from home or visiting laundries to wash and wring clothing, linens, and the like with a two-roller system called a "wringer" or "wrangle" to squeeze excess water out of wet clothes after washing. To dry, one would hang the items on a clothesline. Midwest City was home to a few public laundries, including B&B Laundry. B&B Laundry was owned by E.F. Brown, a native Oklahoman oil driller with Olsen Drilling Co. and a Midwest City resident. It was opened in July 1946. His daughter and son-in-law Virgil W. Porch worked at Tinker Field and lived in Midwest City. (Courtesy of the Midwest City High School History Center.)

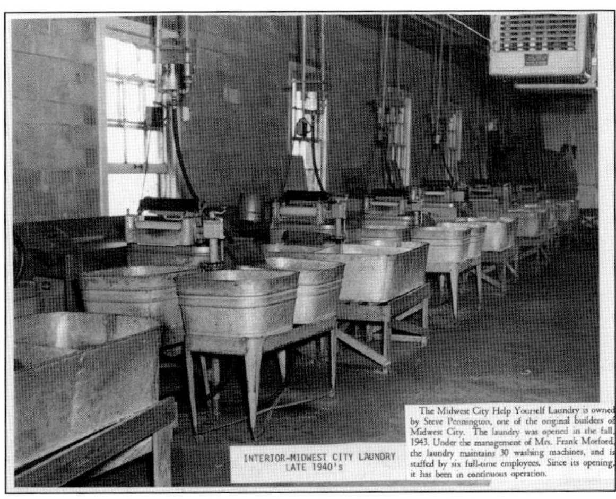

In addition to B&B Laundry, the Midwest City Help Yourself Laundry was owned by one of the original builders of Midwest City, Steve Pennington. The laundry had 30 washing machines and six full-time employees in the late 1940s. (Courtesy of the Midwest City High School History Center.)

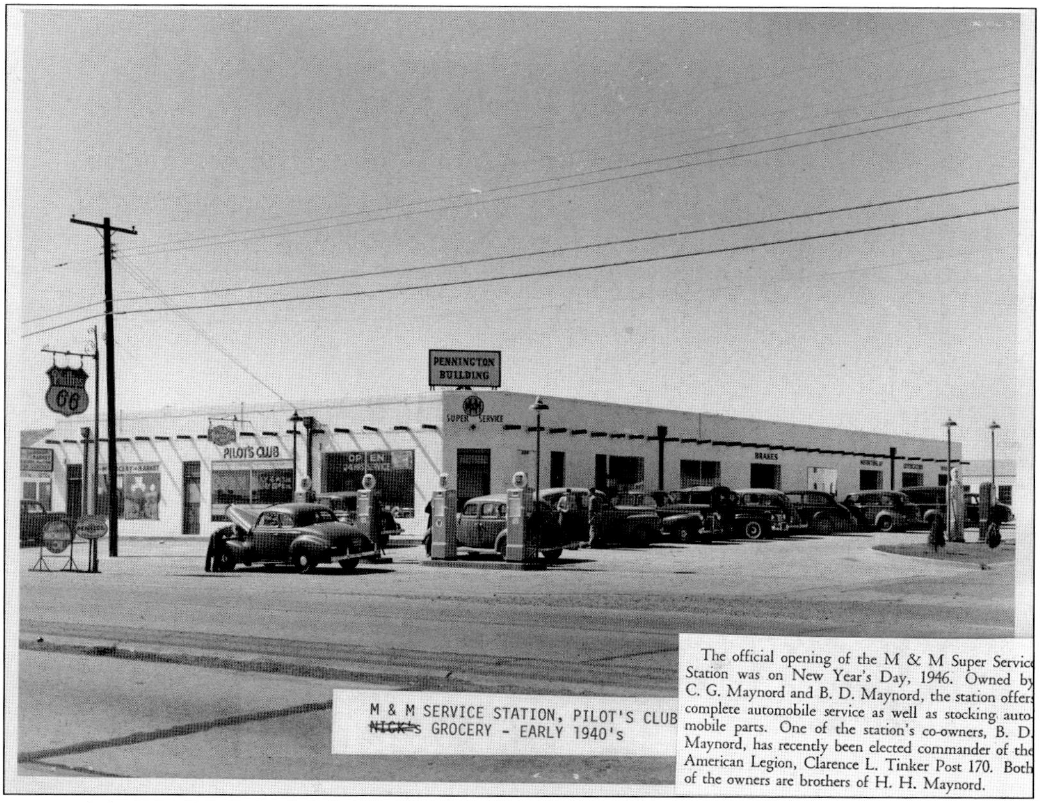

M & M SERVICE STATION, PILOT'S CLUB
~~NICK'~~s GROCERY - EARLY 1940's

The official opening of the M & M Super Service Station was on New Year's Day, 1946. Owned by C. G. Maynord and B. D. Maynord, the station offers complete automobile service as well as stocking automobile parts. One of the station's co-owners, B. D. Maynord, has recently been elected commander of the American Legion, Clarence L. Tinker Post 170. Both of the owners are brothers of H. H. Maynord.

Pictured above is the outside of the M&M Super Service; M&M Grocery and Market; and Midwest City's tavern, Pilot's Club, located on Twenty-Ninth Street in 1943. The description states, "The official opening of the M&M Super Service Station was on New Year's Day, 1946. Owned by C.G. Maynord and B.D. Maynord, the station offers complete automobile service as well as automobile parts. One of the station's co-owners, B.D. Maynord, has recently been elected commander of the American Legion, Clarence L. Tinker Post 170. Both of the owners are brothers of H.H. Maynord." Below is the inside of the Pilot's Club, and the inset reads, "The Pilots' Club, Midwest City's tavern, is owned by H.E. Nelson and managed by H.R. Houston. It was opened for business in January 1946. Houston, who attended the University of Oklahoma, came to Midwest City in June of the same year, after a period of service with the Navy. Both he and the owner of the Pilot's Club live in Midwest City." (Both, courtesy of the Midwest City High School History Center.)

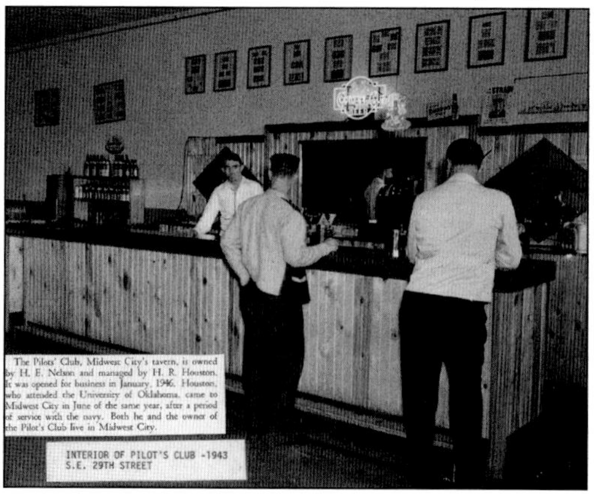

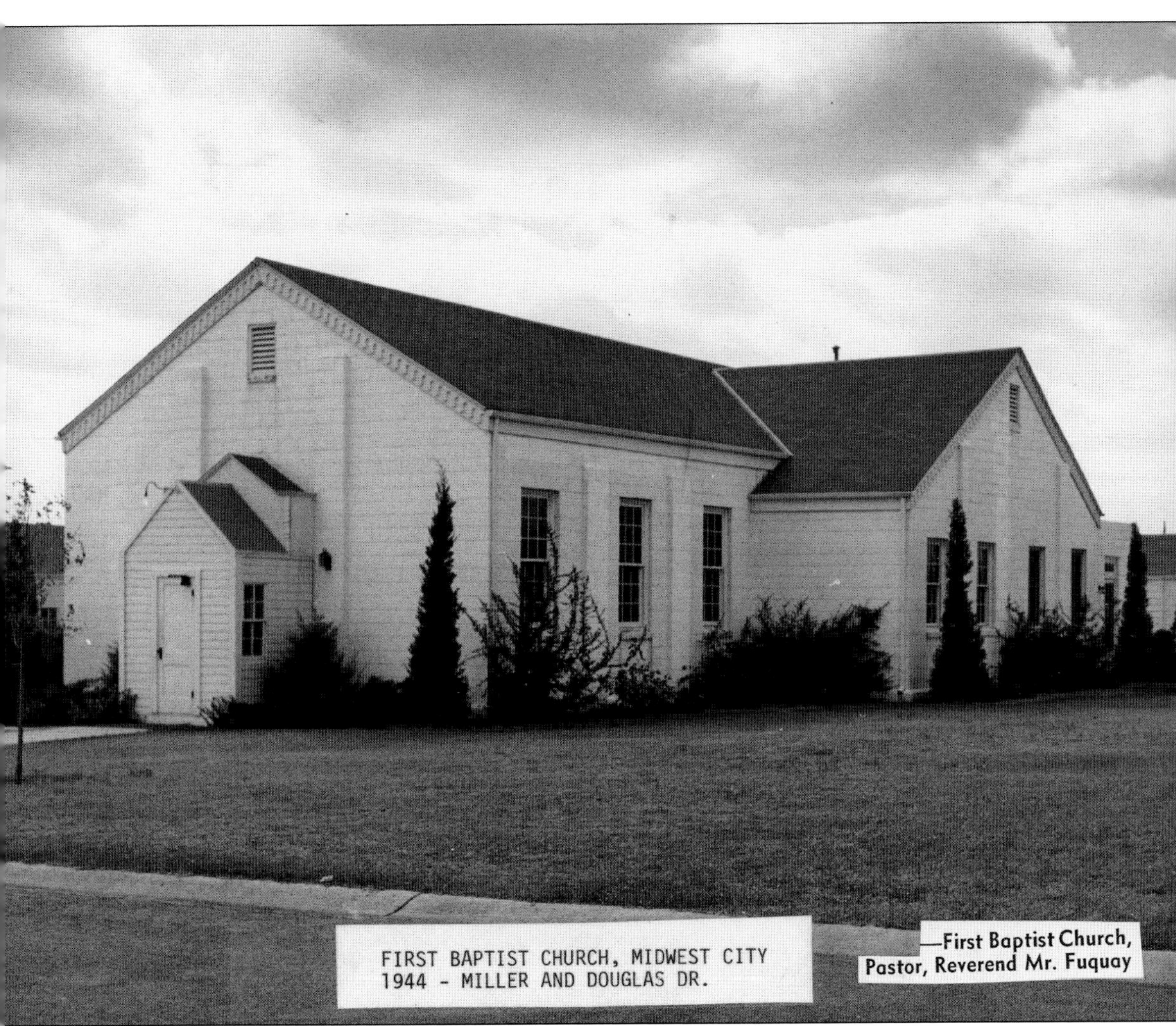

Churches were one of the tenets of Midwest City culture and city design by Bill Atkinson. One of the first churches in the Original Mile, First Baptist Church of Midwest City, was originally located on North Marshall Drive and East Douglas Drive before later moving to Rickenbacker Drive and Kittyhawk Drive. This photograph was taken in 1944, and the church was led by Rev. Murray Fuquay. The church later moved to another building in 1947, where it remained for 70 more years, giving back to the community. (Courtesy of the Midwest City High School History Center.)

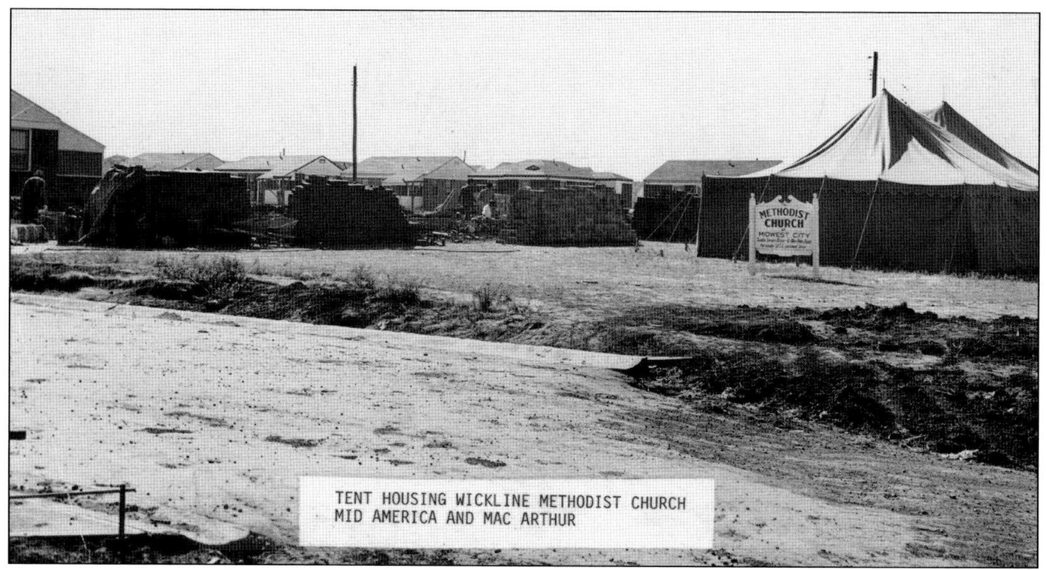

Another early church in Midwest City was Wickline Methodist Church, founded at Mid-America Boulevard and East MacArthur Drive and led by minister D. Allen Polen. It was the home church to the Atkinson family. Many of the city's leaders were a part of this congregation over the years. The original building pictured below still existed as late as the 2020s. (Both, courtesy of the Midwest City High School History Center.)

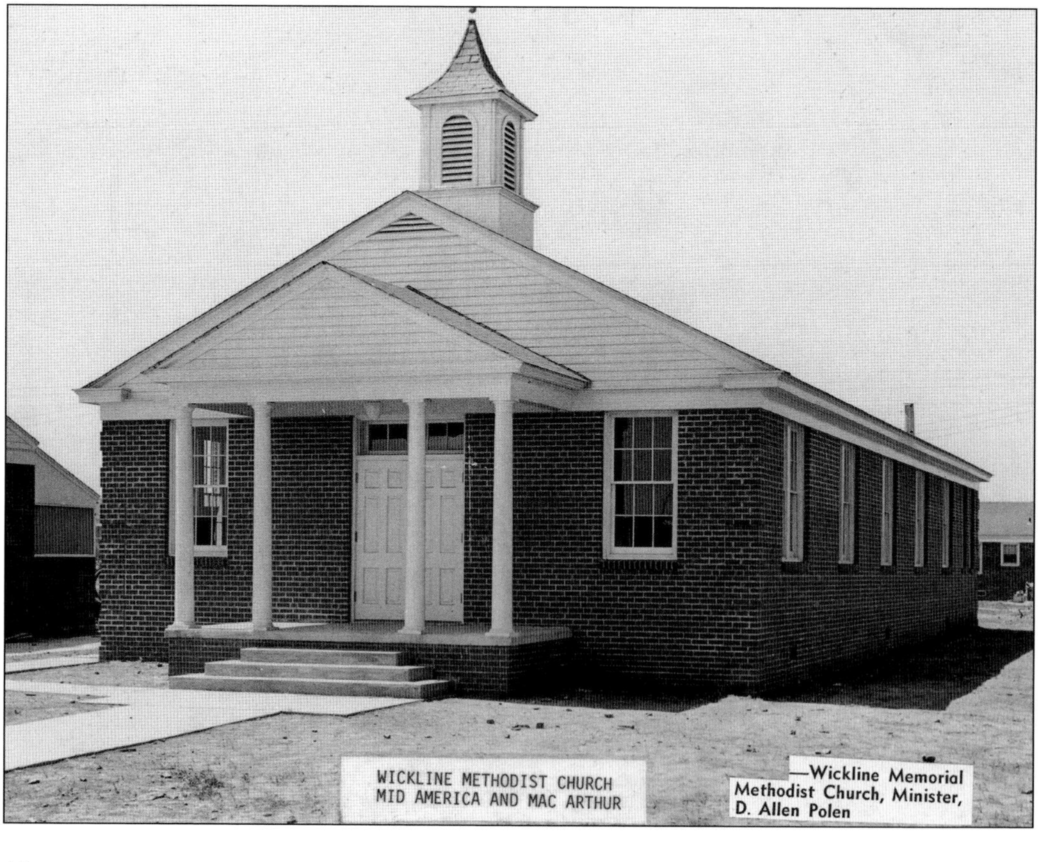

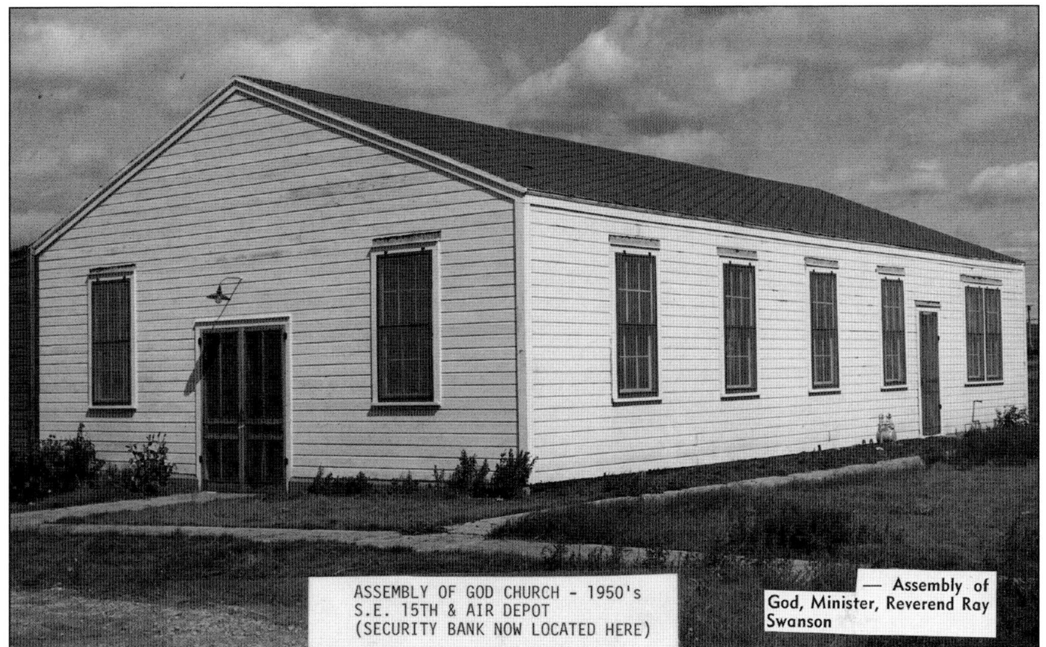

A diverse representation of denominations was present upon the founding of Midwest City as people flocked to take care of the spiritual lives of the new residents. Above is the Assembly of God Church once located on Fifteenth Street and Air Depot Boulevard and led by Rev. Roy Swanson. Below is the First Christian Church off Key Boulevard and East Douglas Drive, led by Rev. Robert G. Nelson. First Christian Church was still in operation at the same location through the 2020s. (Both, courtesy of the Midwest City High School History Center.)

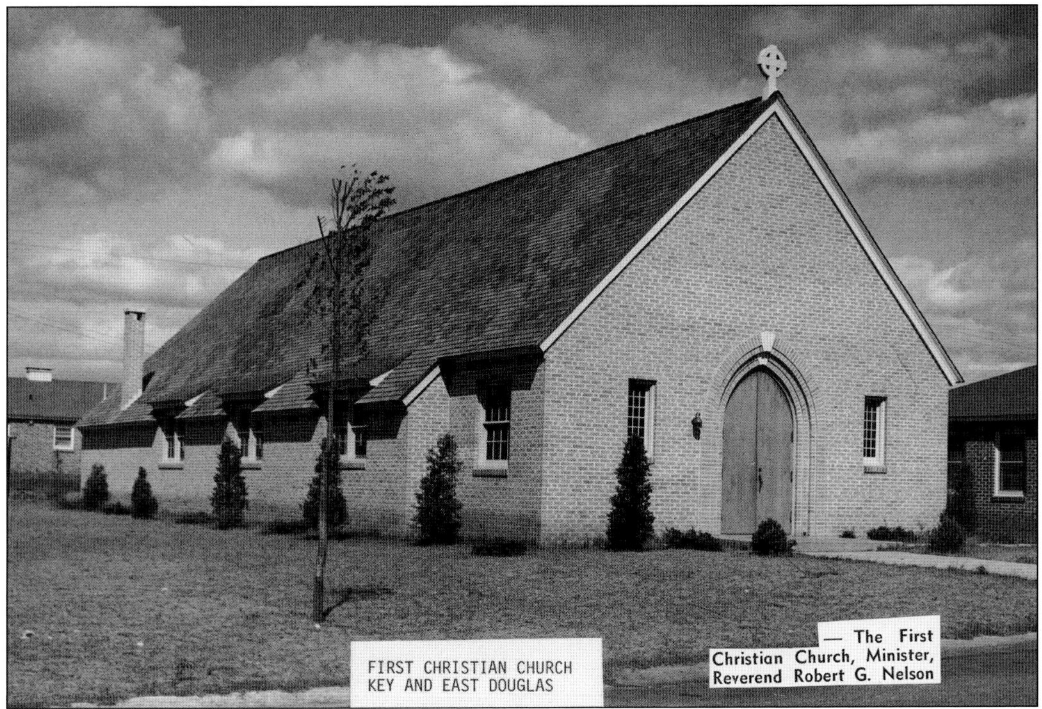

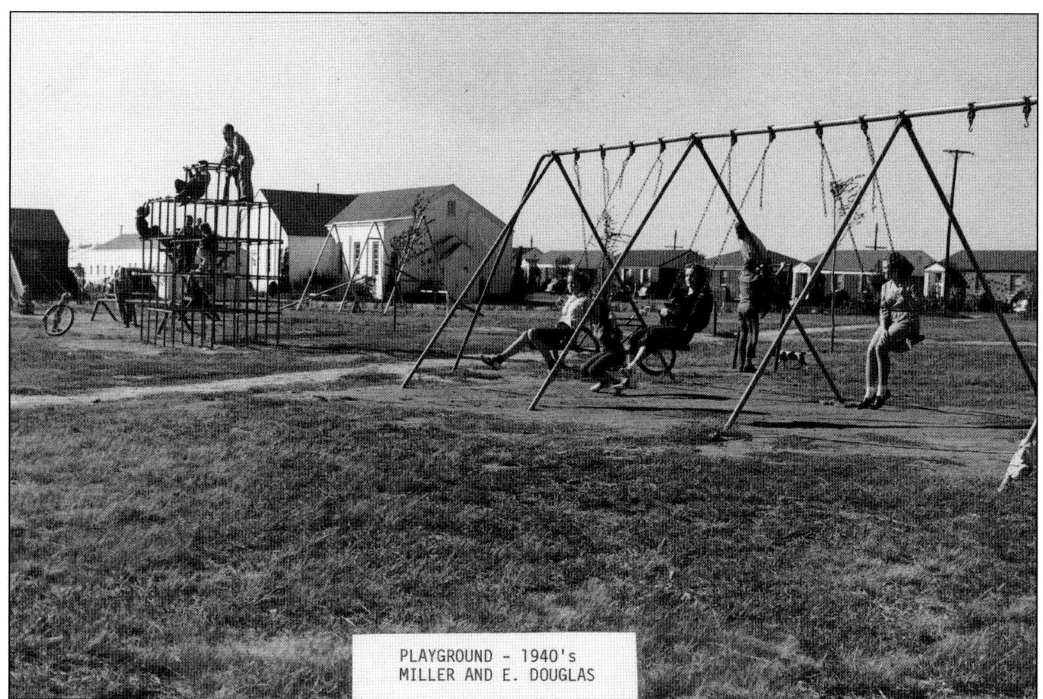

Midwest City prided itself on its parks and their close proximity to the homes and schools. Pictured above is a playground in the Original Mile of Midwest City on Mid-America Boulevard and East Douglas Drive. The white building behind the playground is the original First Baptist Church of Midwest City in the 1940s. The location of the photograph below is unknown but is approximately from the 1950s. (Above, courtesy of the Midwest City High School History Center; below, courtesy of the Oklahoma Historical Society.)

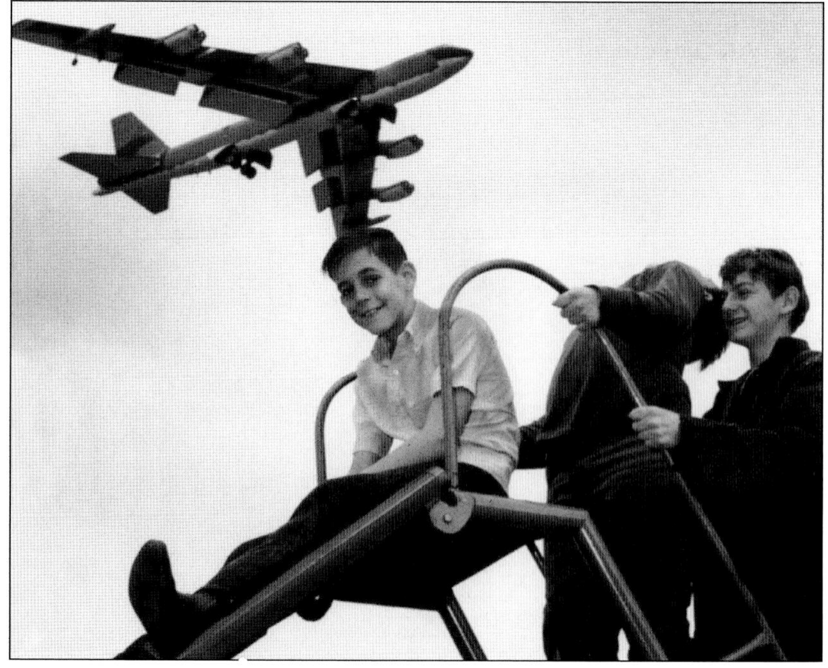

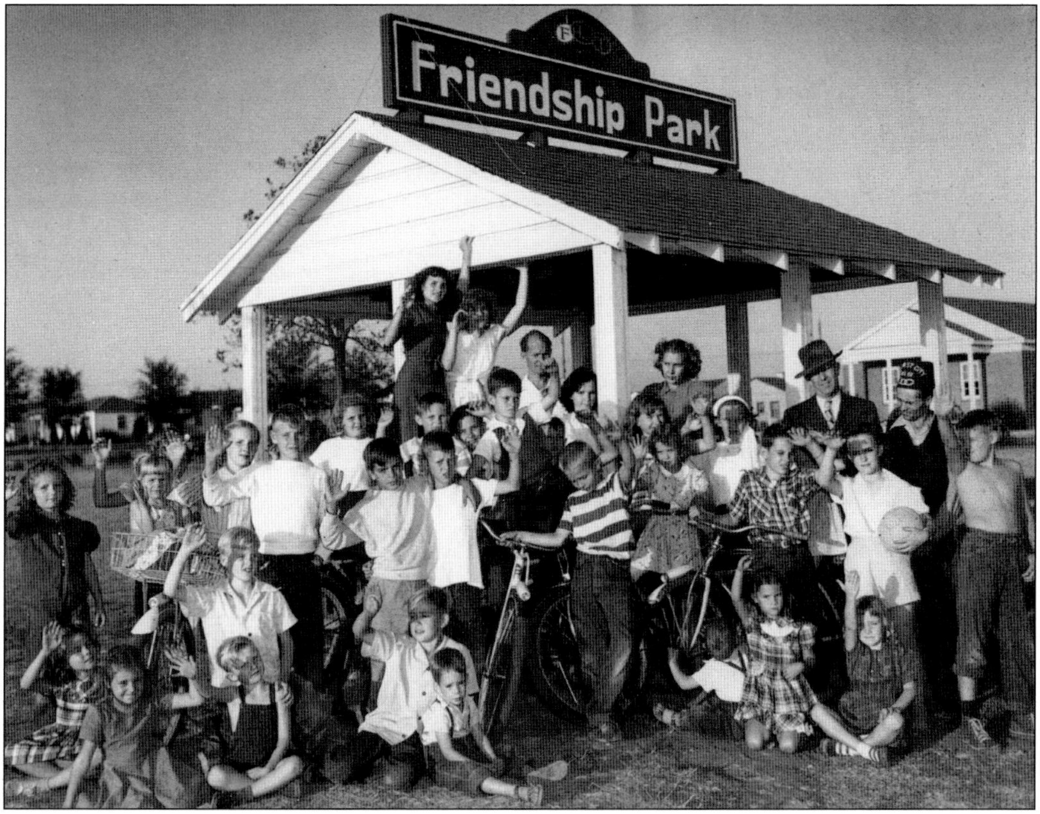

Parks were an essential part of Midwest City values. Families wanted places to recreate and for their children to play. Friendship Park (above) was replaced with Elks Park after a new water tower was installed in 2011. Lions Club Park (below) was located on Midwest Boulevard near the city swimming pool. The pool was later moved to Douglas Drive and East Reno Avenue. As mentioned in the introduction, Midwest City grew to over 30 parks and walking trails by the 2020s, continuing the legacy of outdoor recreation. (Both, courtesy of the Rose State College Foundation.)

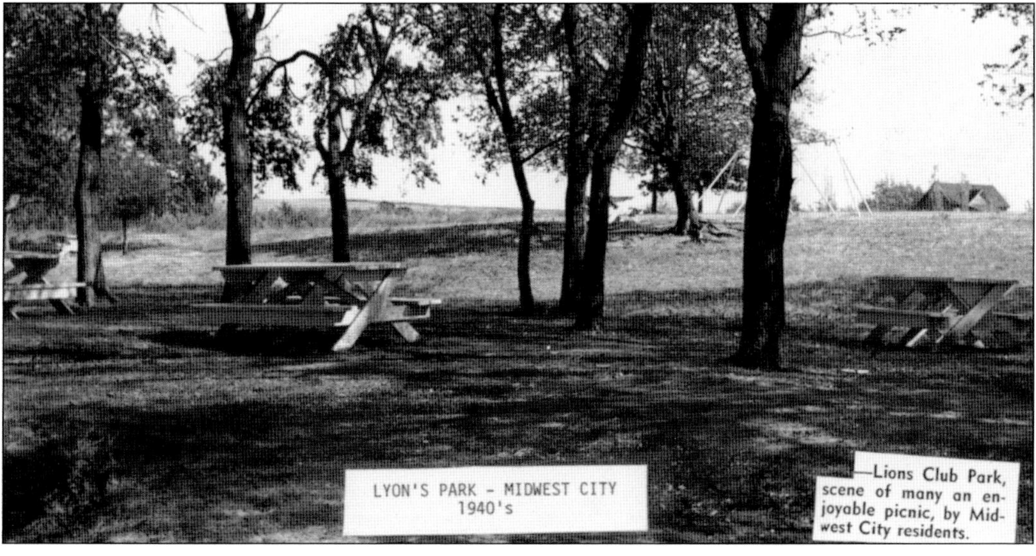

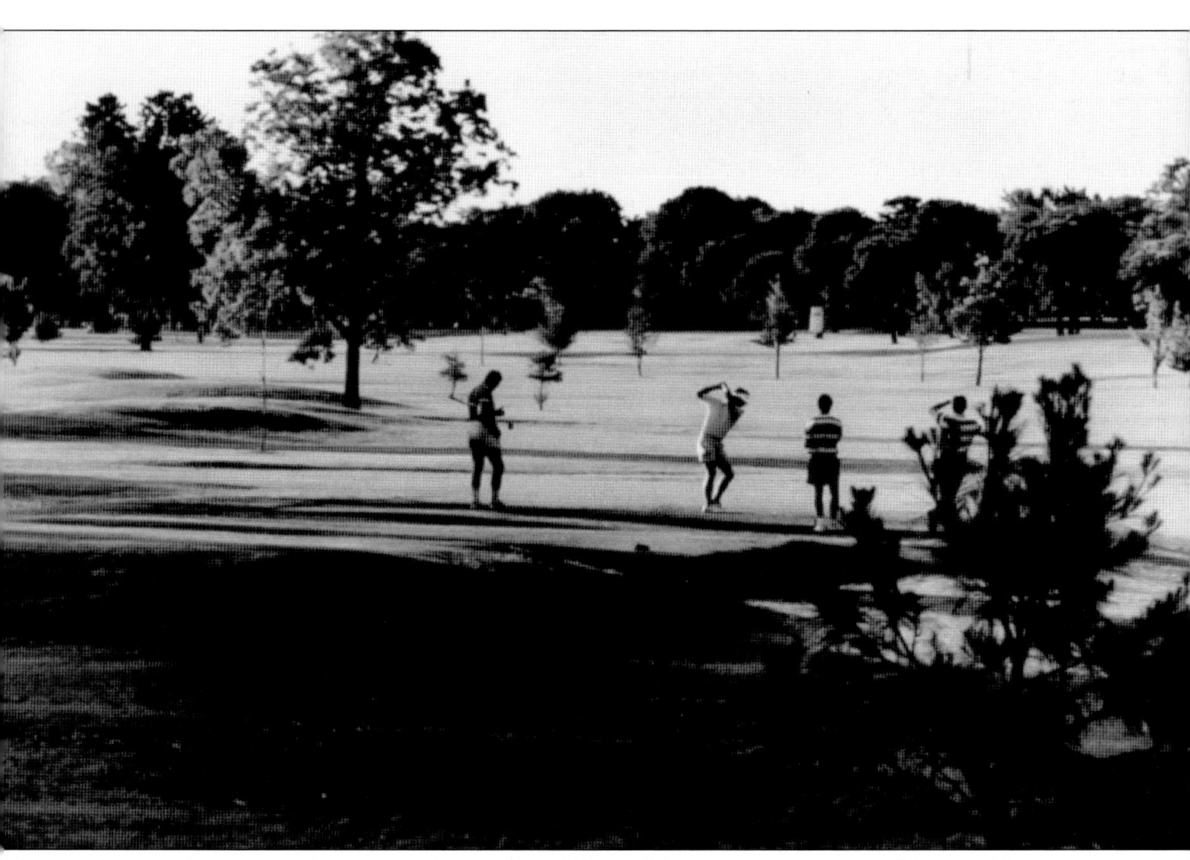

To continue providing amenities to the Midwest City community, an 18-hole golf course was installed in Midwest City and was later named after John Conrad. John Conrad was a Midwest City pharmacist who opened six drugstores throughout the Oklahoma City area, with the first two stores in Midwest City with Ozzie Marr called Conrad-Marr Drug Store. The John Conrad Regional Golf Course was originally designed and built in 1971 by Floyd Farley. It is crafted within 160 acres of challenging tree-lined roughs, bubbling creeks, water features, and rolling hills. The course privileges local golf enthusiasts, competitions, and fundraisers, and many students of golf teams in the area practice there. It received a large reconstruction thanks to the 2018 Moving Forward G.O. Bond Program, which cost $5.1 million. (Courtesy of Oklahoma Historical Society.)

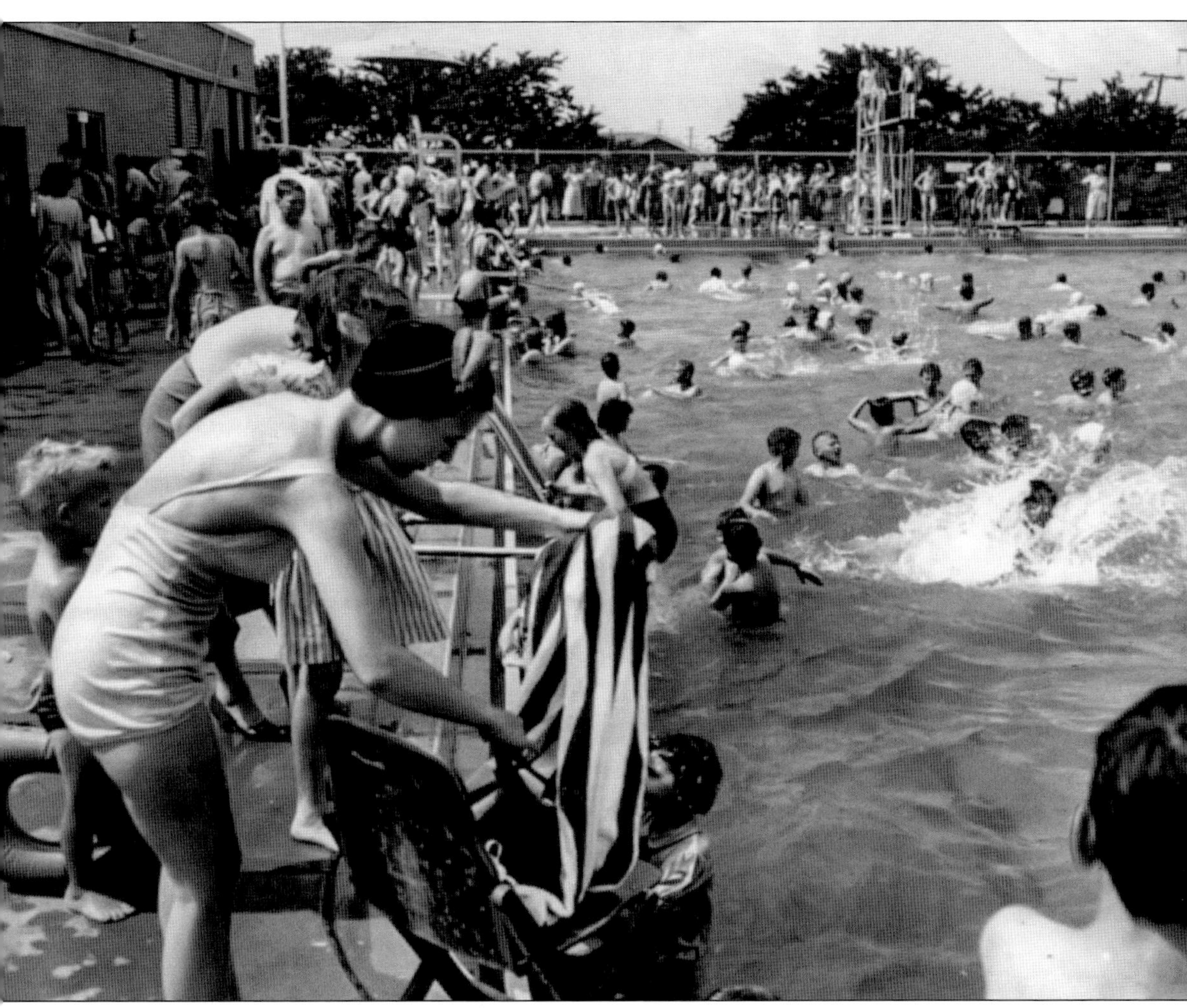

Midwest City had a few public pools in its day, including an exclusive pool for the Elks Golf and Country Club. The first community pool was located in Original Mile. The main public pool was located in Midwest City's Regional Park (formerly called John Conrad Regional Park) and opened in the early 1970s. (Courtesy of the Oklahoma Historical Society.)

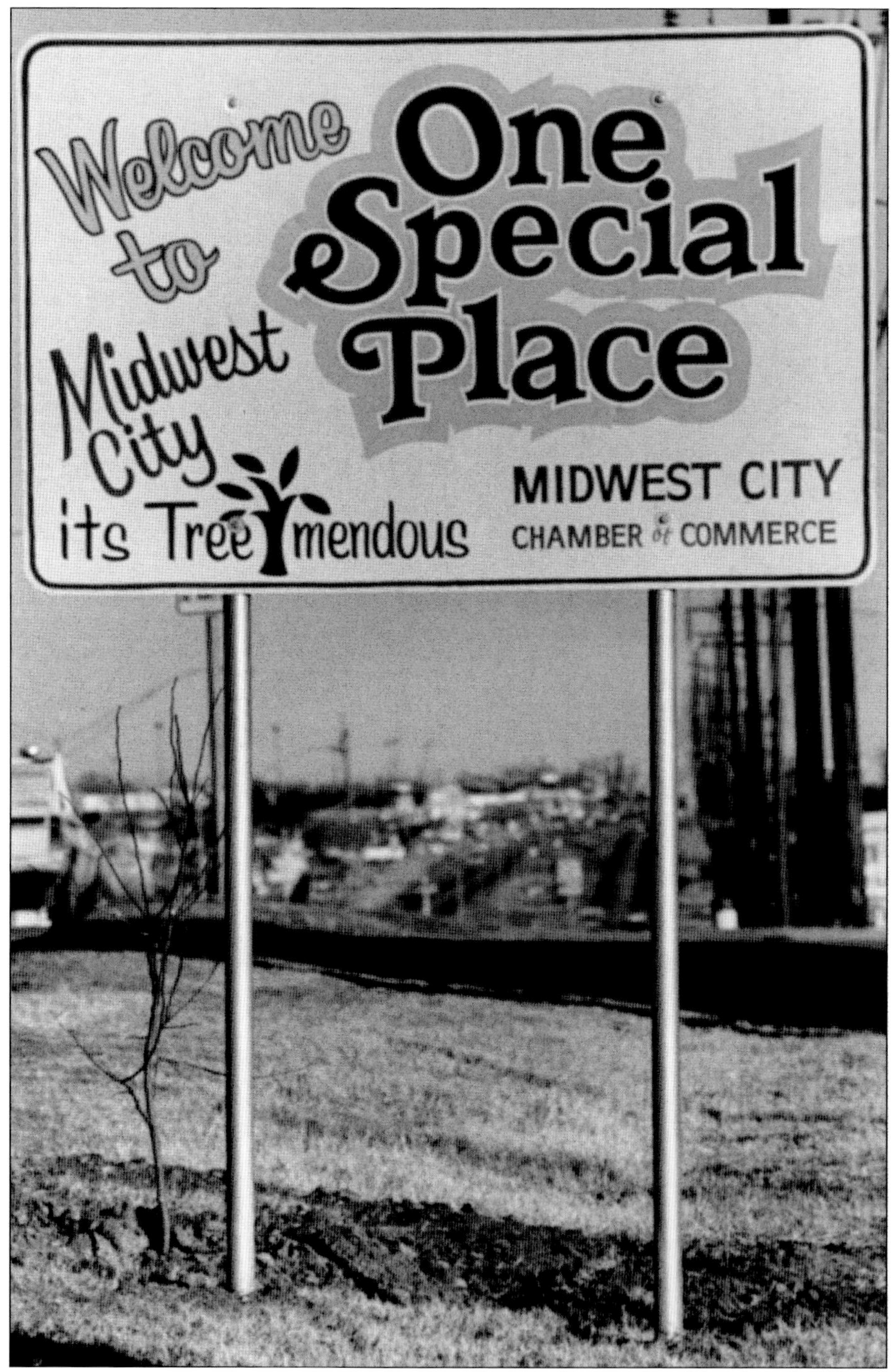

This sign was posted at the entrance of Midwest City and sponsored by the Midwest City Chamber of Commerce. It is unknown if related, but in 1980, Midwest City established a "Tree Board" comprised of residents appointed by the city council to plant new trees and remove dead, dying, diseased, or dangerous trees. Trails and cultivating nature became a focus of the 1980s–early 2000s. (Courtesy of the Rose State College Foundation.)

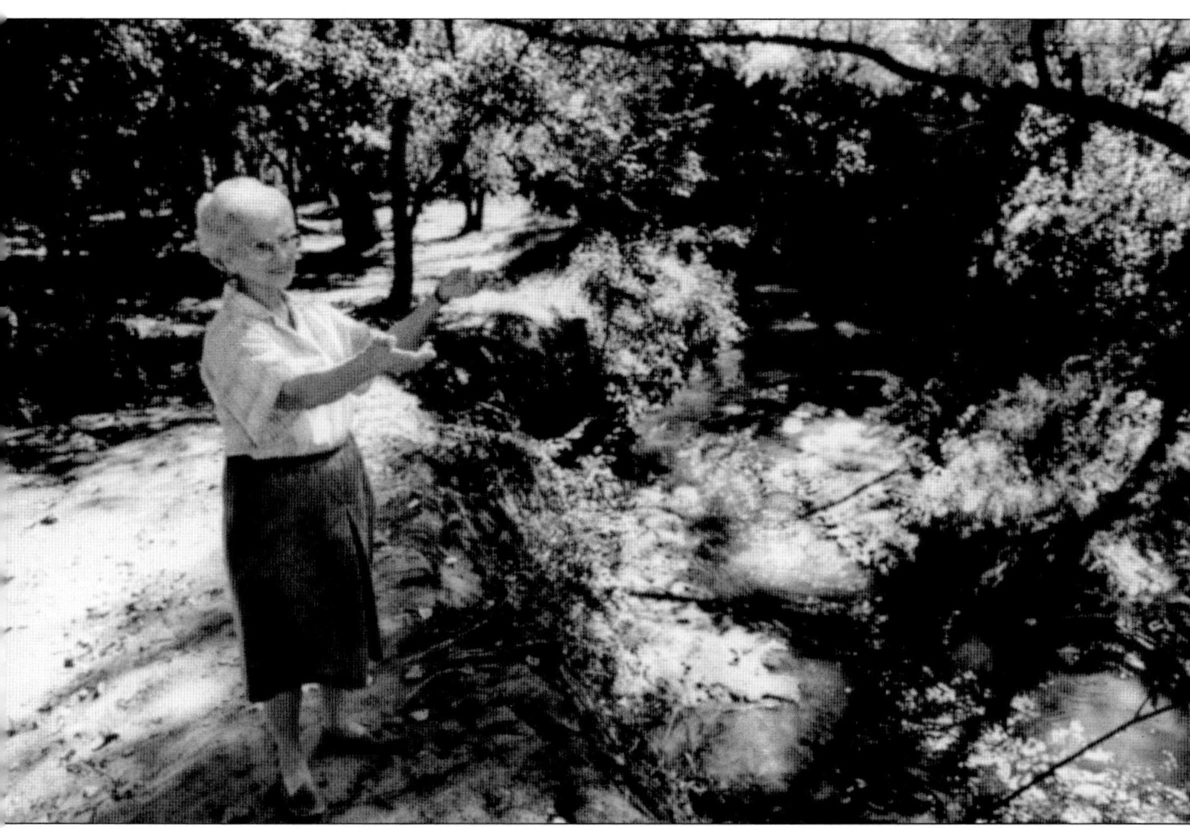

As Midwest City developed over time, residents expressed desires for walking trails and opportunities to be more physically active in nature. Pictured here is Hazel Craddock, devout Midwest City community member and former president of the Midwest City Porcelain Artists, on the MWC (Midwest City) nature trail during a beautification project in 1994. (Courtesy of Oklahoma Historical Society.)

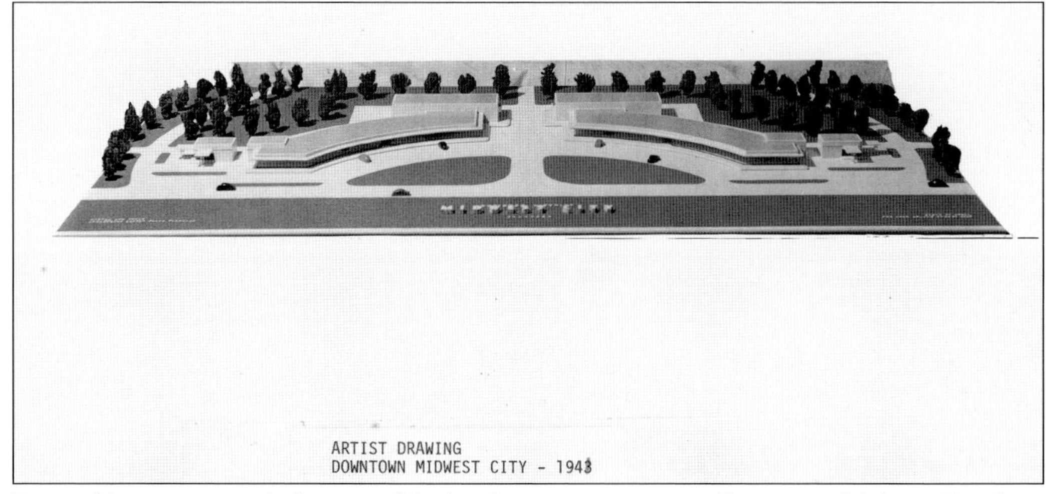

Pictured here is an artist's drawing of the local commerce center in Downtown Midwest City from the 1940s to the 1990s. This was located right across from the Tinker Air Field gate on Twenty-Ninth Street and held many shops essential to the lives of local residents. In the foreground of the image below, a man and his young child window shop in winter during the 1950s at the downtown shopping area in Midwest City. A woman in a fur coat strolls as she perhaps runs errands while observing Christmas decorations in the windows. (Above, courtesy of the Midwest City High School History Center; below, courtesy of Rose State College Foundation.)

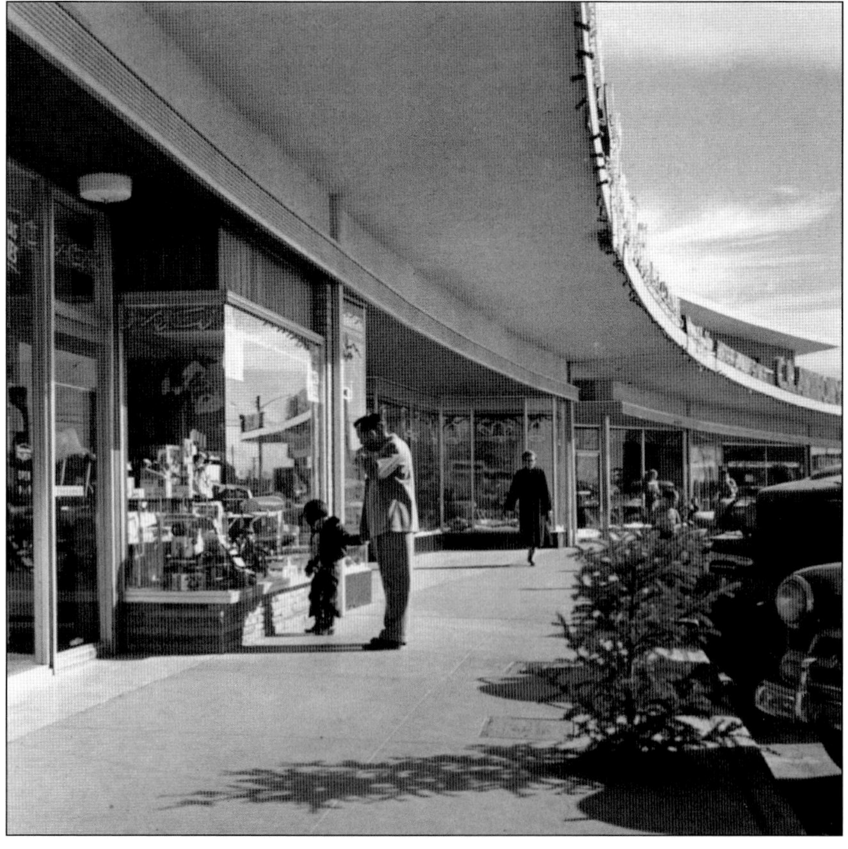

Four

Midwest City Commerce

To be a self-sustaining city, Midwest City had to have its own diversified economy. The Midwest City Chamber of Commerce attracted, invited, and cultivated business life in Midwest City while Atkinson and his team levied connections to bring more influential business leaders to choose Midwest City as their home. The Midwest City Chamber of Commerce developed a strong relationship with Tinker and its rotating base commanders. With new life coming in through Tinker and providing an intriguing opportunity for developers and investors, Midwest City became home to small businesses and industrial corporations. Throughout the years, Midwest City became a flagship city for the surrounding rural areas in health care, shopping, and employment opportunities. With Interstate 40 and Highway 62 cutting through Midwest City, many customers and employees could easily access the area to support the economy. Some businesses came and went, such as the nearby General Motors plant, which was located in Oklahoma City near the border of Midwest City and employed many Midwest City residents. Midwest City was fertile ground for many entrepreneurs, including large brands such as the first Crest Discount Foods, the first Sam's Club in all of the United States, Humpty Dumpty grocery, Conrad-Marr Drug Store, and Hudiburg Chevrolet. In its totality, Midwest City never forgot its roots of supporting Tinker Air Force base with civil-service employees to support national defense alongside military service men and women.

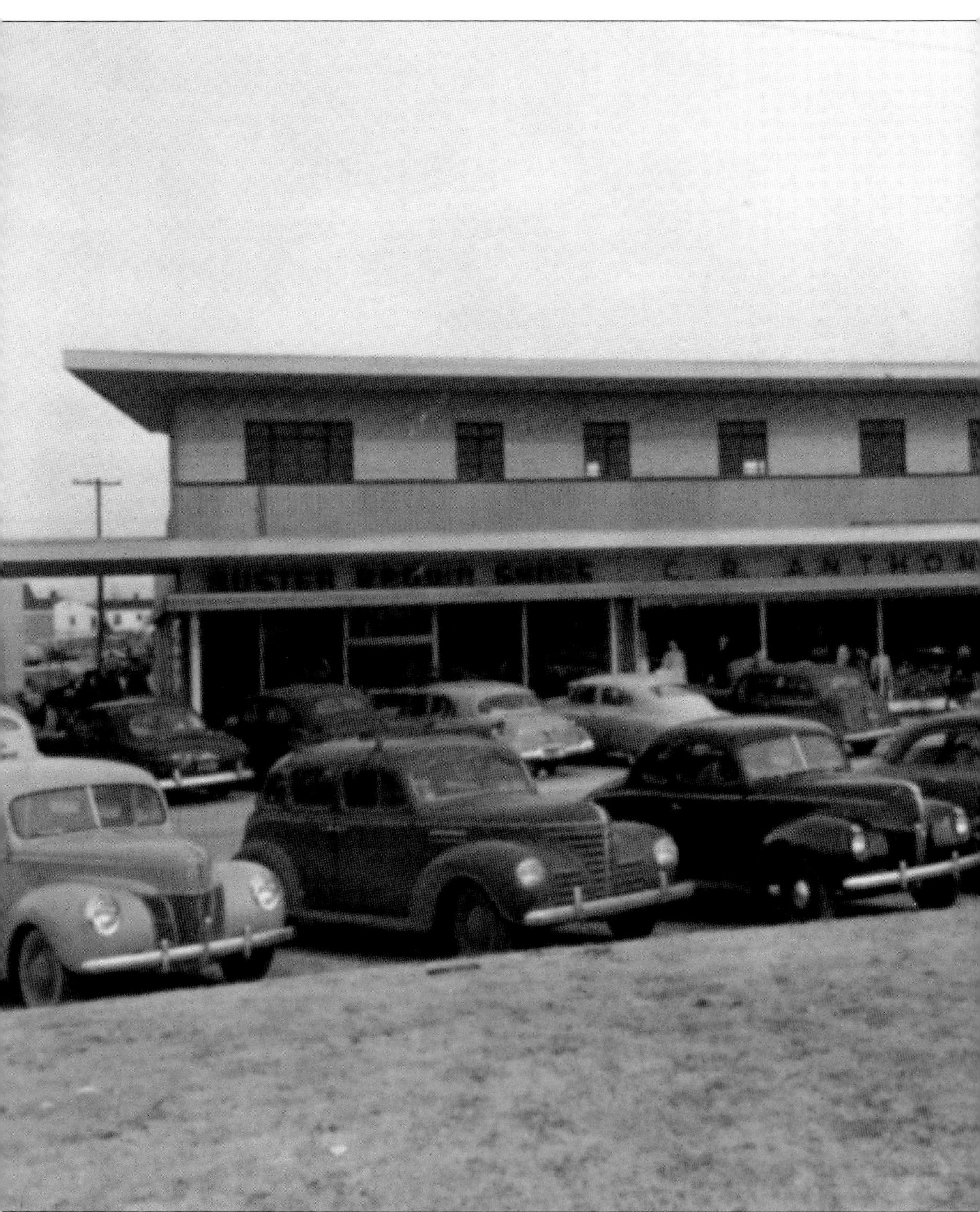

The Midwest City business district consisted of strip shopping centers, small office buildings, and car lots in the 1940s and 1950s. Being one of the visions of Atkinson himself, the area offered a variety of businesses that included 18 stores such as banks, retail, grocery, drugstore, beauty shop,

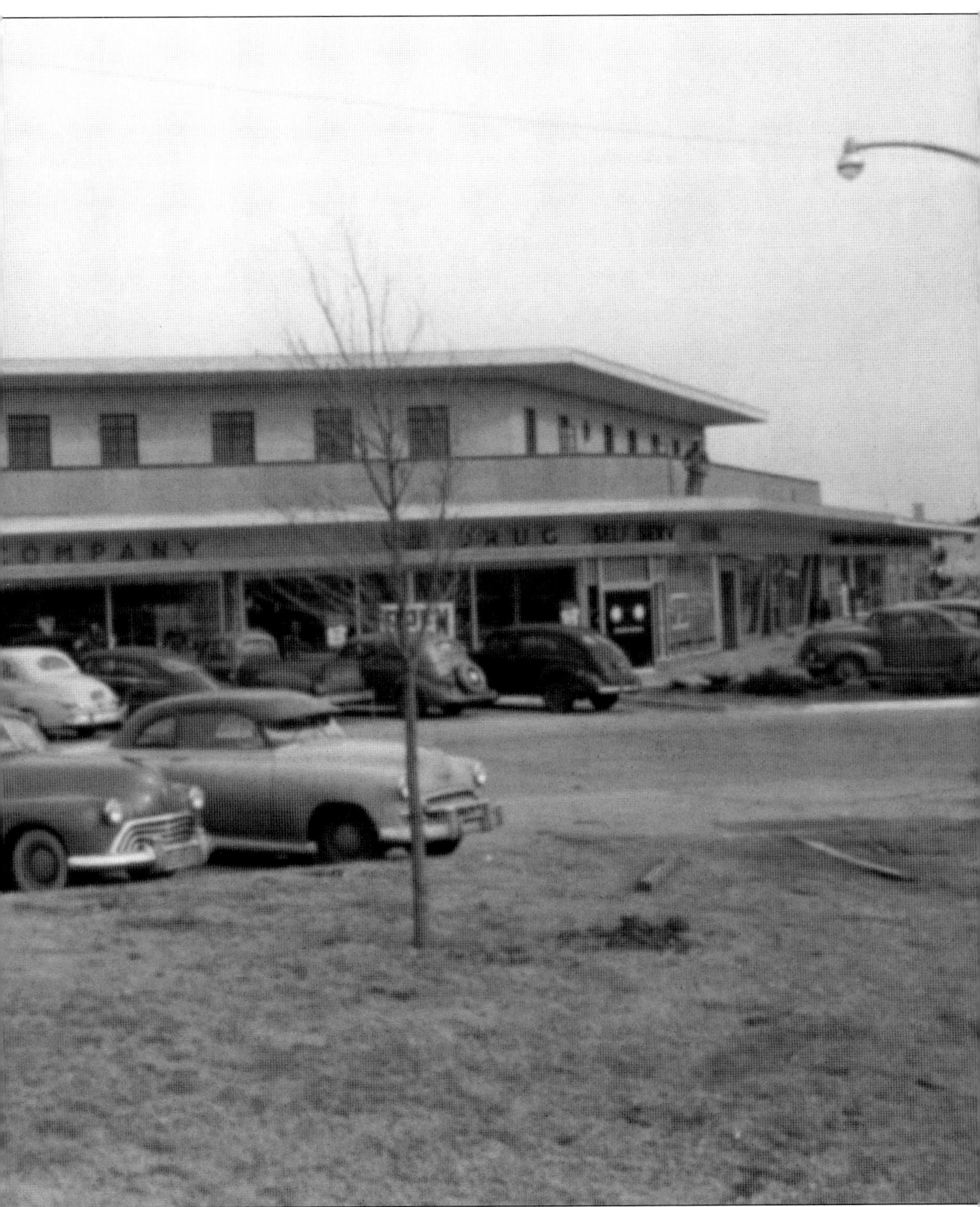

gift shops, and more. It was designed in a semicircular arrangement and was the center of Midwest city living. It was said that any need someone had could be accessed from the Twenty-Ninth Street business district. (Courtesy of Rose State College Foundation.)

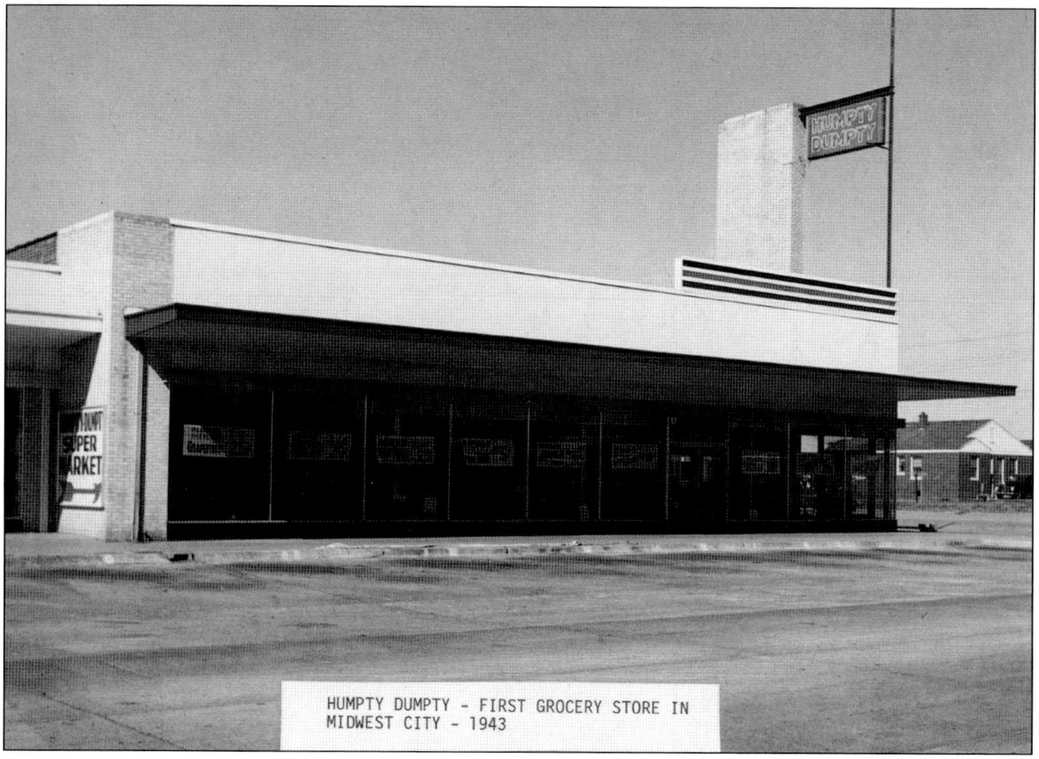

HUMPTY DUMPTY - FIRST GROCERY STORE IN MIDWEST CITY - 1943

As he planned the city, Atkinson personally invited the founder of Humpty Dumpty, Sylvan Goldman, to place his operations in Midwest City, even building a customized location to encourage his investment. This Humpty Dumpty store was one of the first grocery stores in Midwest City and was located off Twenty-Ninth in downtown. In the photograph below, recognizable brands like Folgers can be seen, as can Midwest Citians shopping in the background. One can also see shopping carts, an invention created in Oklahoma by Humpty Dumpty's founder. He created the shopping cart after growing up working in dry goods stores and seeing customers make multiple trips to carry and purchase their items. (Both, courtesy of Midwest City High School History Center.)

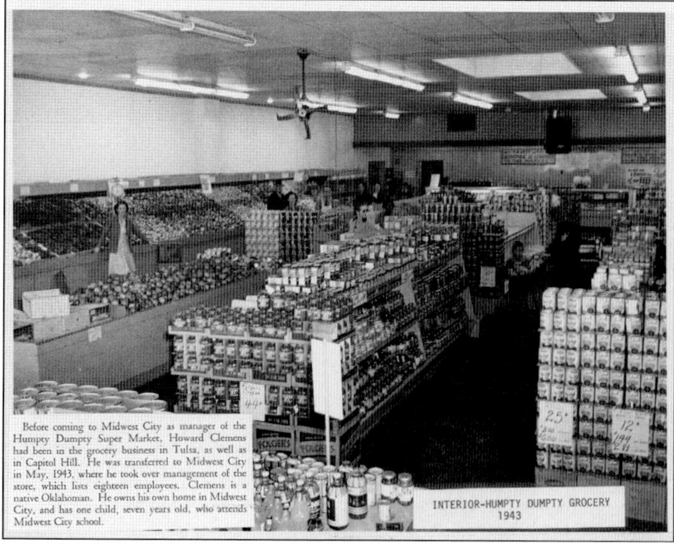

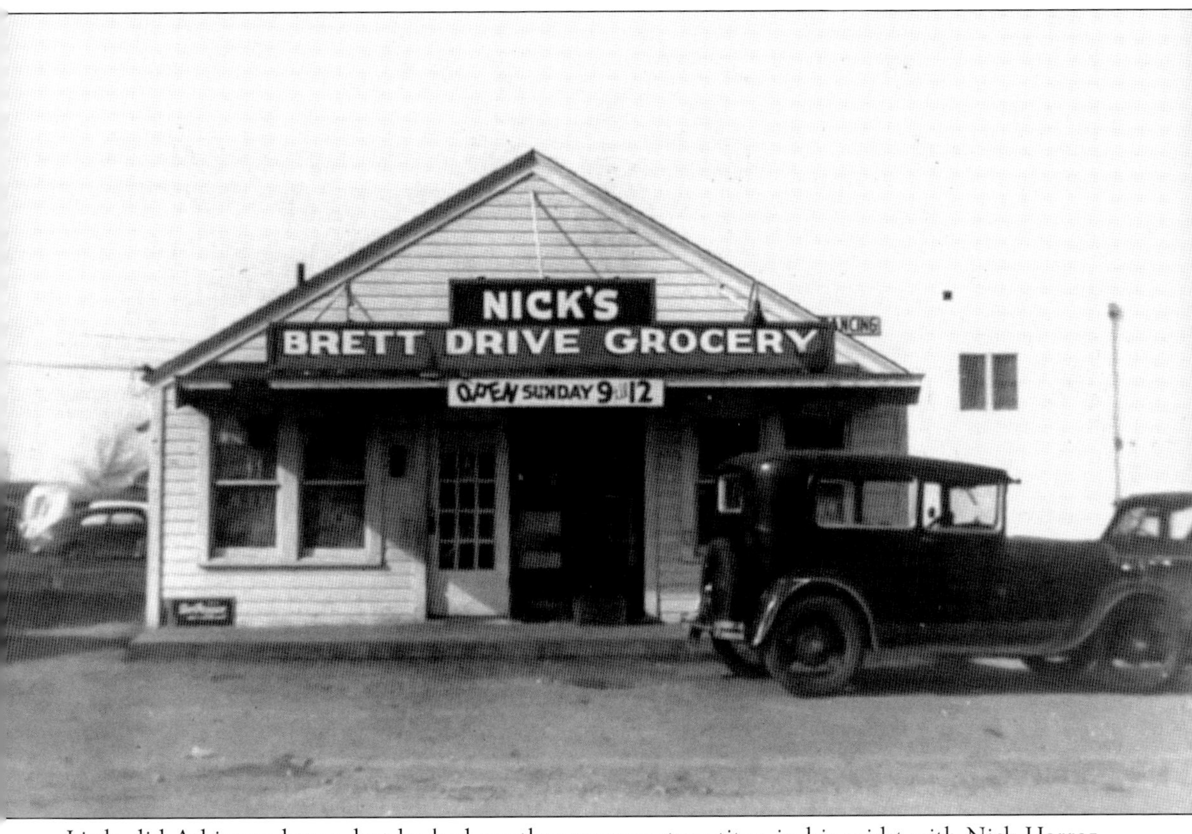

Little did Atkinson know, but he had another grocery store titan in his midst with Nick Harroz of Brett Drive Grocery. Nick Harroz, a veteran fighter pilot, transformed this small drive-thru grocery into a grocery store empire known as Crest Discount Foods, later shortened to Crest Foods. Harroz's store was originally located on Brett Drive, as pictured here in the 1940s. Harroz moved his store in 1964 to the Ridgecrest shopping center on Reno Avenue and found inspiration for a new brand name, a derivative of Ridgecrest from customers shortening the name while writing checks. By the 2020s, Crest had grown to nine locations and was passed down to the next generation of the Harroz family. (Courtesy of the Rose State College Foundation.)

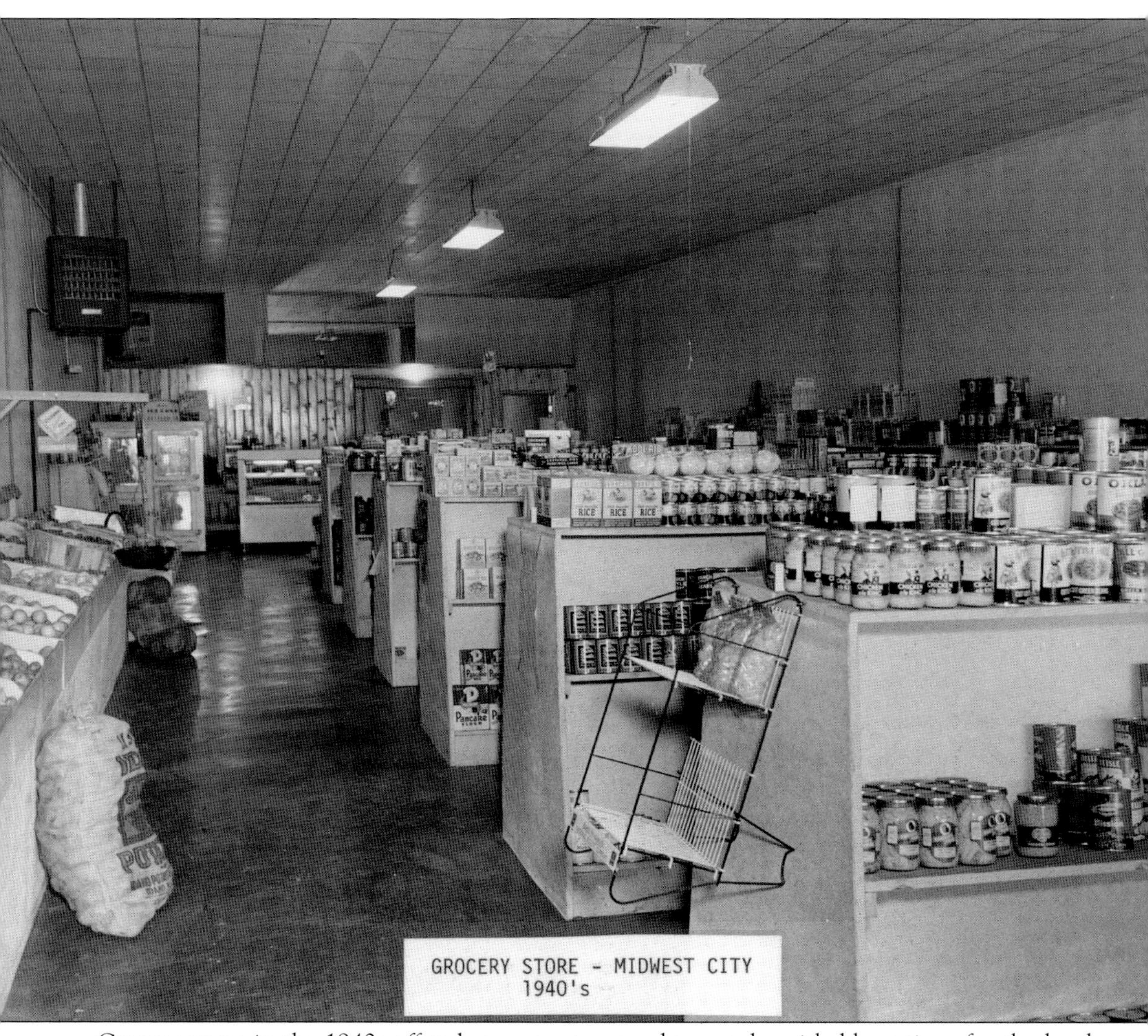

Grocery stores in the 1940s offered many pantry, produce, and perishable options for the local shopper. In this Midwest City store, Texiana Rice boxes, Kool-Aid mixture, cans of ranch-style beans, and Pillsbury Pancake Flour are sold. On the far left side of the photograph in the back of the store, a sign offers ice-cold buttermilk, which was very convenient for the times. (Courtesy of the Midwest City High School History Center.)

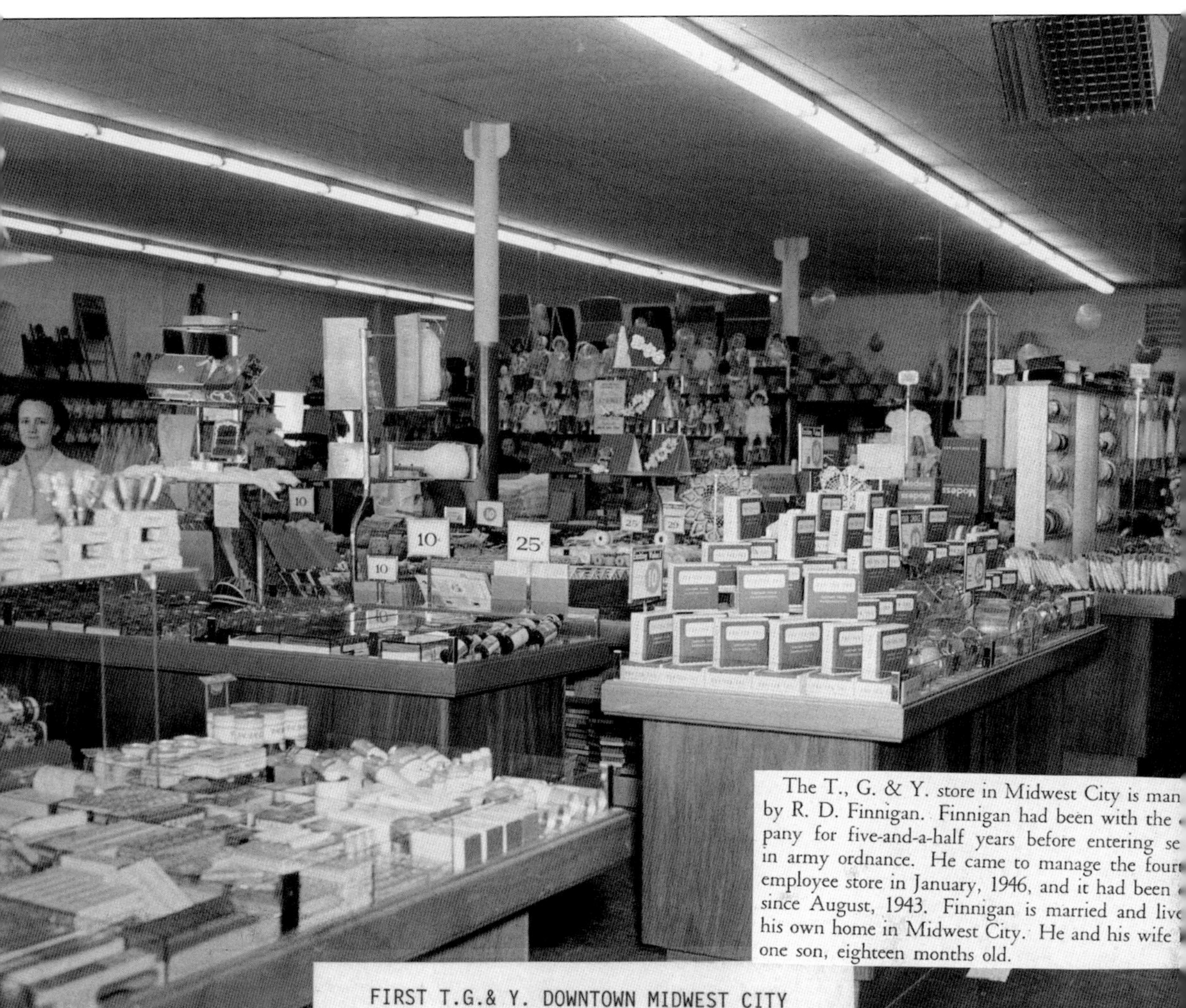

A TG&Y was much like a five-and-dime store (a store that sold items for 5¢, 10¢, and 25¢) and offered a variety of items from children's toys and washboards to accessories and home goods. It was located in the downtown shopping center. (Courtesy of the Midwest City High School History Center.)

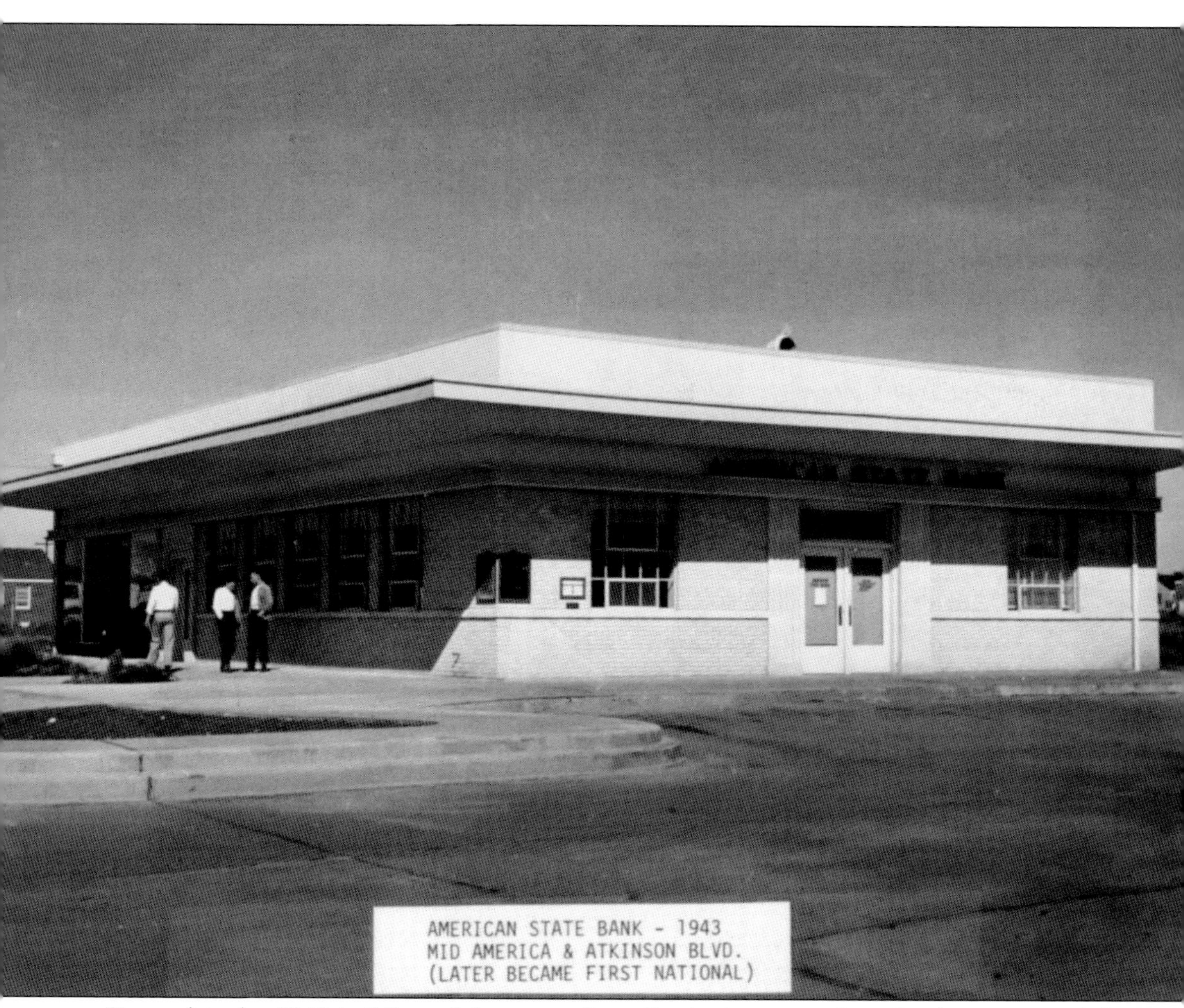

Pictured is the 1943 building of American State Bank. American State Bank was one of the original banks in Midwest City and later became FNB Community Bank. Originally owned by Harold Empie, it was sold to Henry Croak in 1954. In 1962, the name changed to First National Bank of Midwest City. (Courtesy of FNB Community Bank.)

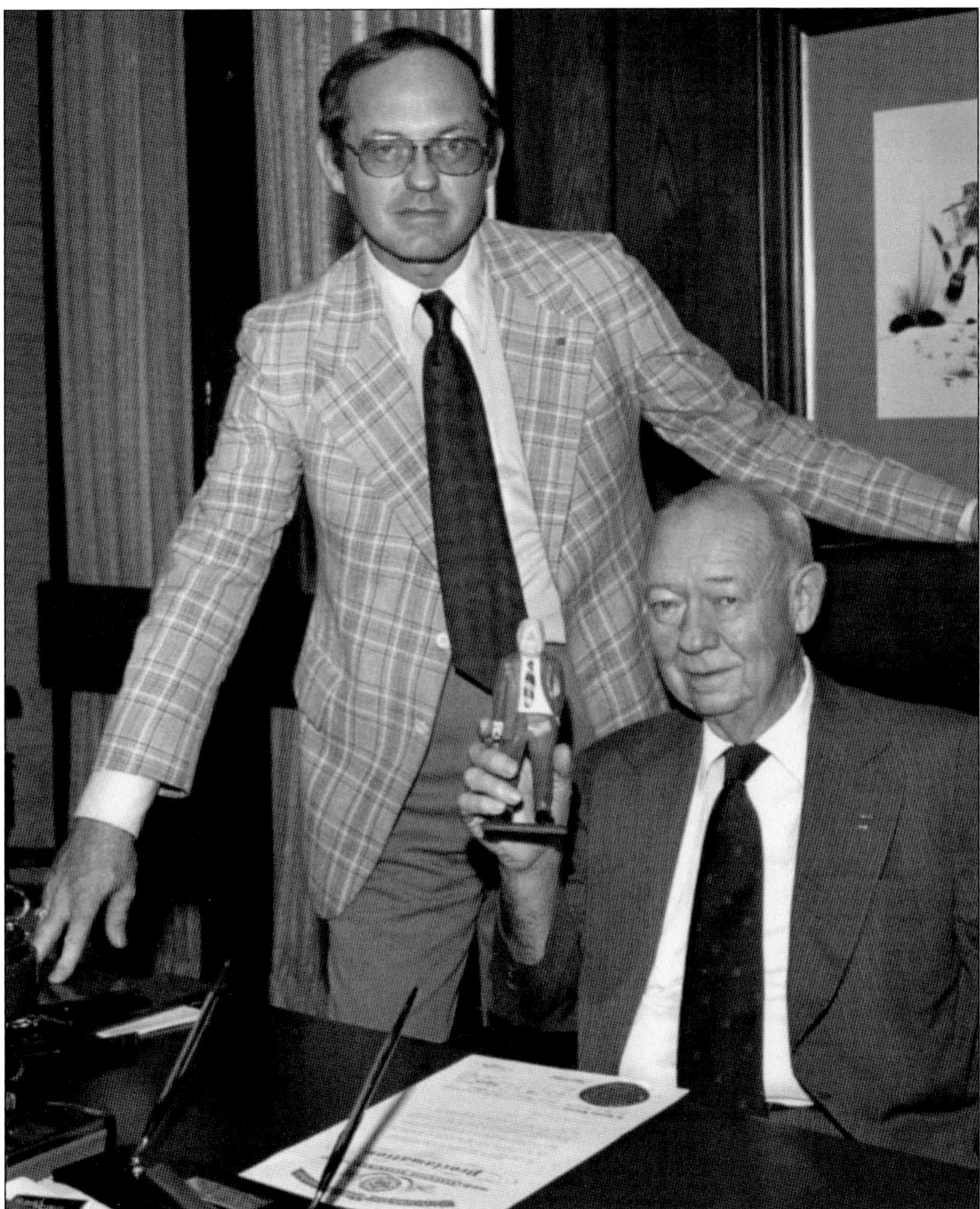

Pictured above is Robert Croak and his father, Henry Croak. Henry passed the business to his son Robert and then Robert to his children, William H. "Bill" Croak, John Croak, and Shelly Croak-Yocham. As of the 2020s, Bill Croak, John Croak, Kyle Croak, and Julie Croak Waddle are continuing their family's legacy. The bank continues to be a supporter of the Midwest City community. (Courtesy of FNB Community Bank.)

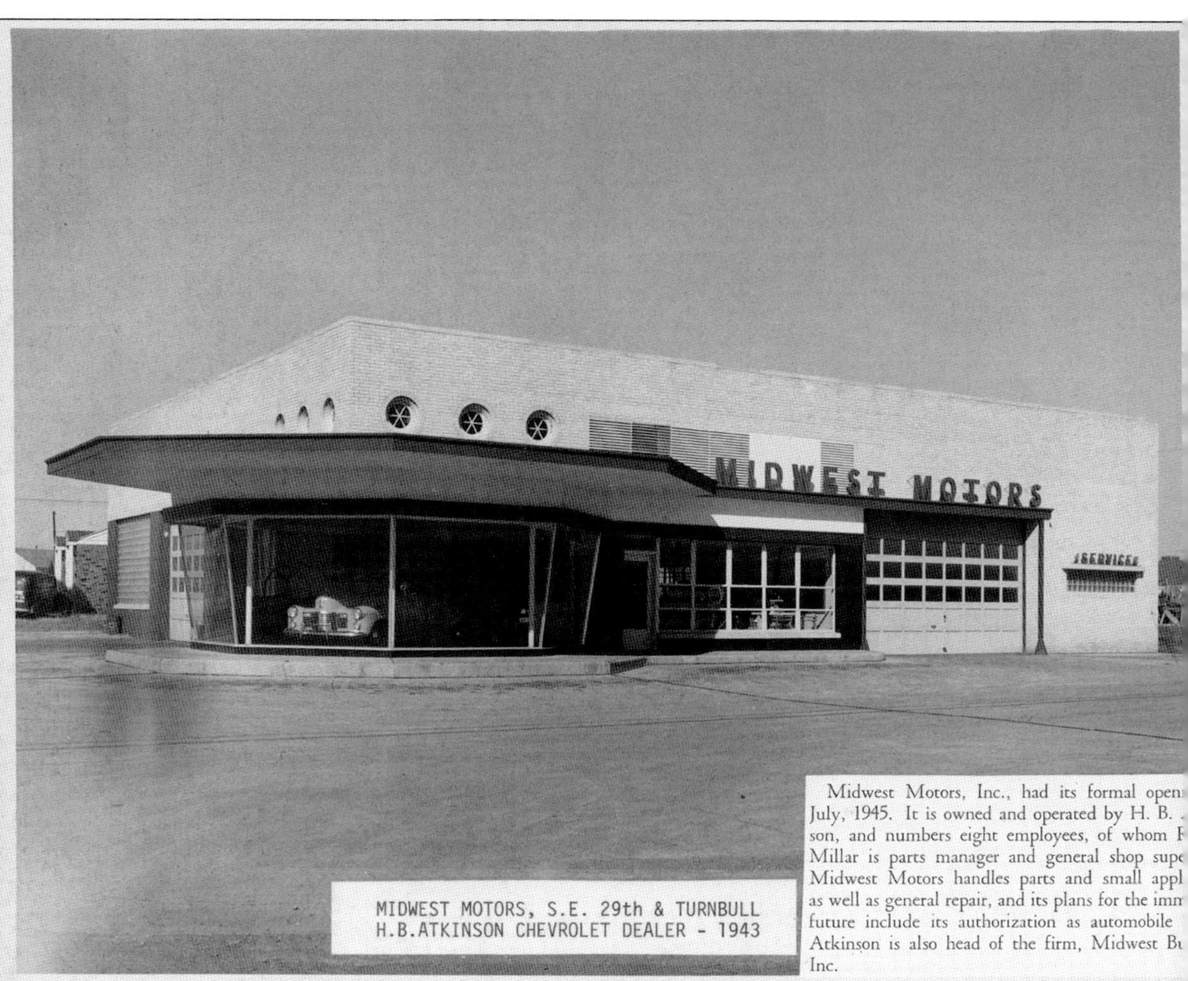

A brother of Bill Atkinson, H.B. Atkinson ran a car dealership in Midwest City. He began his car selling days in Shreveport, Louisiana, and even became the president of the Chevrolet Salesmen Organization in the New Orleans Zone. With the help of a supportive mentor, he took his skills to Midwest City in 1942 when his brother began development. Midwest Motors was the town's first auto garage; it was later called H.B. Atkinson Chevrolet Company. It was sold to Paul Hudiburg of Hudiburg Chevrolet Company in 1957. (Courtesy of the Midwest City High School History Center.)

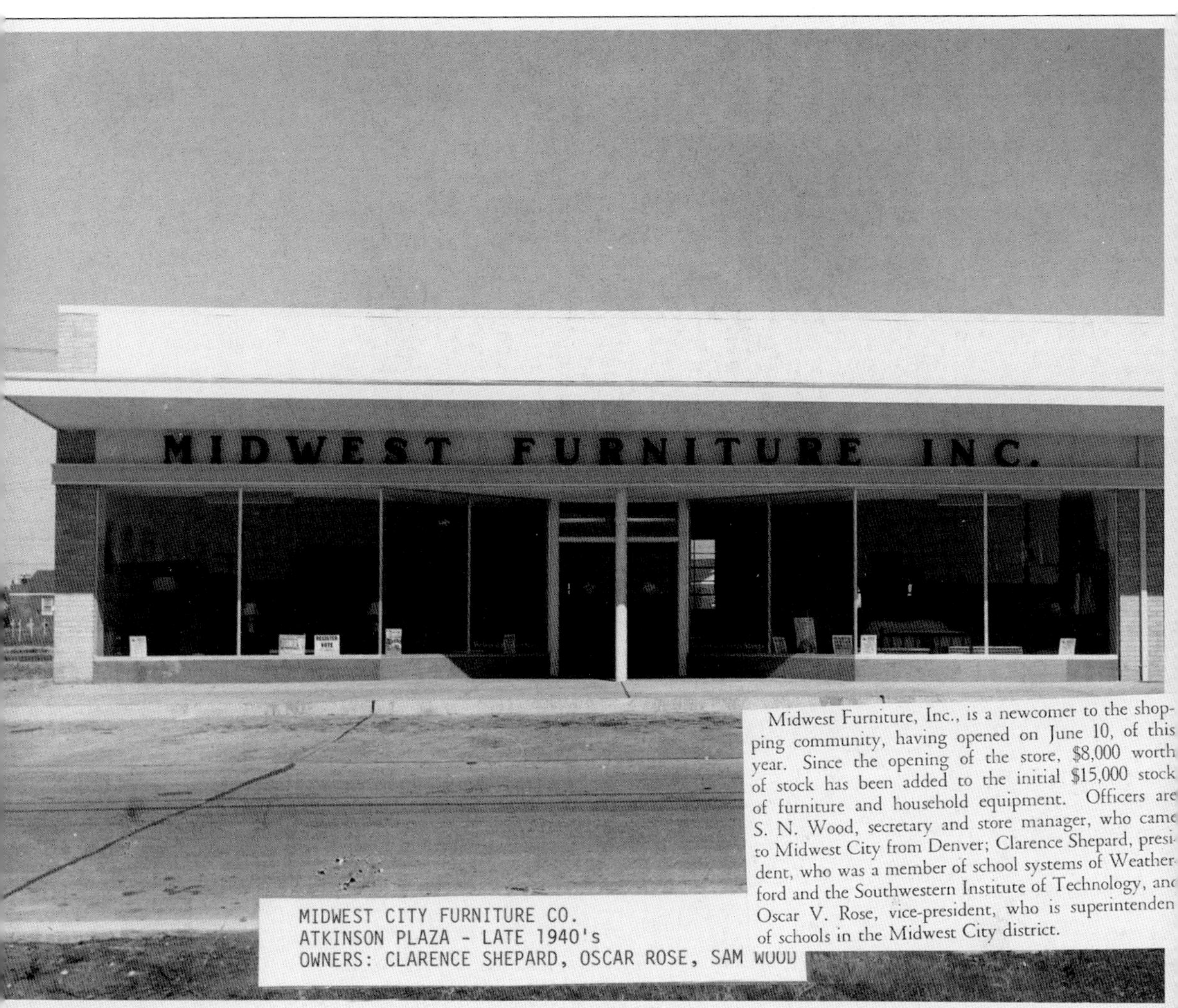

Atkinson Plaza held many stores, including Midwest Furniture Inc. in the late 1940s on Fifteenth Street near Lockheed Drive. The owners were Clarence Shepard, Oscar V. Rose (founder of Rose State College), and Sam Wood. Midwest City Furniture opened with $15,000 in stock of furniture and household equipment. Rose was the vice president of the officers, overseeing the business for a time. (Courtesy of the Midwest City High School History Center.)

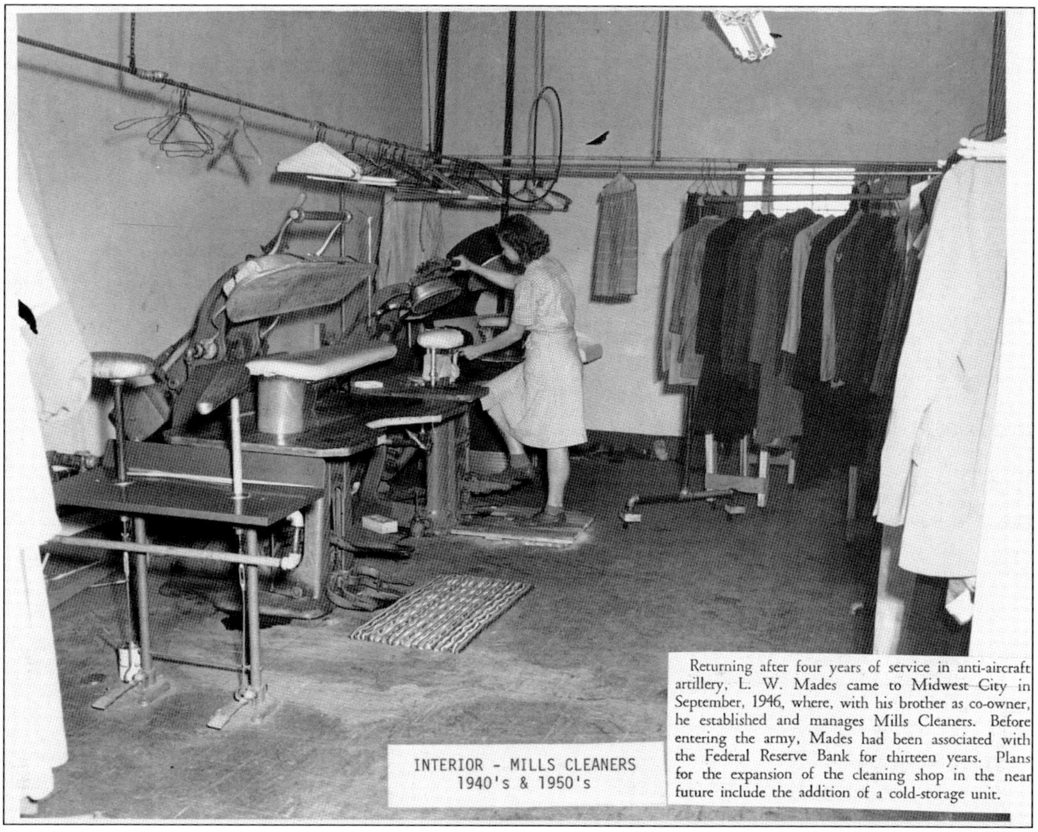

INTERIOR - MILLS CLEANERS
1940's & 1950's

Returning after four years of service in anti-aircraft artillery, L. W. Mades came to Midwest City in September, 1946, where, with his brother as co-owner, he established and manages Mills Cleaners. Before entering the army, Mades had been associated with the Federal Reserve Bank for thirteen years. Plans for the expansion of the cleaning shop in the near future include the addition of a cold-storage unit.

In addition to Midwest Cleaners on Marshall Drive and Twenty-Ninth Street, Mills Cleaners served Midwest City residents in West Atkinson Plaza. Additional original businesses in the plaza included American State Bank, Bomber Inn Café, Conrad-Marr Drug Store, Midwest City Beauty and Barber Shop, Bills Fine Pasties, TG&Y, and a Humpty Dumpty grocery store. Another observation to note in the photograph below is the telephone number of Mills Cleaners, 3-3393. In the early 1950s, there was a two-letter, five-number system, and Midwest City phone numbers began with "PE," meaning "Pershing," followed by a telephone exchange. This helped switchboard operator know where to transfer the call. (Both, courtesy of the Midwest City High School History Center.)

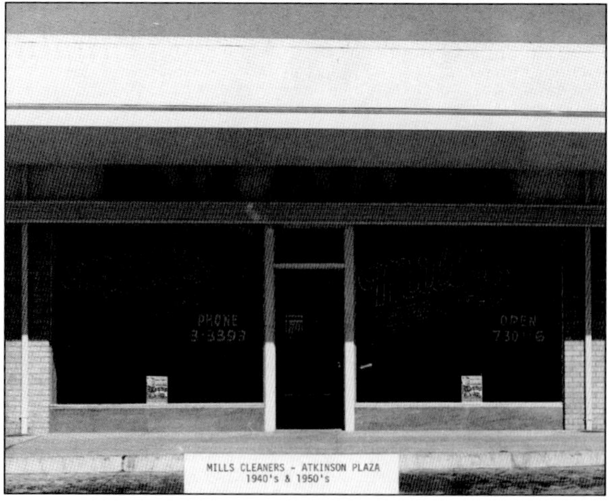

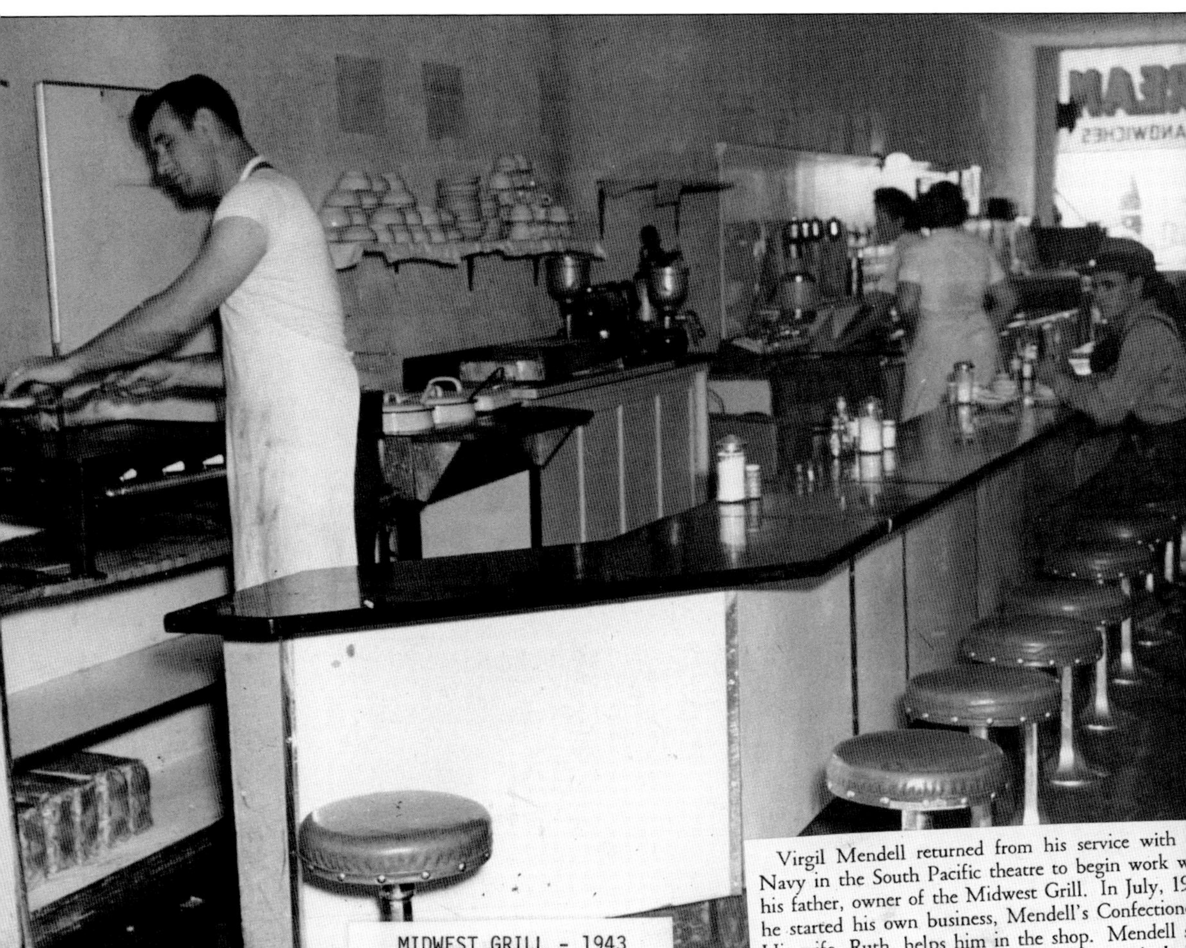

Seen here is the Midwest Grill. Documents show that Virgil Mendell (possibly pictured here), the son of the owner of Midwest Grill, returned from his service with the Navy in the South Pacific theater to begin work with his father. In July 1946, Mendell started his own business, Mendell's Confectionery. His wife, Ruth, helped him in the confectionery shop. (Courtesy of the Midwest City High School History Center.)

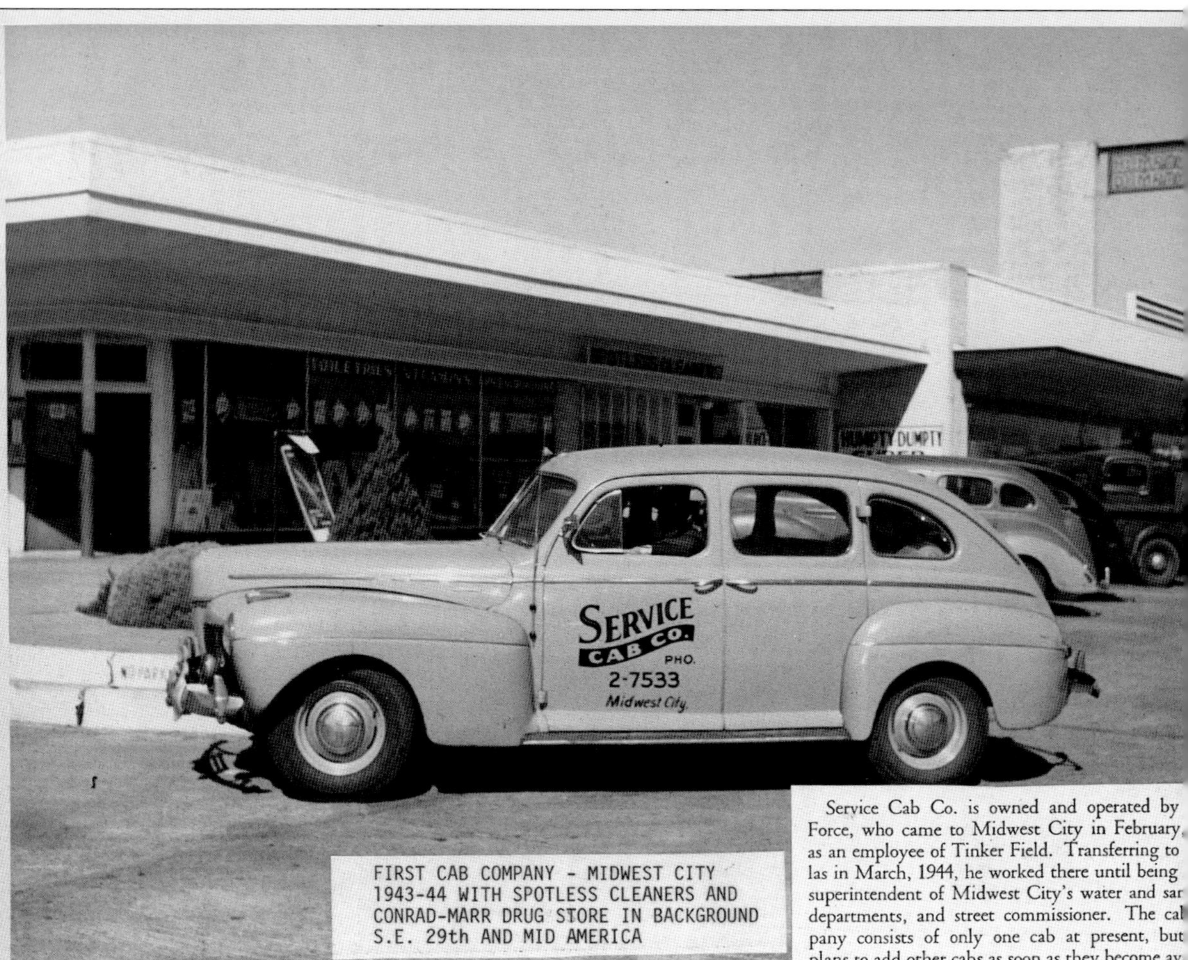

This vehicle belonged to the first cab company in Midwest City, Service Cab Co., in the early 1940s. In the background, one can see Spotless Cleaners, Conrad-Marr Drug Store, and the Humpty Dumpty grocery store in downtown Midwest City. The cab company was owned and operated by L.C. Force, who originally came to Midwest City in 1943 as an employee of Tinker Field. He transferred to the Douglas Aircraft Company plant in 1944 and then became the superintendent of Midwest City's water and sanitation departments and street commissioner. (Courtesy of the Midwest City High School History Center.)

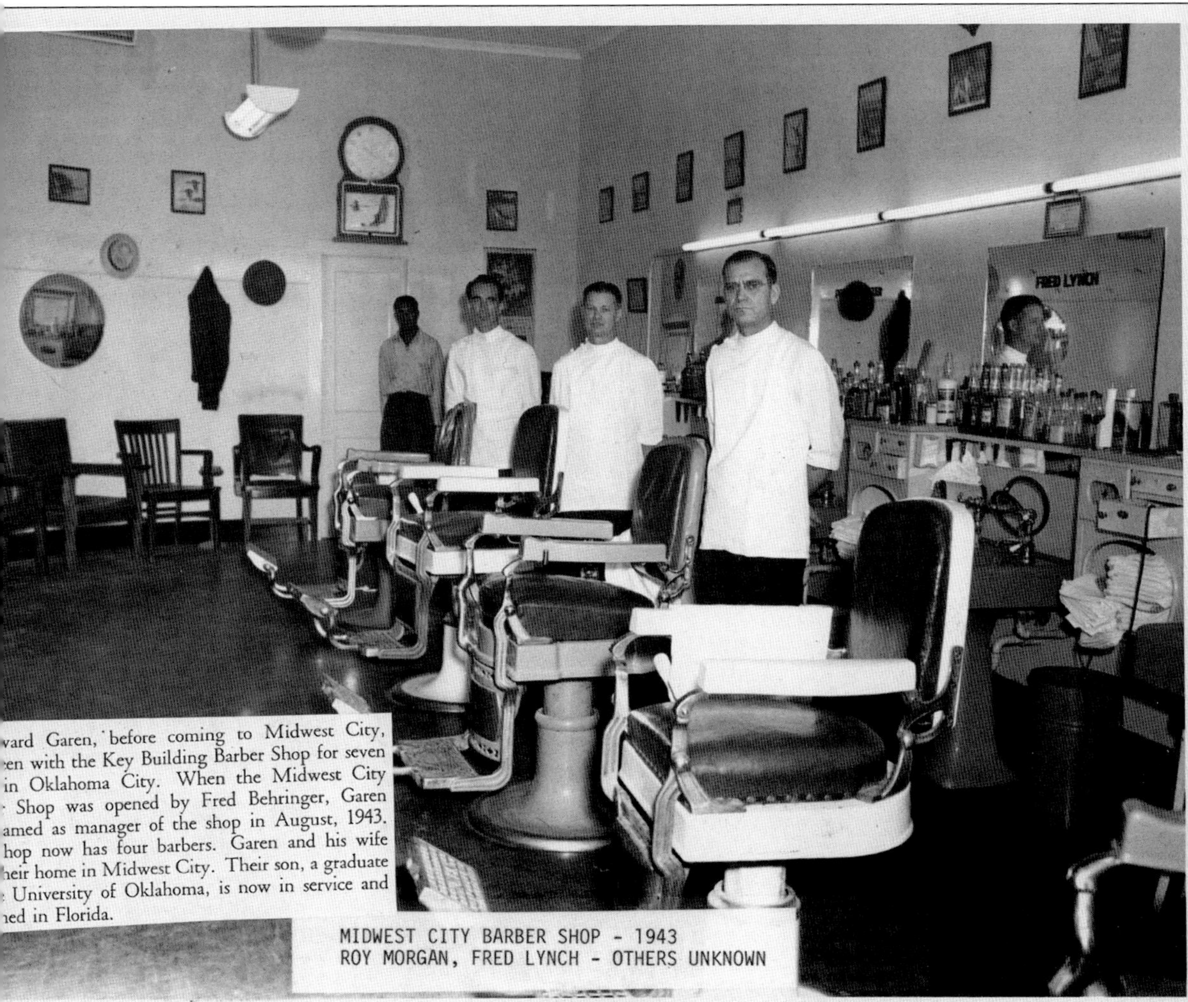

Just as Midwest Beauty Shop served Midwest City residents with their hair needs, so did Midwest City Barber Shop. Pictured here in 1943 are barbers Roy Morgan (first chair) and Fred Linch (second chair). This barbershop was opened by Fred Behringer. Howard Garen, manager of the shop, and his wife owned their home in Midwest City, and their son served in the military. (Courtesy of the Midwest City High School History Center.)

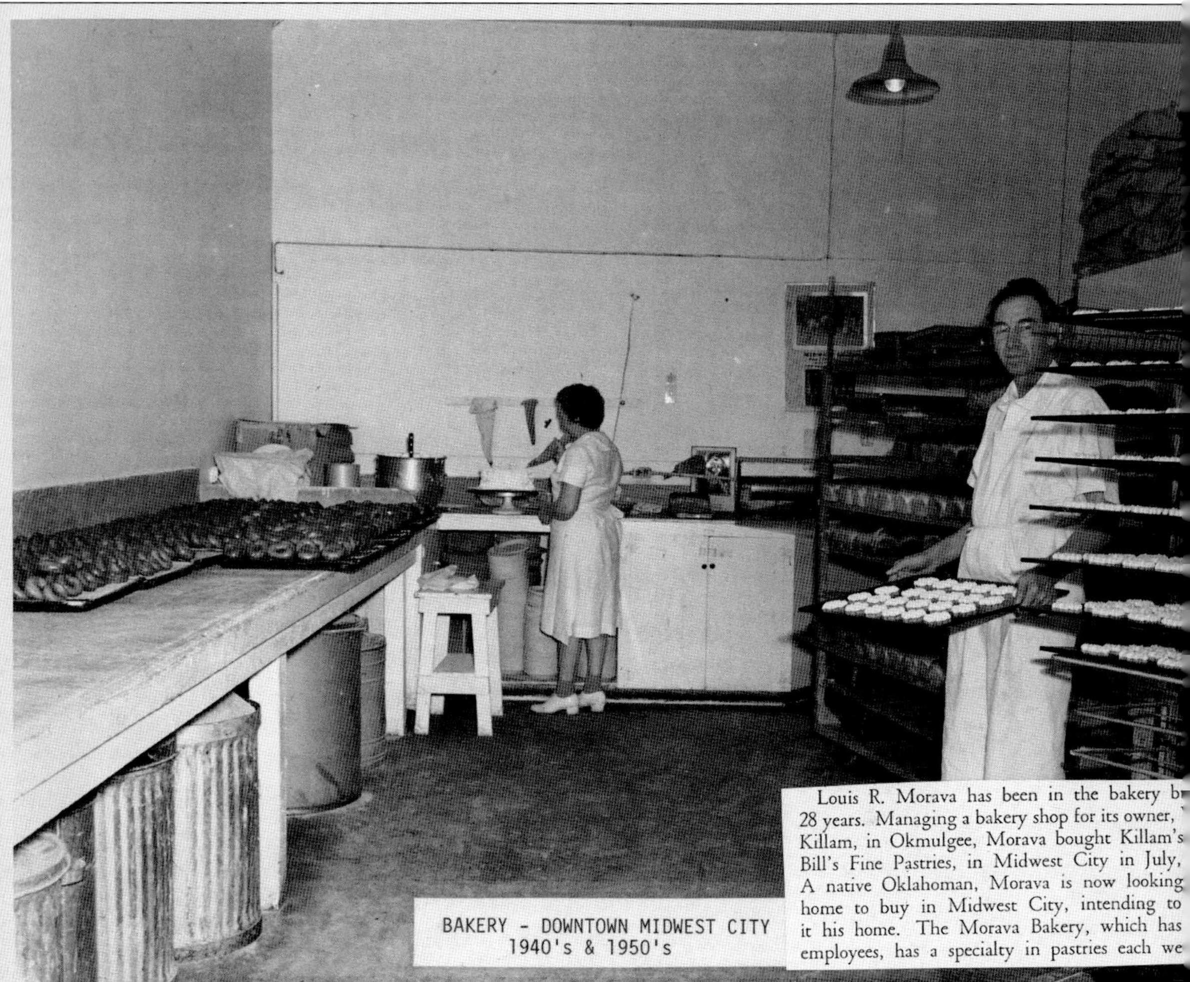

The Morava Bakery was located in downtown Midwest City in the 1940s and 1950s. Louis R. Morava had served in the baking industry for over 28 years at the time of this photograph. Morava bought Bill's Fine Pastries in Midwest City in July 1946. Morava was from Oklahoma and looking for a home to buy in Midwest City. The Morava Bakery had seven employees and a weekly pastry special. (Courtesy of the Midwest City High School History Center.)

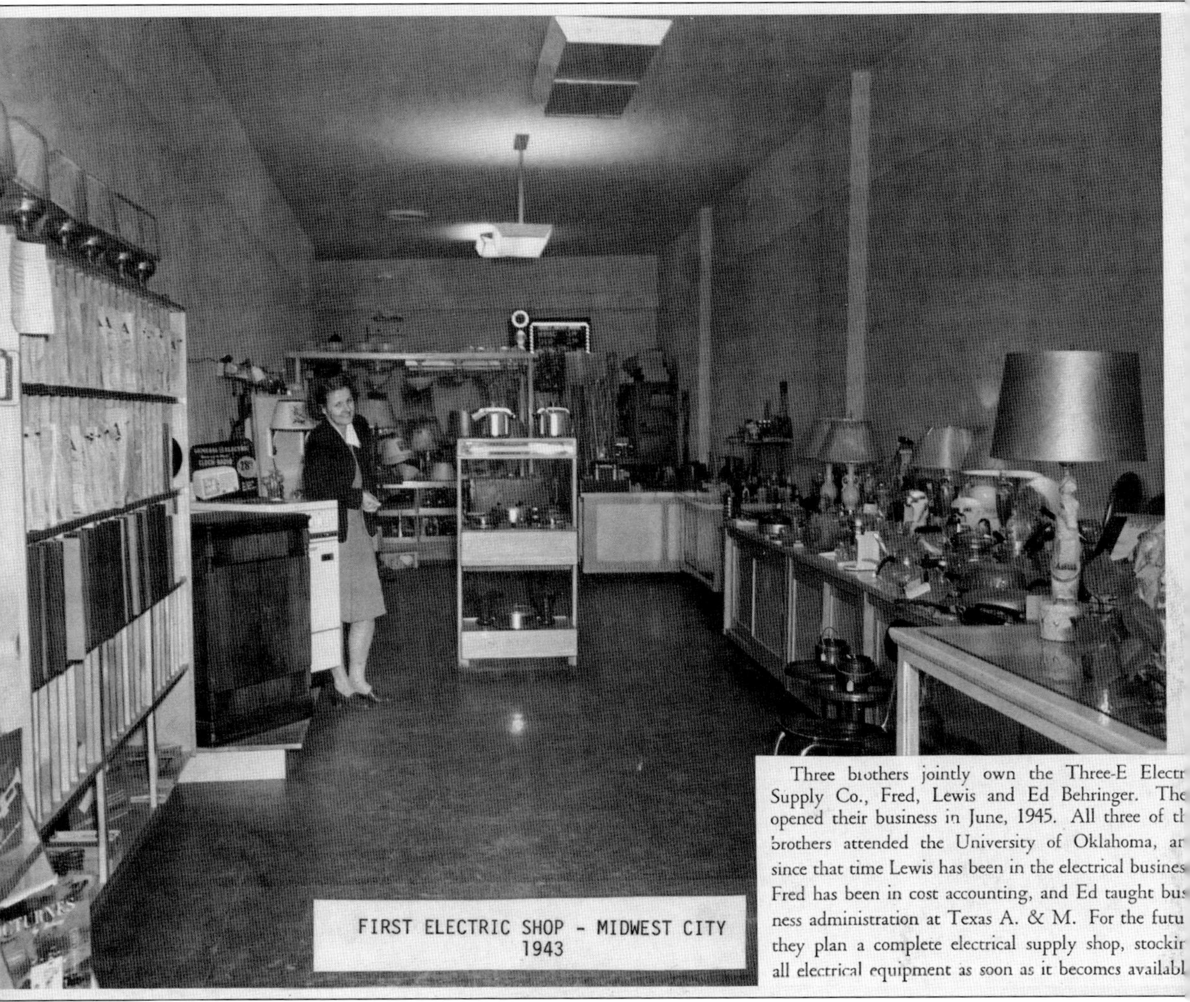

The first electric shop in Midwest City, the Three-E Electric Supply Co., sold electronics like radios, lamps, wiring, and vinyl records and prominent brands such as General Electric. Three brothers—Fred, Lewis, and Ed Behringer—opened this Midwest City business in 1945. (Courtesy of the Midwest City High School History Center.)

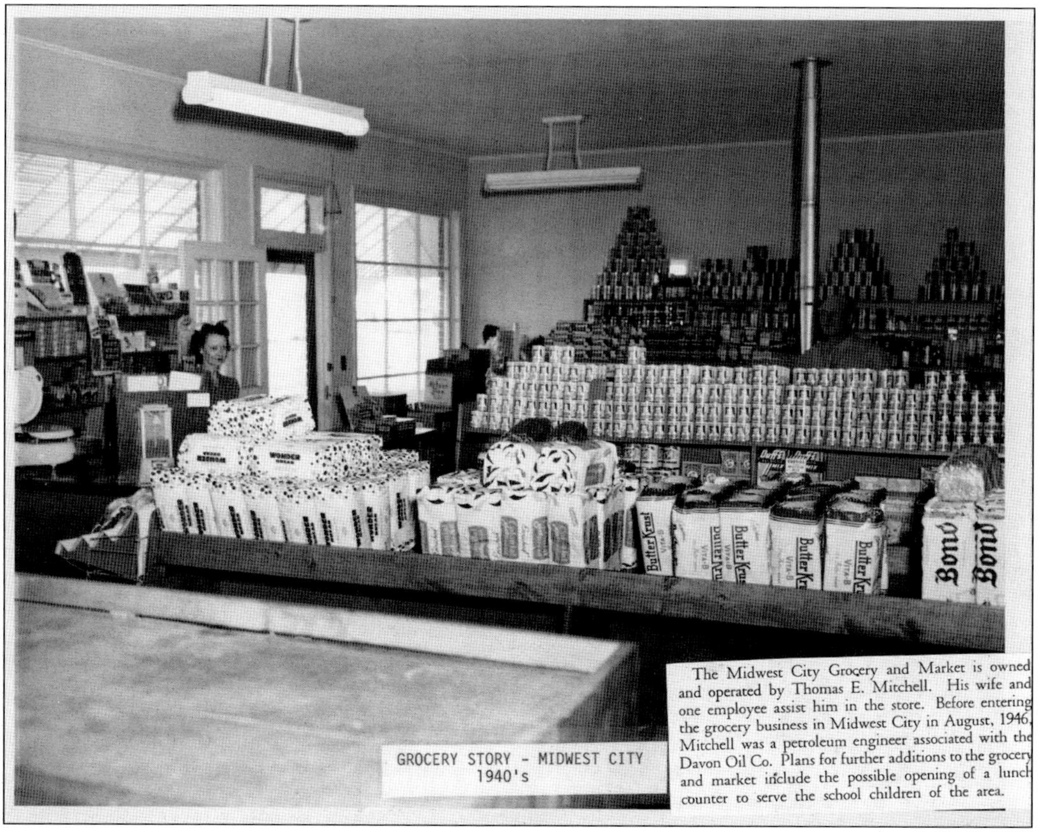

GROCERY STORY - MIDWEST CITY
1940's

The Midwest City Grocery and Market is owned and operated by Thomas E. Mitchell. His wife and one employee assist him in the store. Before entering the grocery business in Midwest City in August, 1946, Mitchell was a petroleum engineer associated with the Davon Oil Co. Plans for further additions to the grocery and market include the possible opening of a lunch counter to serve the school children of the area.

Alongside the Humpty Dumpty, other grocery store owners planted their businesses in Midwest City. Above is the Midwest City Grocery and Market, owned and operated by Thomas E. Mitchell. Below is the Midwest City Grocery Mart located at 601 North Key Boulevard. It was a smaller convenience store deeper in the Original Mile for locals. It was later expanded to the south of the building and remained in operation at least through the 2020s. (Both, courtesy of Midwest City High School History Center.)

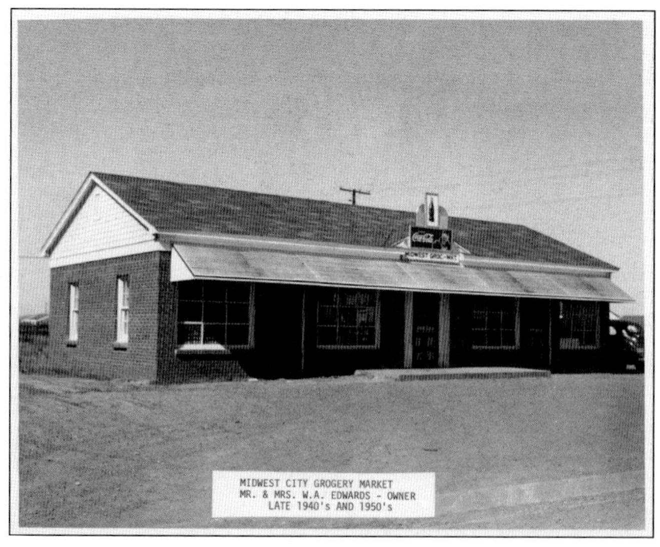
MIDWEST CITY GROGERY MARKET
MR. & MRS. W.A. EDWARDS - OWNER
LATE 1940's AND 1950's

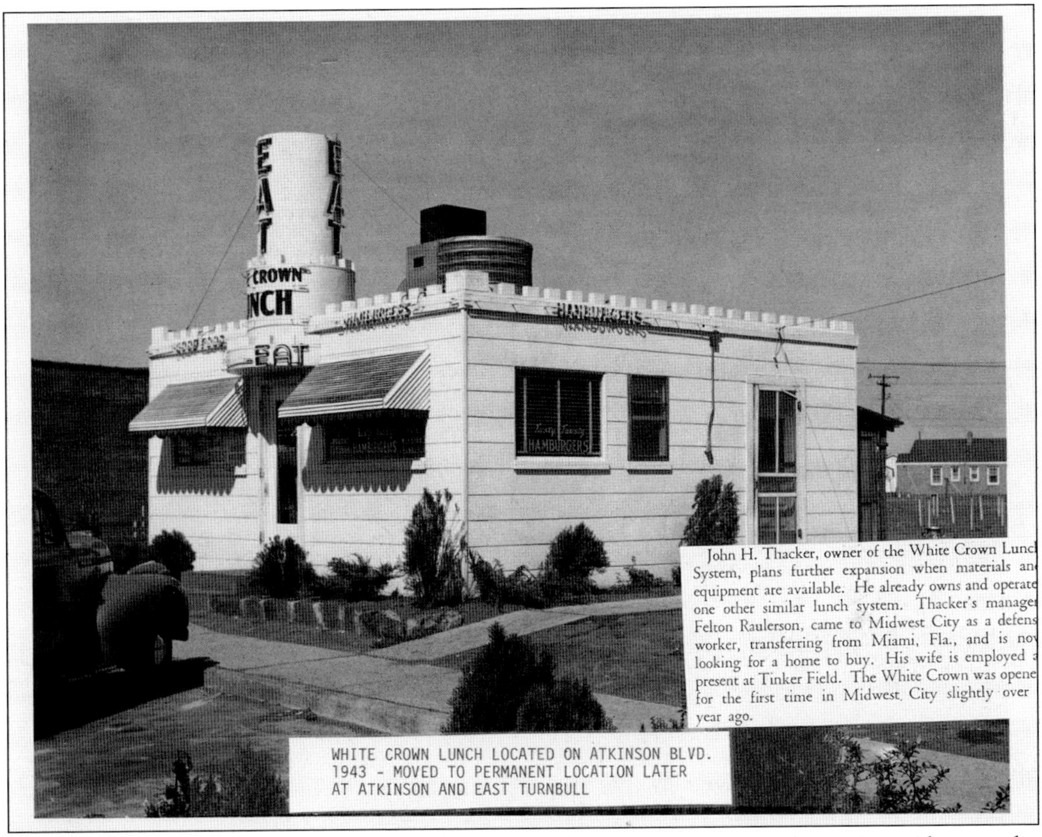

John H. Thacker, owner of the White Crown Lunc System, plans further expansion when materials an equipment are available. He already owns and operate one other similar lunch system. Thacker's manage Felton Raulerson, came to Midwest City as a defens worker, transferring from Miami, Fla., and is no looking for a home to buy. His wife is employed a present at Tinker Field. The White Crown was opene for the first time in Midwest City slightly over year ago.

WHITE CROWN LUNCH LOCATED ON ATKINSON BLVD.
1943 - MOVED TO PERMANENT LOCATION LATER
AT ATKINSON AND EAST TURNBULL

Residents had many options for food and dining with the building of Midwest City. Above is the White Crown Lunch located on Atkinson Boulevard in 1943. Below is Mac's Bar-B-Que, formerly Eddie's Drive In. (Both, courtesy of Midwest City High School History Center.)

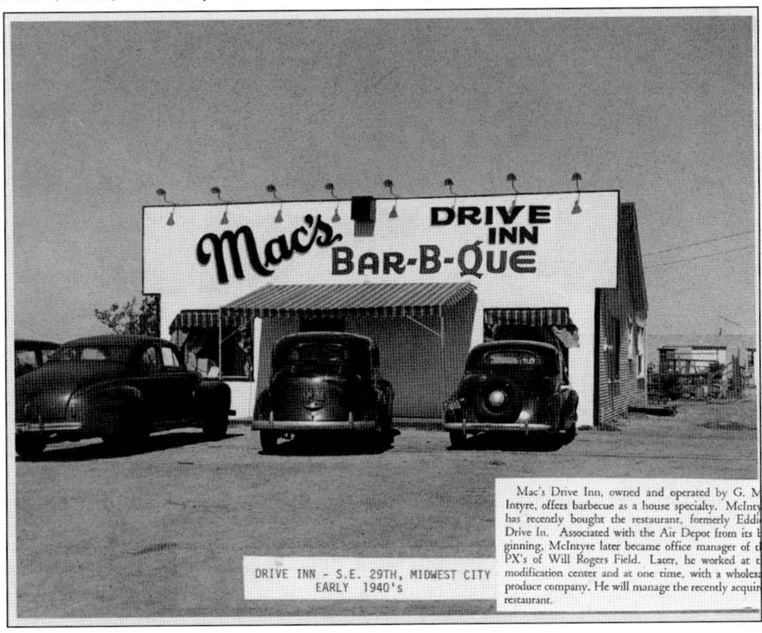

DRIVE INN - S.E. 29TH, MIDWEST CITY
EARLY 1940's

Mac's Drive Inn, owned and operated by G. M Intyre, offers barbecue as a house specialty. McInty has recently bought the restaurant, formerly Eddi Drive In. Associated with the Air Depot from its b ginning, McIntyre later became office manager of t PX's of Will Rogers Field. Later, he worked at t modification center and at one time, with a wholes produce company. He will manage the recently acquir restaurant.

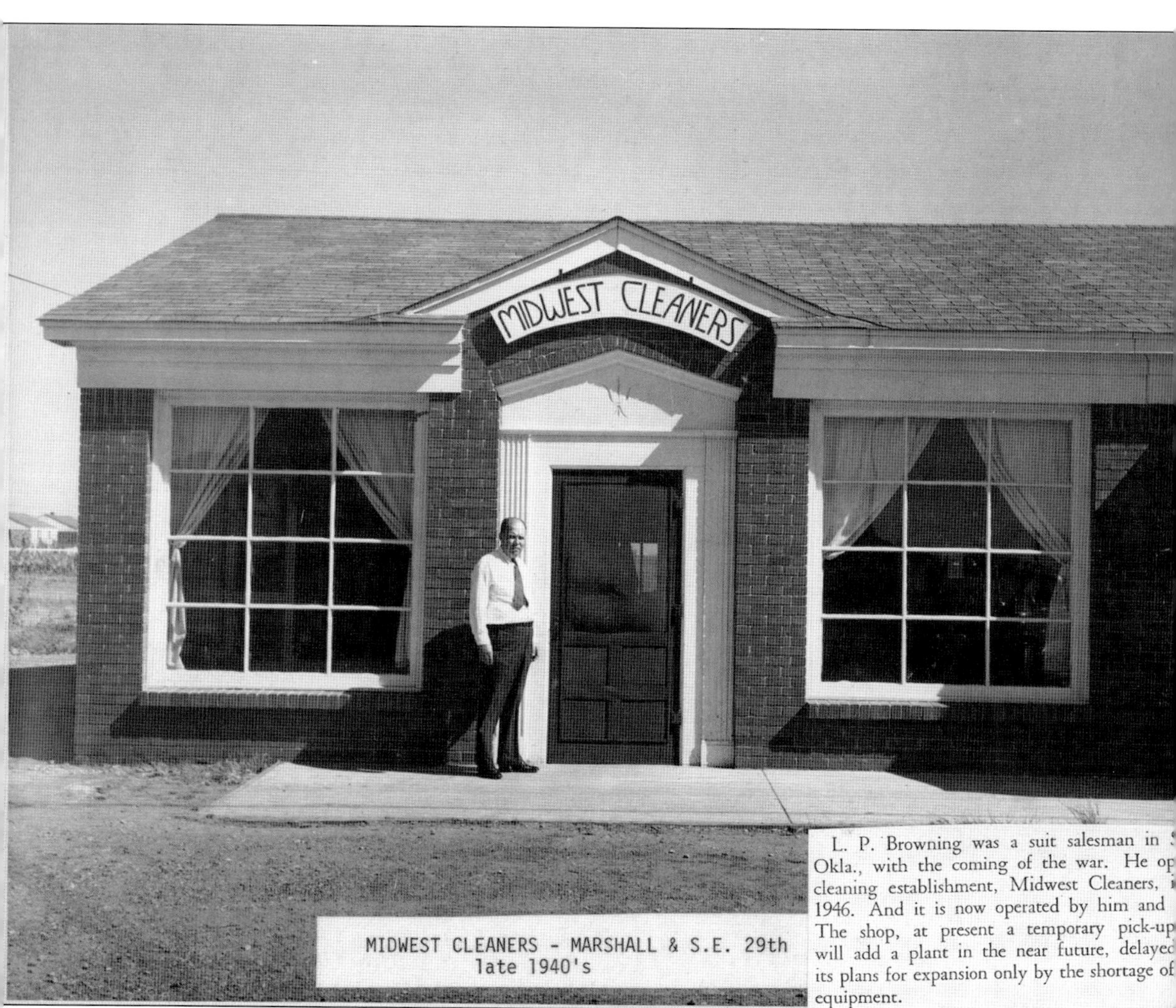

Among the self-service laundries, there were also laundry cleaners. Midwest Cleaners was located off Marshall Drive and Southeast Twenty-Ninth Street during the late 1940s. L.P. Browning was a suit salesman in Shawnee, Oklahoma, with the coming war. He opened his cleaning establishment, Midwest Cleaners, in late 1946. (Courtesy of the Midwest City High School History Center.)

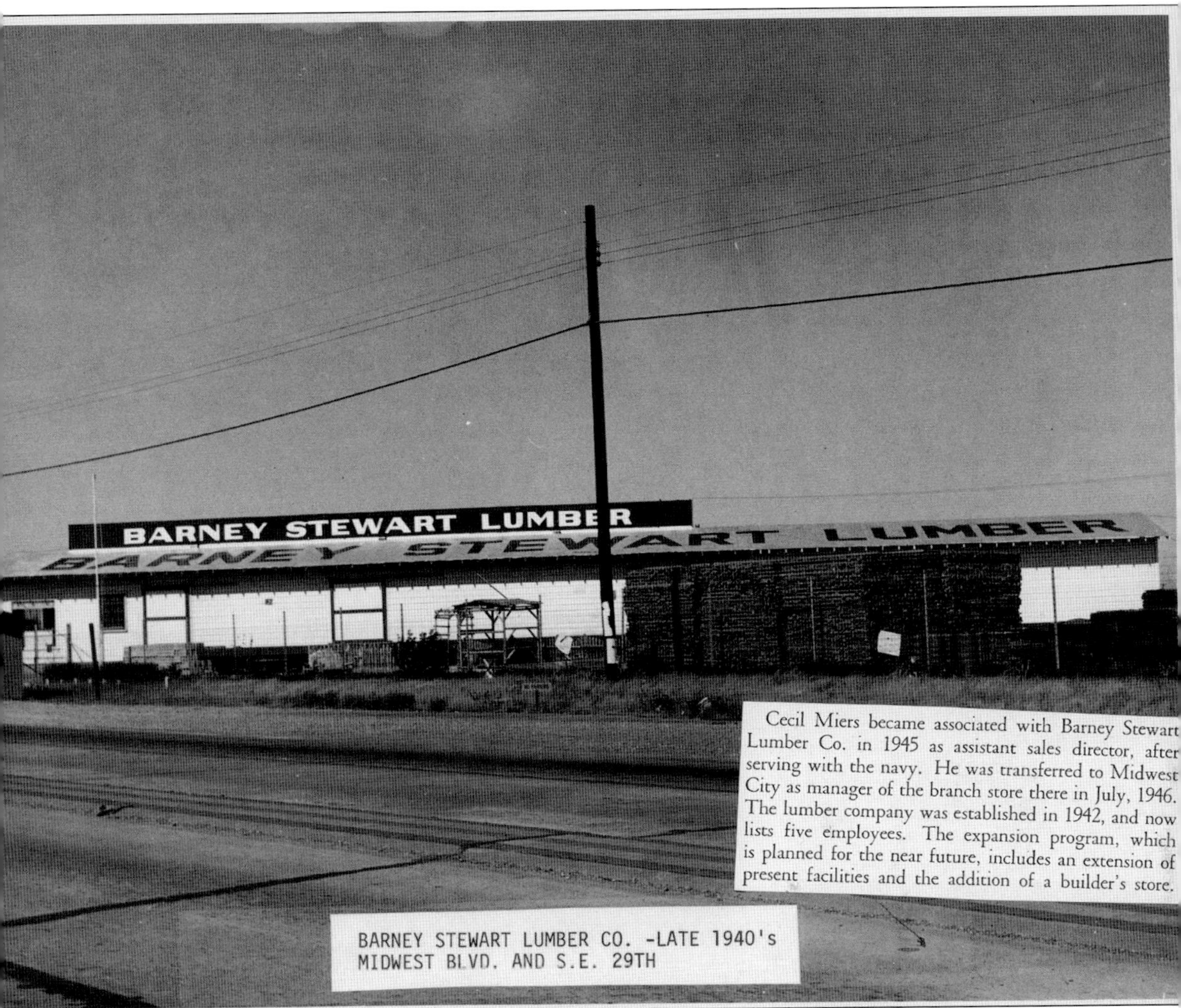

Another businessman had the same idea as Atkinson and opened up another lumberyard. Located on Midwest Boulevard and Twenty-Ninth Street, only one mile from Atkinson's lumber company, Barney Stewart Lumber Co. was established in Midwest City in 1942. (Courtesy of the Midwest City High School History Center.)

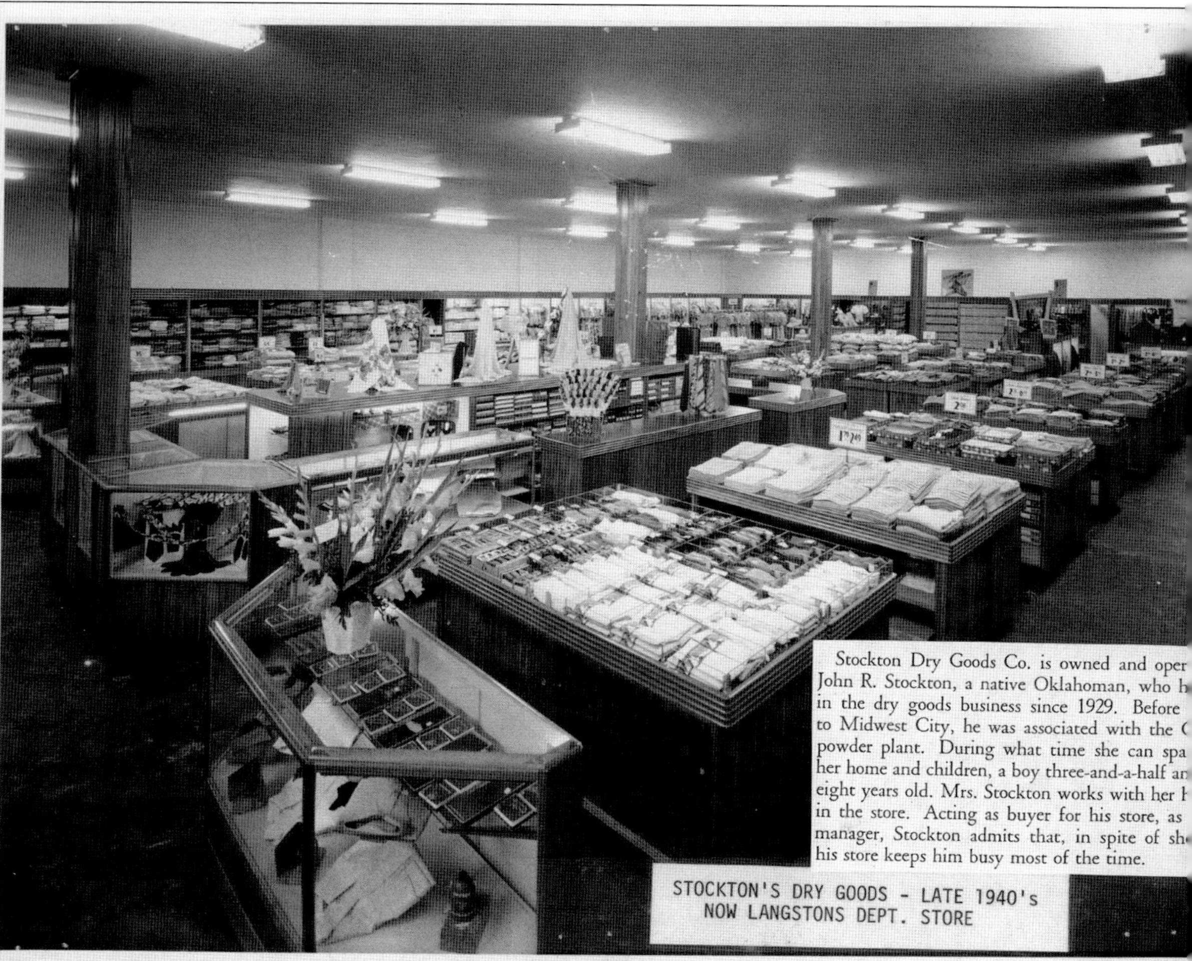

Stockton Dry Goods Co. was a department store in early Midwest City. The business was owned and operated by John R. Stockton, who had been in the dry goods business since 1929. It offered clothing, shoes, men's ties, and other apparel. It was owned and operated by Stockton and his wife, who opened grocery stores in 1947 that went on to have multiple locations. John Stockton retired in 1980 and passed away in 1995. (Courtesy of Midwest City High School History Center.)

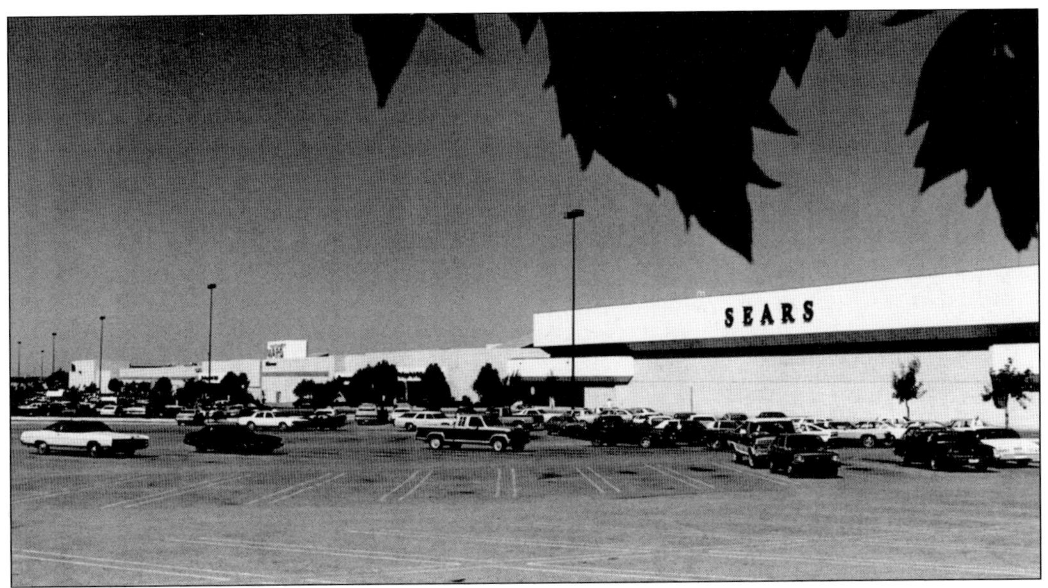

Heritage Park Mall was Midwest City's first mall. Opened in 1978, it offered an array of stores such as Dillard's, Sears, and Montgomery Ward. Located on the corner of Reno Avenue and Air Depot Boulevard, it was a destination for many rural communities in eastern Oklahoma County and drew quite a crowd on its grand opening. To celebrate the grand opening, there were celebrity appearances by Billy Carter, Ed McMahon of *The Tonight Show*, soccer star Kyle Rote Jr., and Olympic runner Jim Ryun. (Above, courtesy of Oklahoma Historical Society; below, courtesy of Rose State College Foundation.)

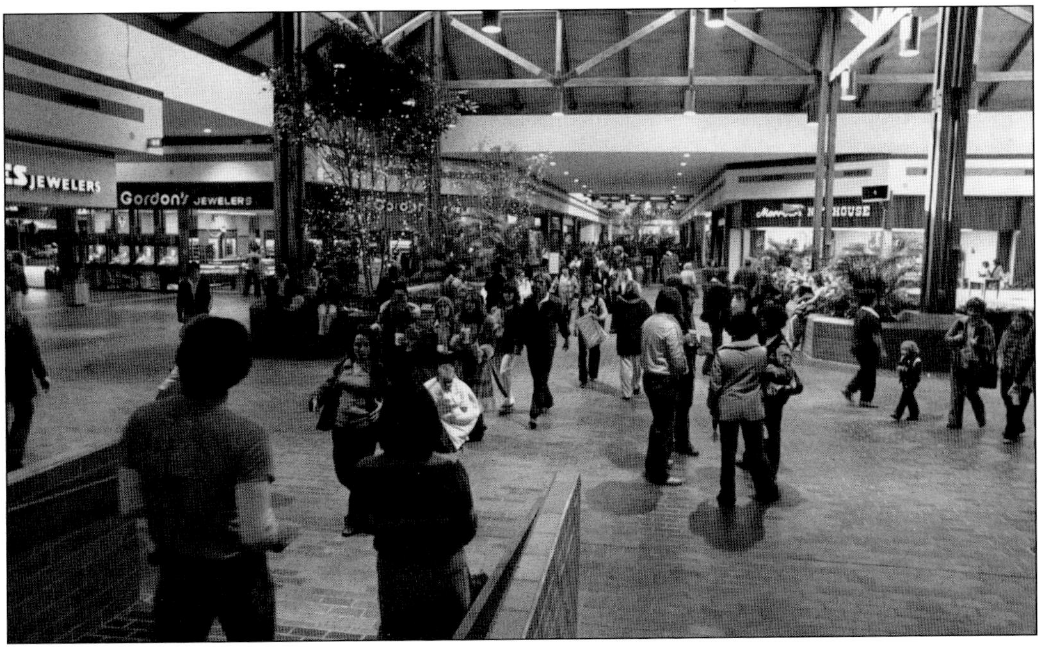

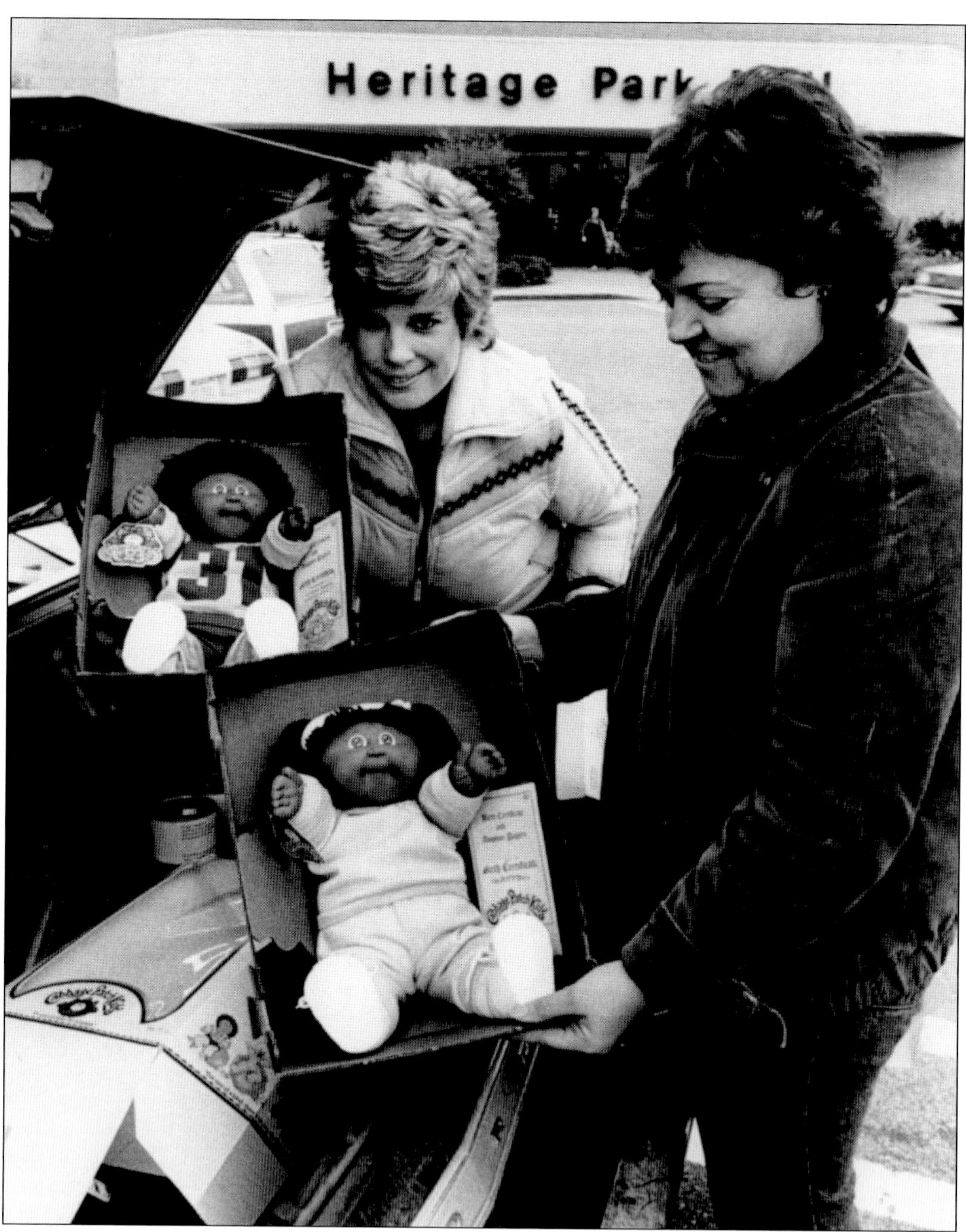

Customers Dorothy Grimes (left) and Shirley Bellwe (right) show off their newly purchased and wildly popular Cabbage Patch Kids outside of Heritage Park Mall in November 1981. Shopping malls gained popularity in the 1980s and 1990s but later saw a decline across the nation. Heritage Park Mall was one of those economic victims as the seasons changed in the economy, and it closed in February 2010 after 30 years of being a community staple. (Courtesy of Oklahoma Historical Society.)

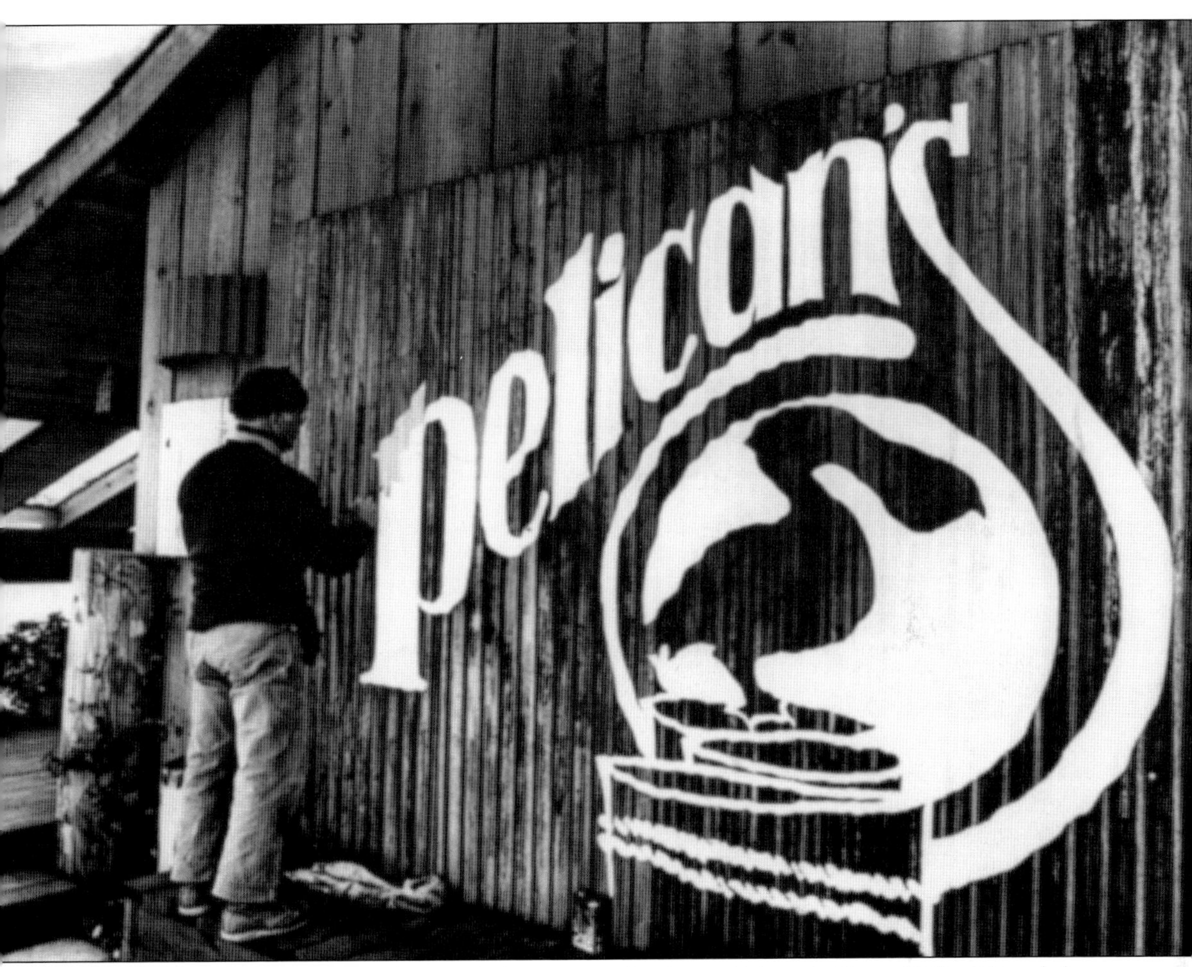

Jim Dolezel, a Vietnam vet, and Tim Thelin run a tight ship at Pelican's. Since 1980, Pelican's has served seafood to the Midwest City community. The restaurant is a local supporter of community initiatives and fundraisers and promotes local business networking. (Courtesy of Oklahoma Historical Society.)

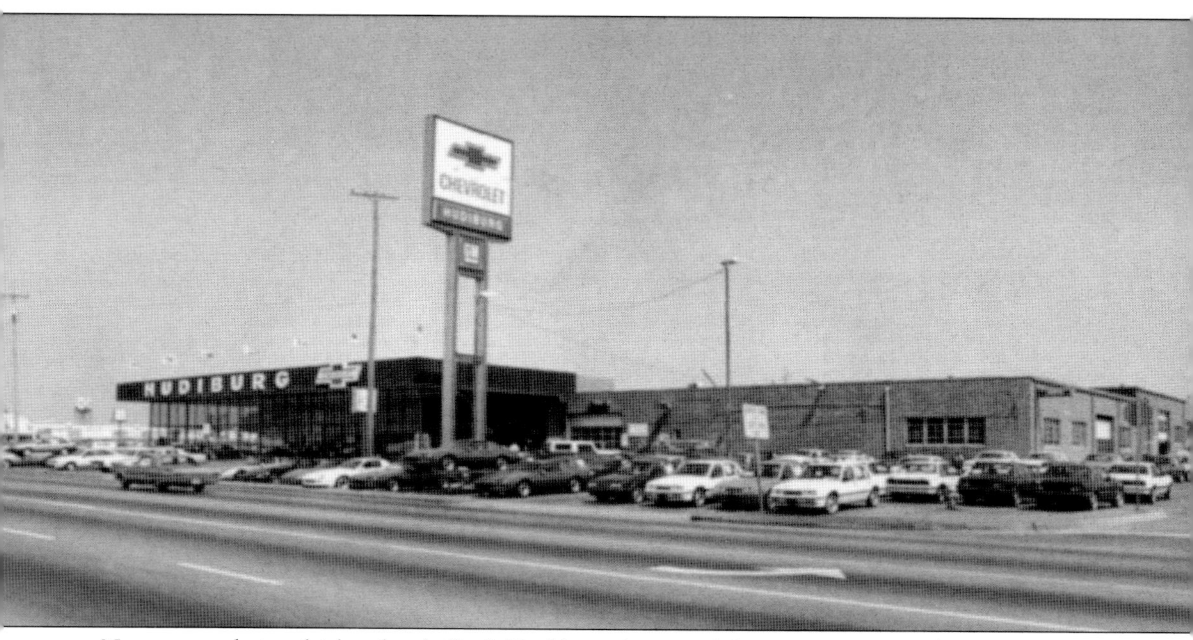

Never completing high school, Paul Hudiburg leveraged his entrepreneurial spirit and began selling used cars and tractors in Prague, Oklahoma, with his business, Prague Farm Equipment. In 1957, he broke ground on Hudiburg Chevrolet. Little did he know that this business with one dealership and eight employees would one day grow into one of the most prominent car dealership companies in the state of Oklahoma. Under the leadership of his son David, Hudiburg grew the business to the Hudiburg Auto Group, including Chevrolet, Buick, Toyota, Ford, and Subaru by the 2020s. (Courtesy of Rose State College Foundation.)

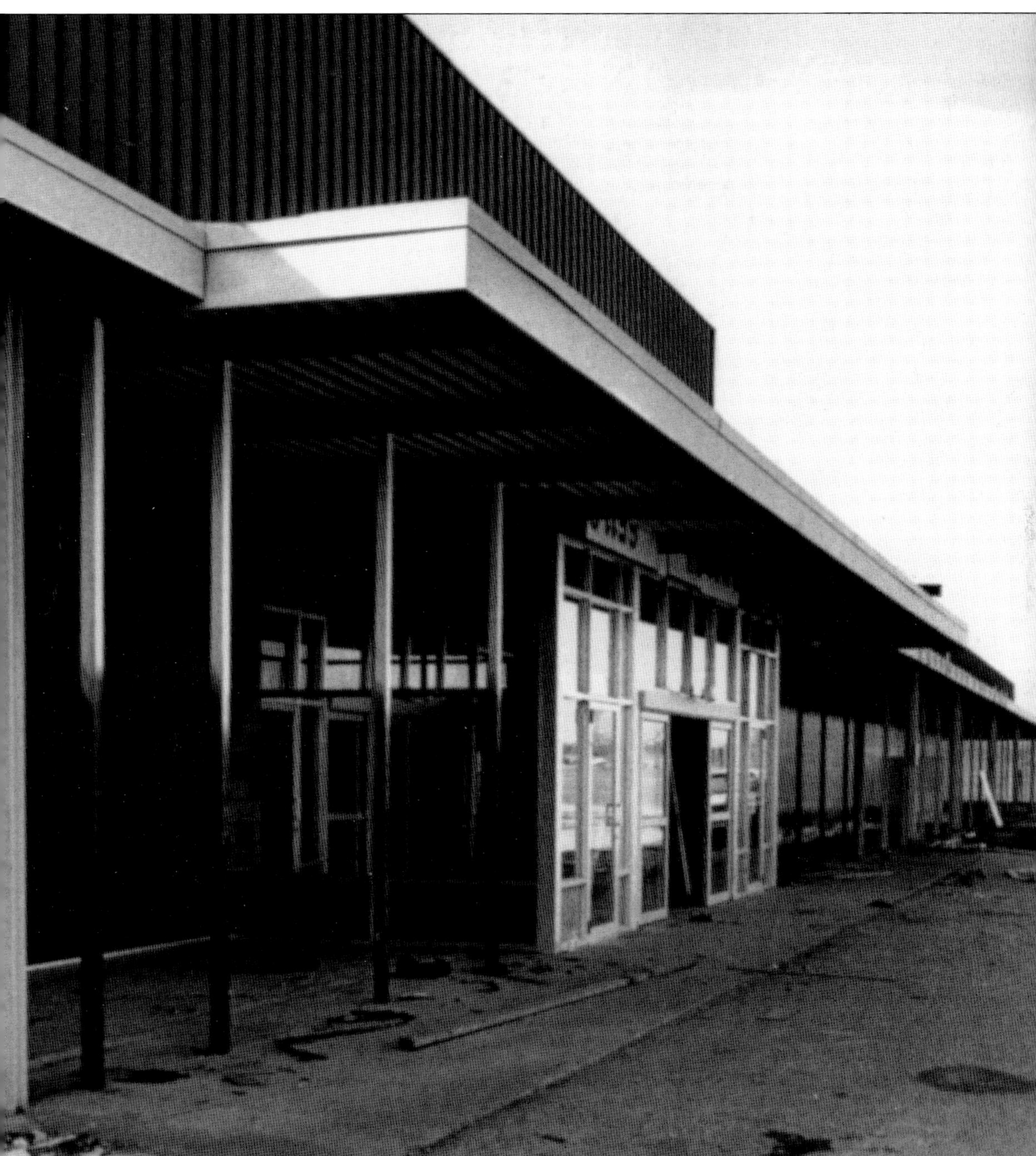

Midwest City remained fertile ground for businessmen such as Nick Harroz of Crest Foods, Paul Hudiburg of Hudiburg Chevrolet, and Sylvan Goldman of Humpty Dumpty grocery stores as Sam Walton tried his hand at planting a new concept in Midwest City. In 1983, the very first Sam's Wholesale Club was born in Midwest City on the corner of Tinker Diagonal Street and Twenty-Ninth Street. The Sam's Club brand grew to over 599 stores in 45 states and Puerto Rico by the early 2020s. This photograph shows the facility Sam's had remodeled. (Courtesy of the Oklahoma Historical Society.)

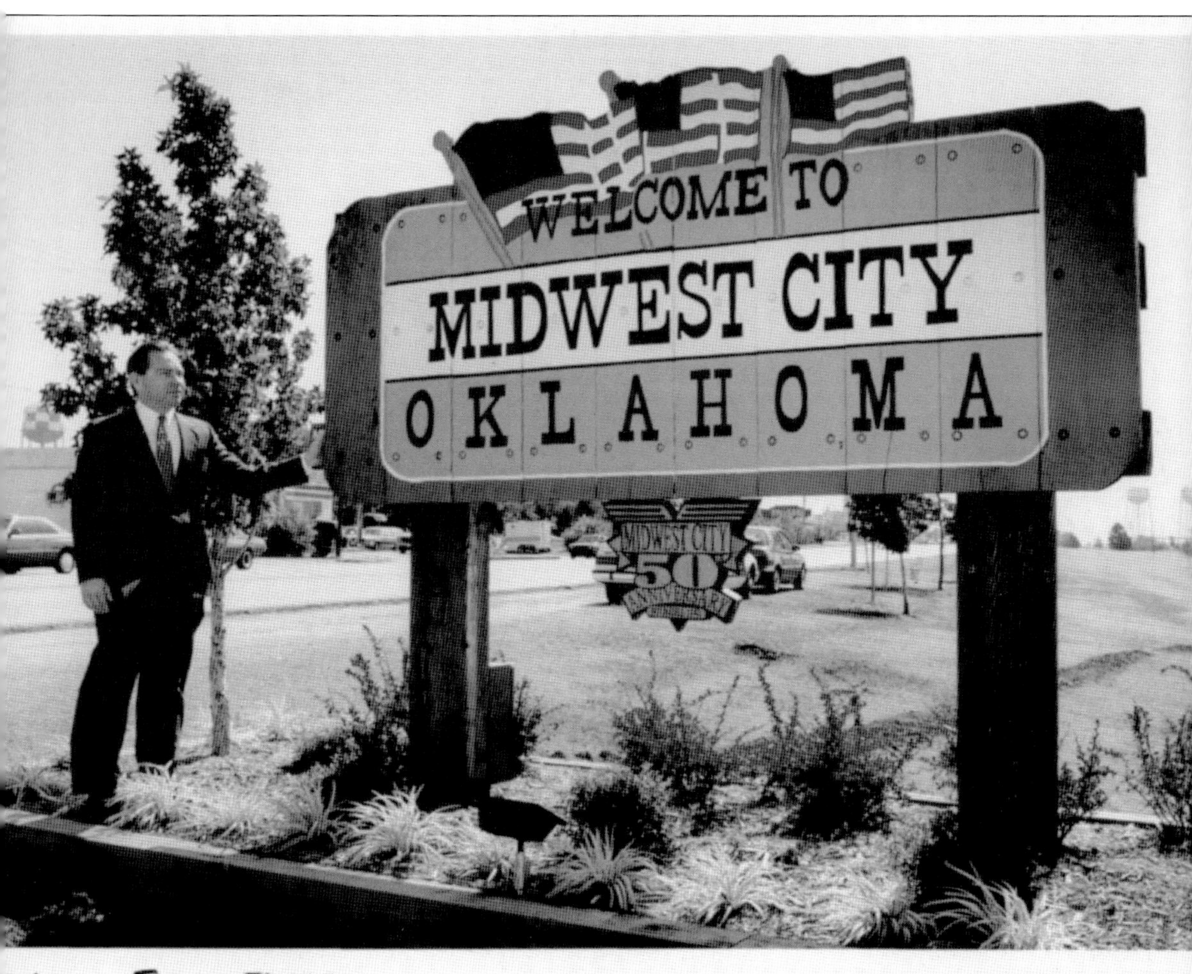

Pictured here is Mayor John Johnson, who served as mayor of Midwest City in the 1990s. He stands beside an iconic sign of Midwest City for visitors entering the city. Midwest City mayors are permitted to serve two four-year terms in office by vote of the people. The first mayor of Midwest City was R.S. Dawson. (Courtesy of Oklahoma Historical Society.)

Five

Provide, Protect, and Preside

Midwest City, though small at first, had a task on its hands. As an independent city, it needed to create and build infrastructure in law enforcement, emergency services, legislation and oversight, disaster response, and public works like waste management. At first, most of the city stayed within the Original Mile, including the municipal buildings. The city was incorporated on March 11, 1943. Operating under a board of trustees, it enacted a charter for the city in 1948, and the first meeting of the Midwest City City Council was held the following January 1949. It continued to expand, including 1,000 additional acres in 1959. The first mayor of Midwest City was R.S. Dawson. Midwest City government oversaw an expanding city that would later extend to 24.5 miles square. Another much-needed service was a local, well-equipped hospital for the region. As Midwest City was a flagship city for local eastern townships and counties, a closer and more advanced medical facility was required to improve health outcomes and increase the response time of emergency services. Thus, Midwest City Memorial Hospital was birthed in 1964. Over the following decades, as the city grew, the municipal buildings became outdated, and it was time for increased capacity of municipal departments and facilities. In the 1970s, new municipal buildings were constructed to meet the growing needs and responsibilities of the city. In 1998, the Hospital Authority Trust was formed and began awarding grants to community organizations and businesses, funding many community-building projects. After many changed hands of the hospital, SSM Health agreed to lead operations and expand the Midwest City hospital district in 2021. As a support city for Tinker Air Force Base, the government has helped support the infrastructure for the residential, commercial, social, spiritual, educational, and recreational needs of the city. Midwest City grew from 10,166 in 1950, to 36,058 in 1960, to 52,267 in 1990, and 58,406 by the early 2020s.

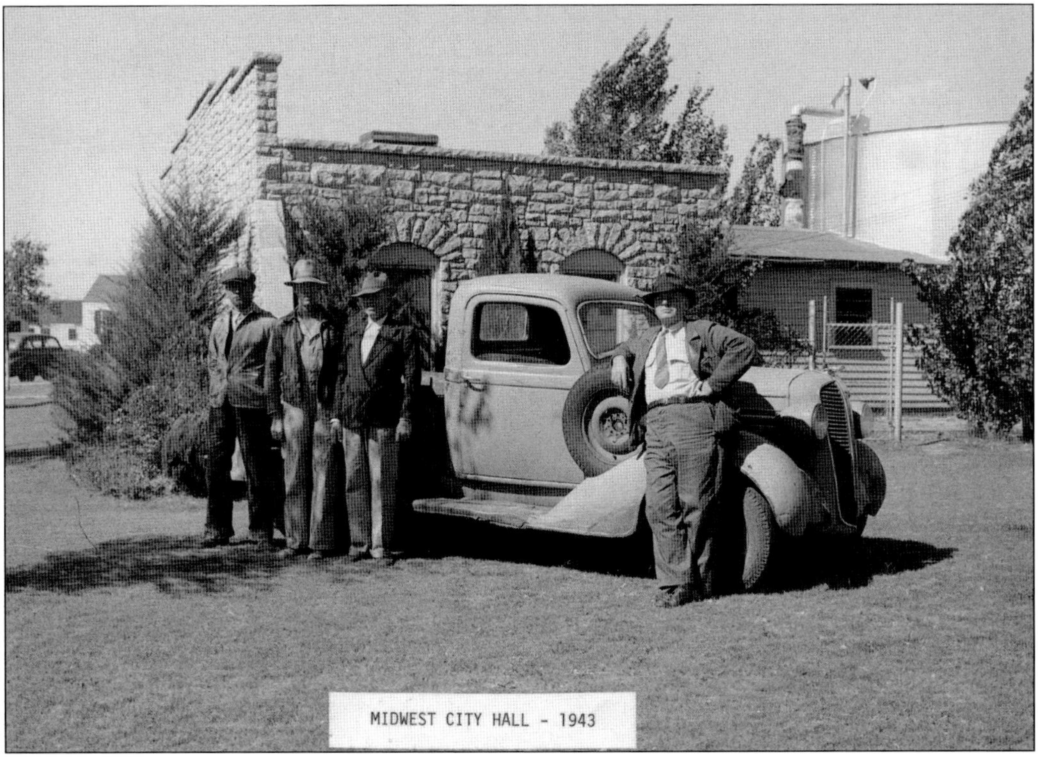

MIDWEST CITY HALL - 1943

Pictured are workmen in front of the original Midwest City Hall building around 1943. The original municipal complex for Midwest City was in the Original Mile behind the shopping center on Mid-America Boulevard. It was later moved to the corner of East Reno Avenue and Midwest Boulevard. In the 1970s, an updated senior center, library, Nick Harroz Community Center, Midwest City Police Department, Midwest City Fire Department, and additional medical offices for the Midwest Memorial Hospital were built around this complex. (Both, courtesy of the Rose State College Foundation.)

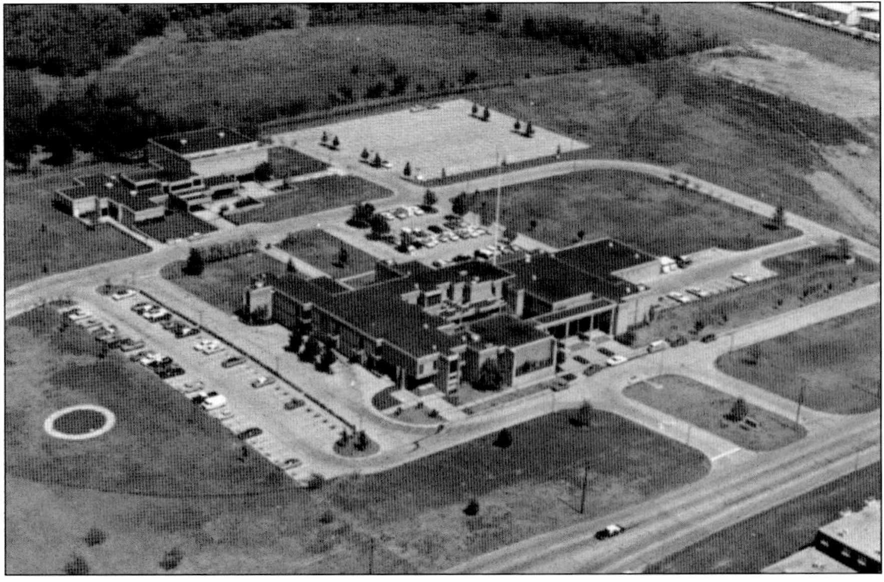

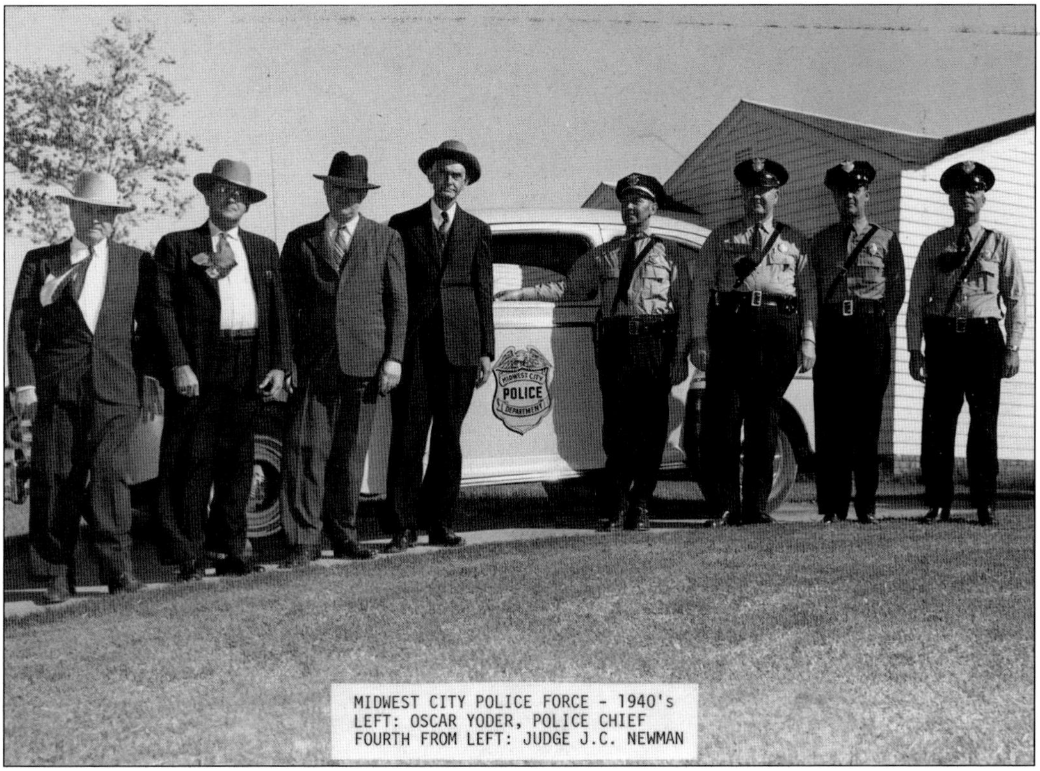

MIDWEST CITY POLICE FORCE - 1940's
LEFT: OSCAR YODER, POLICE CHIEF
FOURTH FROM LEFT: JUDGE J.C. NEWMAN

The Midwest City Police Department began with one man, J.B. Beaird, being appointed as town marshal by Atkinson in 1943; he would use his own vehicle for reimbursement. In 1948, Midwest City chartered a police force by appointing the first chief of police, Oscar Yoder (above, far left). By 1950, the force bought its first motorcycle for $799, and by 1957, it had hired 25 officers. In 1960, Midwest City officers would receive basic law enforcement training from the Oklahoma Highway Patrol. Below is a photograph of police patrol vehicles in the 1980s. Public safety was a consistent focus in the city of Midwest City. (Above, courtesy of Midwest City High School History Center; below, courtesy of Rose State College Foundation.)

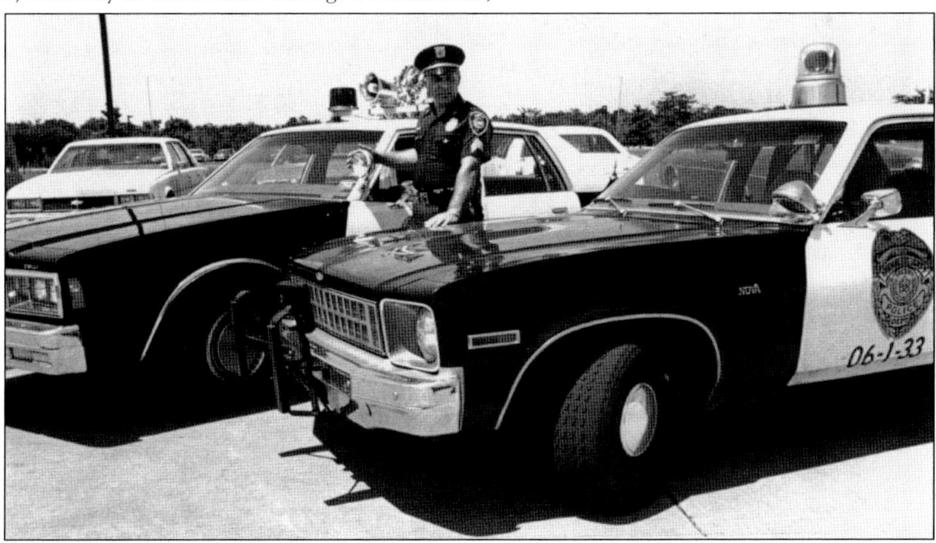

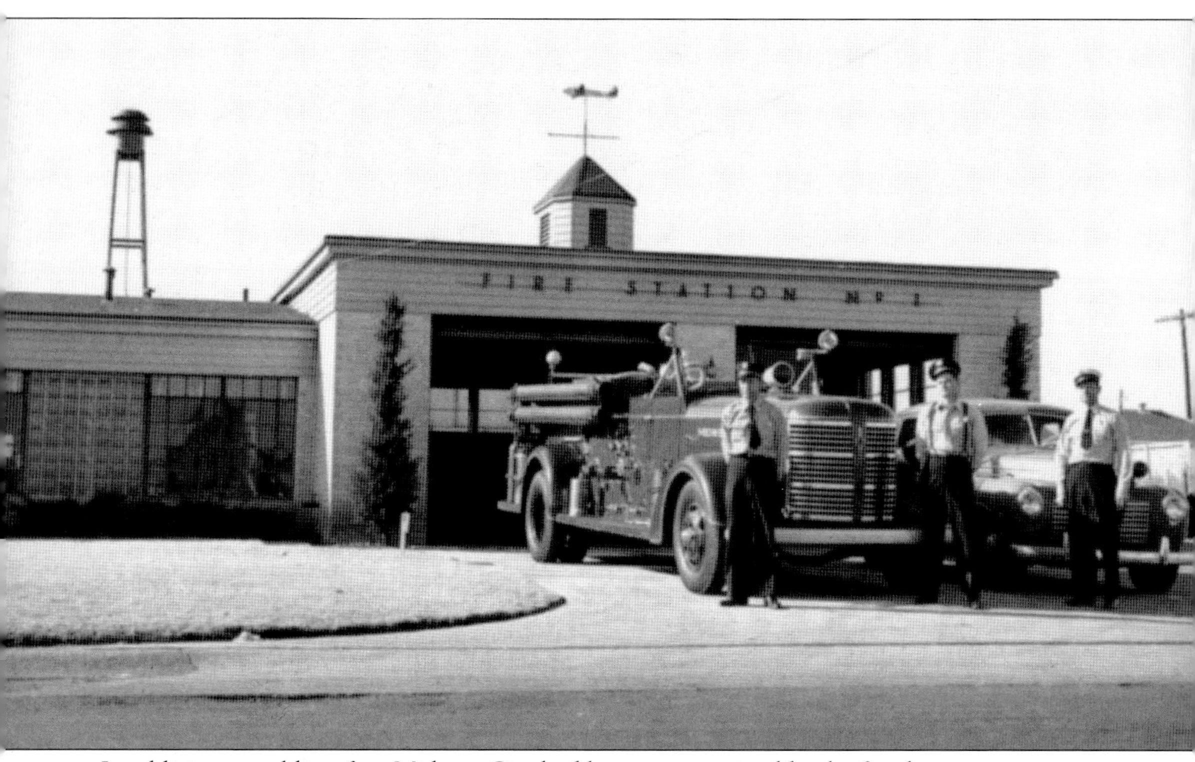

In addition to public safety, Midwest City had hometown teams like the fire department to protect against fire suppression, emergency medical response, disaster management, and public education. This photograph is of fire station No. 1, located in the Original Mile municipal complex. The first fire chief was G.E. Zimmerman. Fire station No. 1 moved with the municipal buildings off Reno Avenue and Midwest Boulevard in the 1970s, and the station in the Original Mile was repurposed as fire station No. 2 until it was demolished. In 2009, fire stations Nos. 2, 3, 4, and 6 were built. In 1983, Midwest City Fire formed the first hazmat team in the state, ensuring every fire suppression personnel was trained as a hazmat technician. (Courtesy of the Rose State College Foundation.)

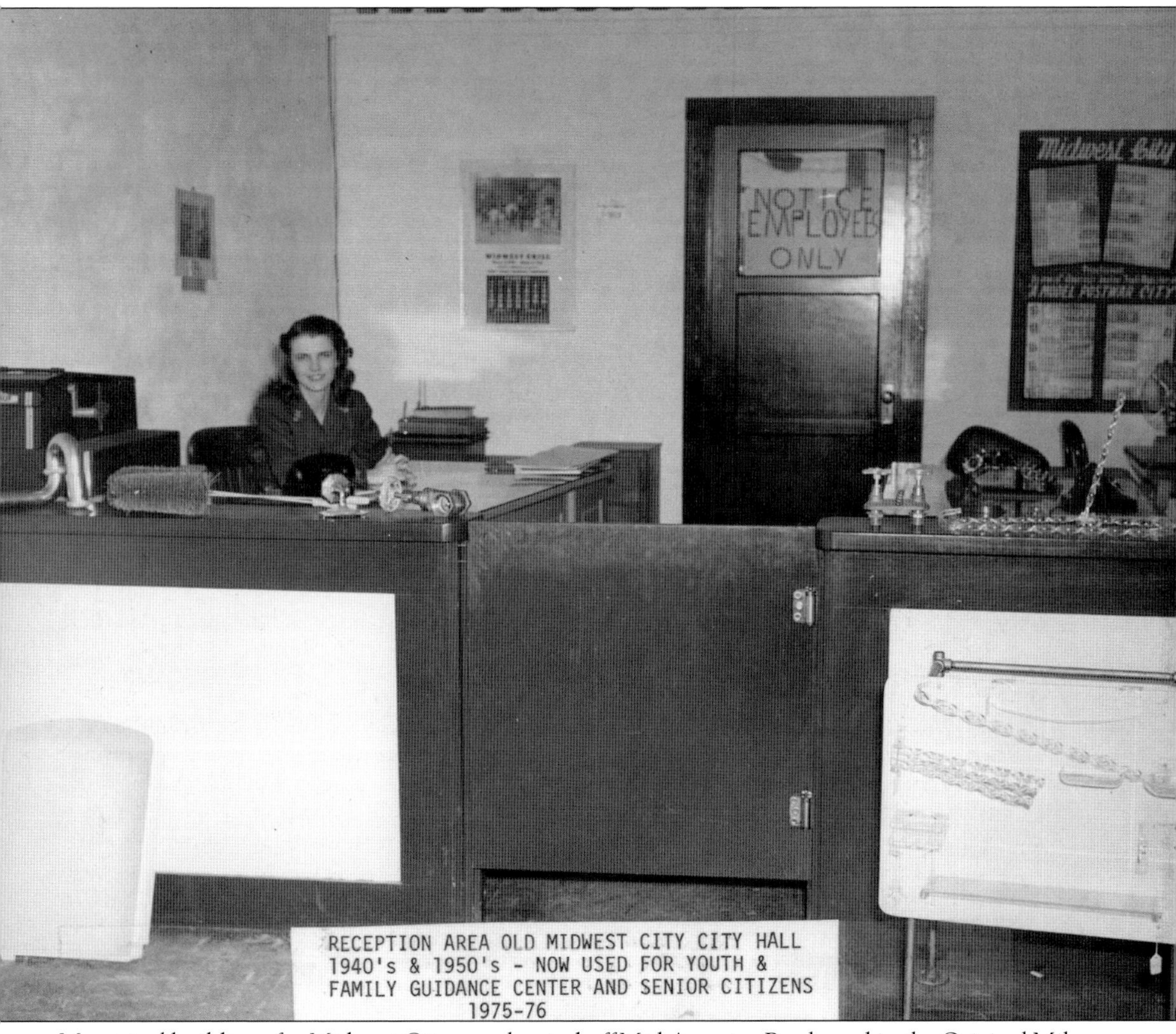

Municipal buildings for Midwest City were located off Mid-America Boulevard in the Original Mile behind the downtown shopping area. As bigger buildings were constructed on Midwest Boulevard and Reno Avenue, the structures were repurposed, such as the old Midwest City Hall. After the buildings began to decay, they were torn down, and the lot sat empty for quite some time before a park was dedicated to the community in honor of W.P. "Bill" Atkinson in 2023. (Courtesy of Midwest City High School History Center.)

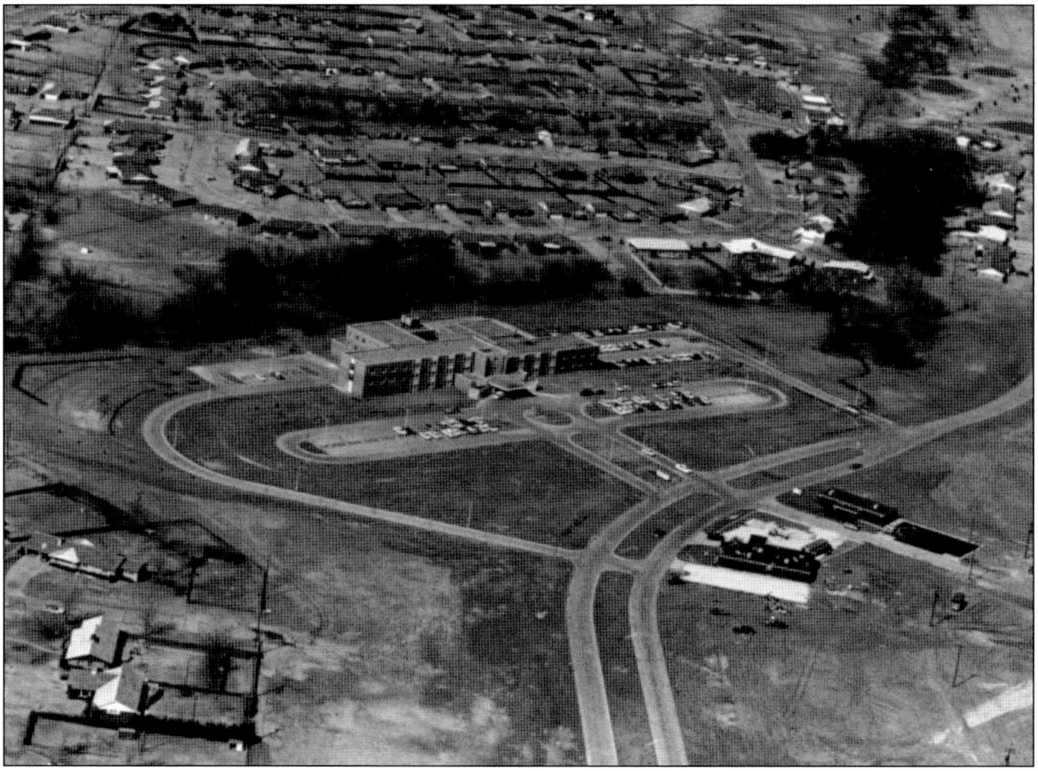

Midwest City's first hospital, Midwest City Memorial Hospital, was dedicated on October 6, 1962. This hospital began as a public hospital owned by the City of Midwest City as a 70-bed facility. It was the nearest hospital for many rural eastern Oklahoma County residents. The aerial view above was captured around 1964. The hospital was funded through voter bond money. The hospital staff photograph below celebrates the second anniversary of the hospital opening in 1966. It remained a public hospital until 1996, when it was leased to a private health care company, Health Management Associates. It would then change hands of health care organizations twice more before SSM Health St. Anthony Hospital-Midwest became the operators in the 2020s. (Above, courtesy of Oklahoma Historical Society; below, courtesy of Rose State College Foundation.)

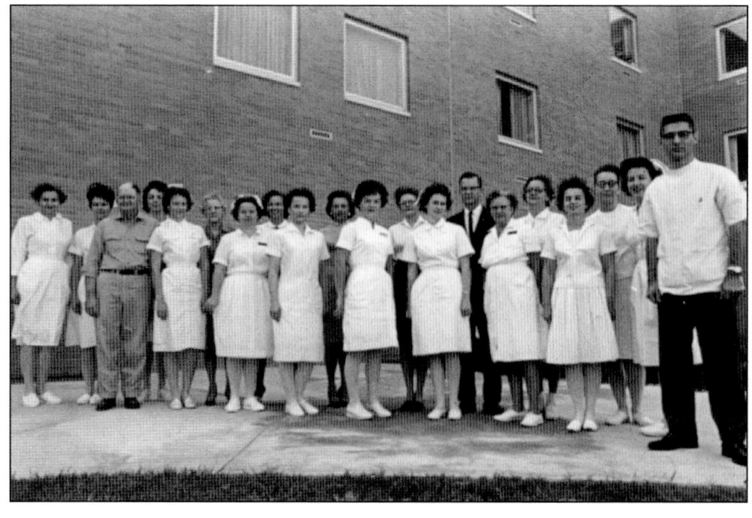

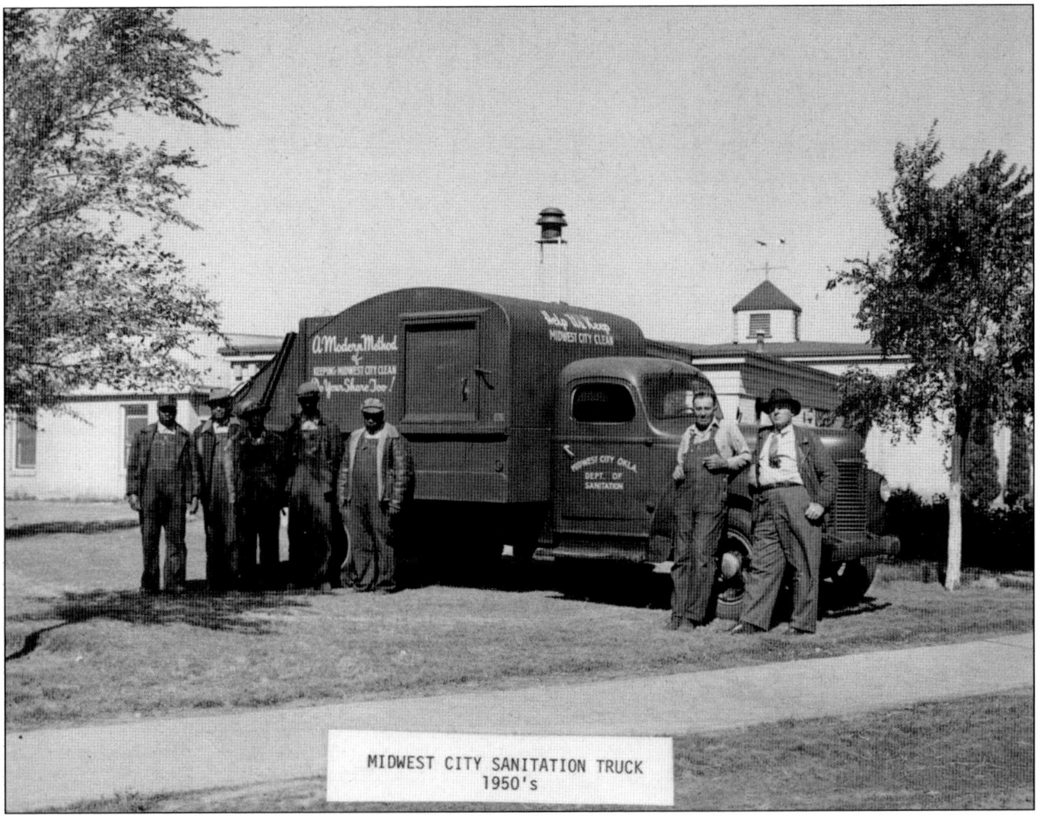

MIDWEST CITY SANITATION TRUCK
1950's

Above, these waste management workers stand in front of a Midwest City sanitation truck in the 1950s. Pictured are five black men on the left and two white men on the right. In the 1940s and 1950s, there were no black families residing in Midwest City, as it was designed for white middle-class families. Black workers would commute into Midwest City from mostly black communities in Oklahoma City for employment opportunities. (Both, courtesy of Midwest City High School History Center.)

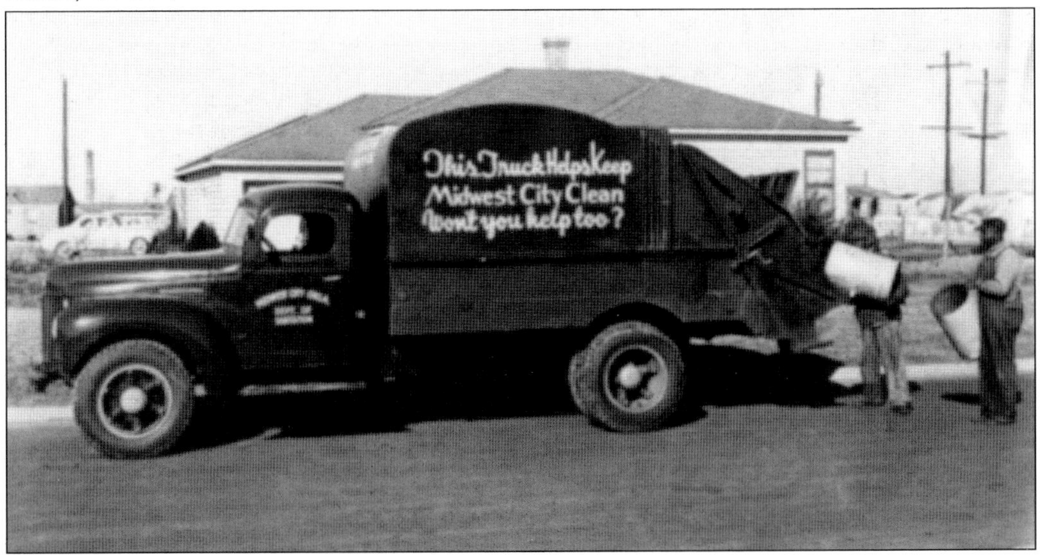

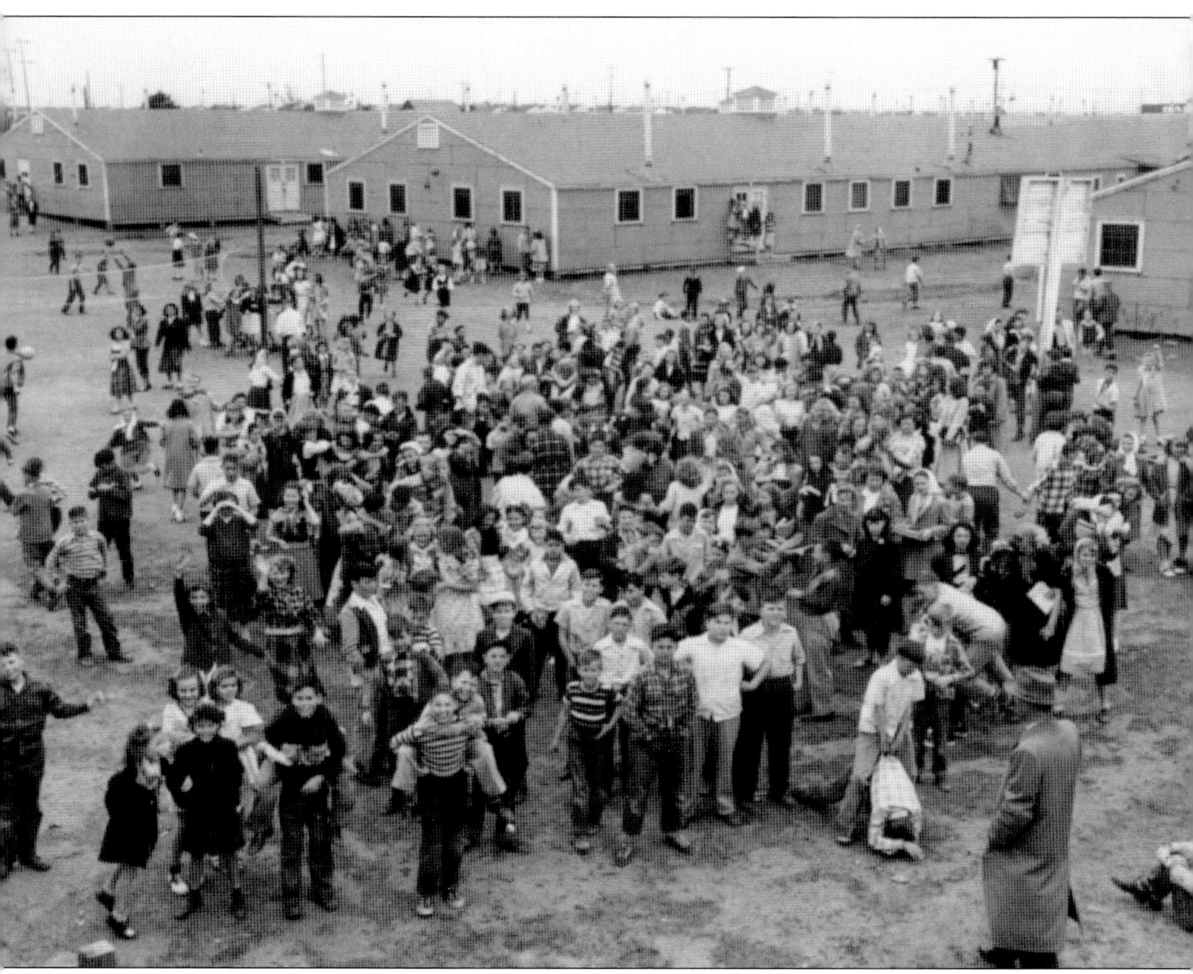

Fourth-, fifth-, and six-grade children happily gather after school for a candid photograph outside of the prefabricated buildings in the 1940s. In the foreground is a staff member named Mr. Melton, who later became a principal in the Mid-Del Schools. Barracks were used as temporary classrooms while the brick school building was being erected. (Courtesy of Rose State College Foundation.)

Six

Changing the Face of Education

Midwest City achieved more than serving its citizens by building schools for its incoming residents. Yes, if Midwest City was going to be successful, it had to have a good quality education system. But the leaders, Oscar V. Rose and J.E. Sutton, not only built a new school system from the ground up, they also changed the education system for every base support town in the United States through their work in legislation in Washington, DC. As many families moved to the new up-and-coming city, a school was needed as soon as possible. Originally, the first school—called Midwest City School—was held in prefabricated hutments in a field of mud with five teachers and 125 students. .

Before the new district was founded, a district called Sooner School District and a Soldier Creek School District fed into Capitol Hill High School of Oklahoma City schools. When Oscar Rose created Midwest City School, he wanted to have classes through 12th grade so that students from Sooner and Soldier Creek did not have to be bused a long distance for high school.

After much work and sacrifice, Mid-Del School District became the fourth-largest school district in Oklahoma at its peak. The district lines of the school district morphed over the years and, by the 2020s, included Del City, Midwest City, Forest Park, Oklahoma City, Choctaw, and Tinker Air Force Base.

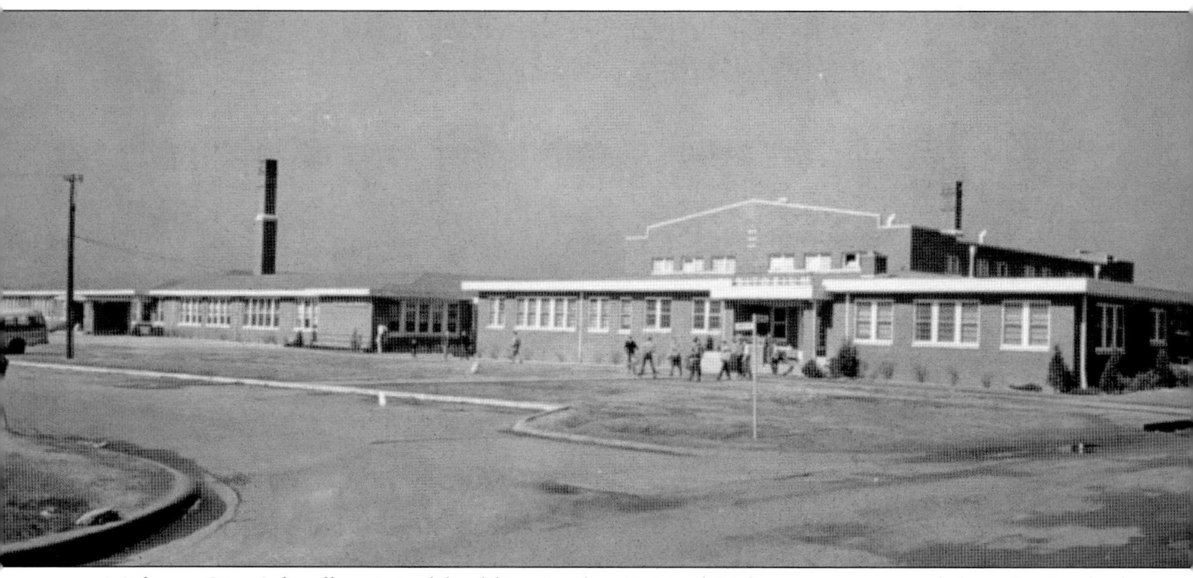

Midwest City School's original building in the Original Mile was repurposed for a junior high school named John Jarman Junior High School. Originally, it held nursery students through 12th grade. Due to an explosion of growth of the city, elementary students were moved off the campus into new buildings in 1946 and 1947, and the property held two different schools, a junior and high school, until a new high school structure was erected. There was also a public library on-site. By the second year, the school had 38 teachers and 1,250 students, according to a study by Meacham & Associates in 1992. (Courtesy of the Midwest City High School History Center.)

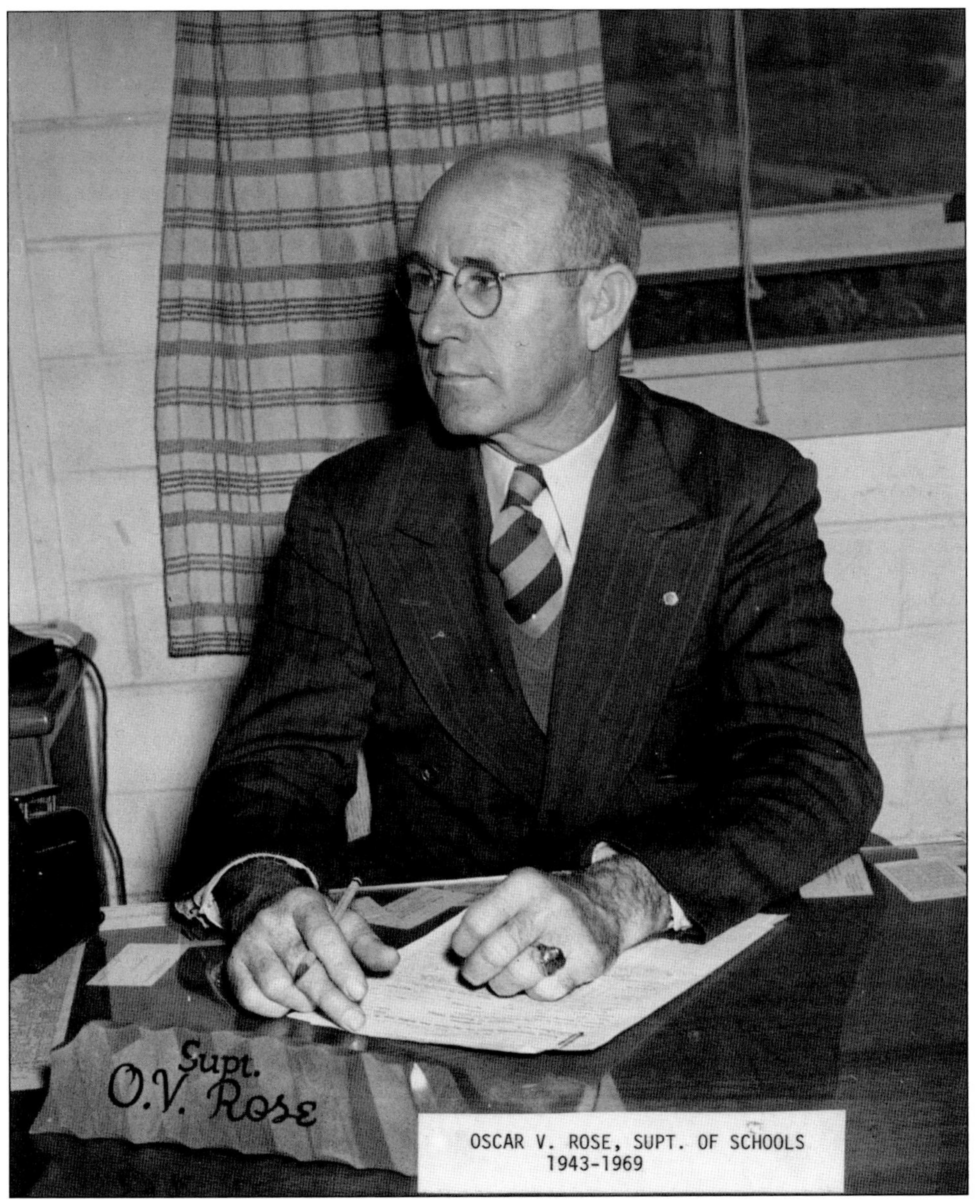

Rose State College is named after this significant man, Oscar V. Rose. Rose served as superintendent of Mid-Del Schools from the founding of the city of Midwest City in 1943 until 1969. The junior college was named in 1970. Working closely with Midwest City School principal J.E. Sutton, Rose helped build a vision and foundation for generations of public education in the Midwest City/Del City area. In 1950, Rose and Sutton both advocated and helped pioneer a federal education fund called "Impact Aid" from the Lanham Act of 1941. Fifteen years later in 1965, Rose met Pres. Lyndon B. Johnson after the signing of the Elementary and Secondary Education Act, now known as "No Child Left Behind," which allowed Rose and Sutton to use federal grants in a broader way to create equal opportunity for students to have a quality education. Upon Rose's death in 1970, house speaker Carl Albert reflected, "No single person has done as much to make the case for children living in federally impacted areas as Oscar Rose." (Courtesy of the Midwest City High School History Center.)

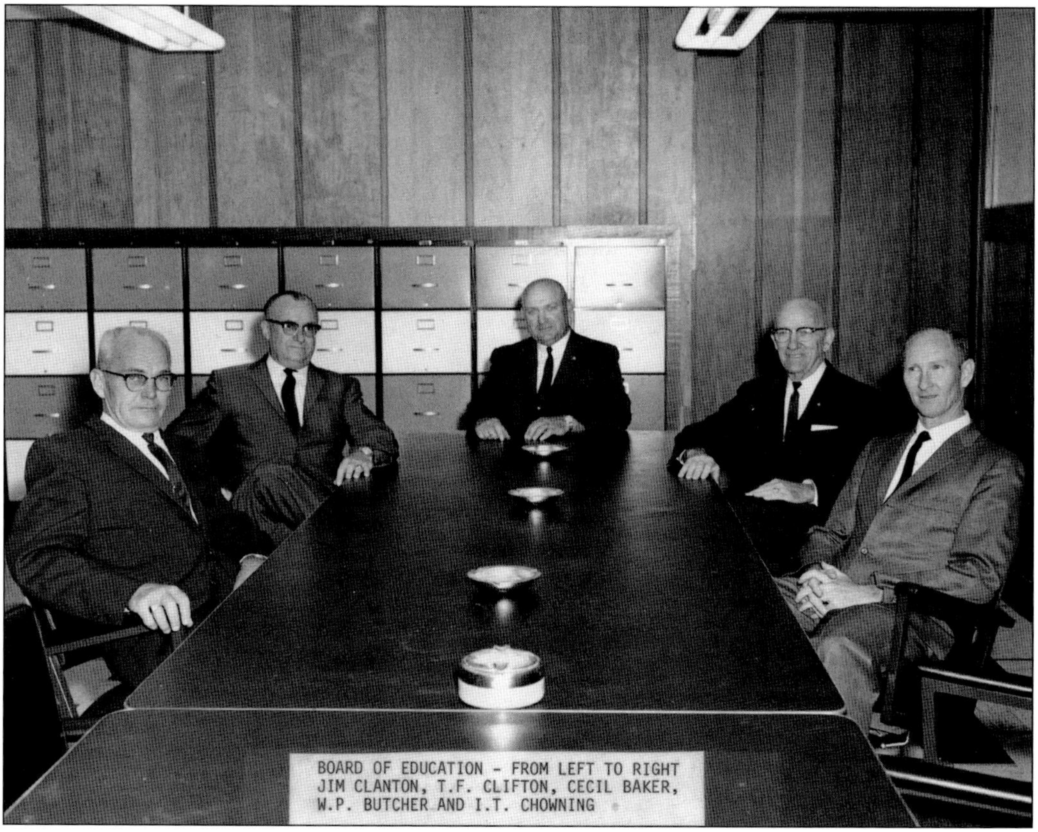

The Midwest City/Mid-Del School Board is pictured above during the 1950s. From left to right are Jim Clanton, T.F. Clifton, Cecil Baker, W.P. Butcher, and I.T. Chowning. Below is the meeting room at the Mid-Del Board of Education. The Mid-Del School System joined together early on in the late 1940s as Del City was founded not long after Midwest City. The joint school system was a result of both schools' athletic programs. As each school district was very competitive but shared school buses for events, an agreement was reached to place the name Midwest City-Del City Schools on the buses in 1970. It was then later shortened to Mid-Del School System. (Both, courtesy of Midwest City High School History Center.)

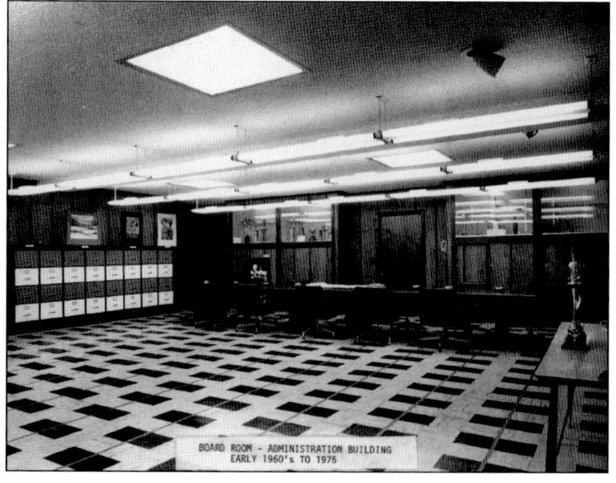

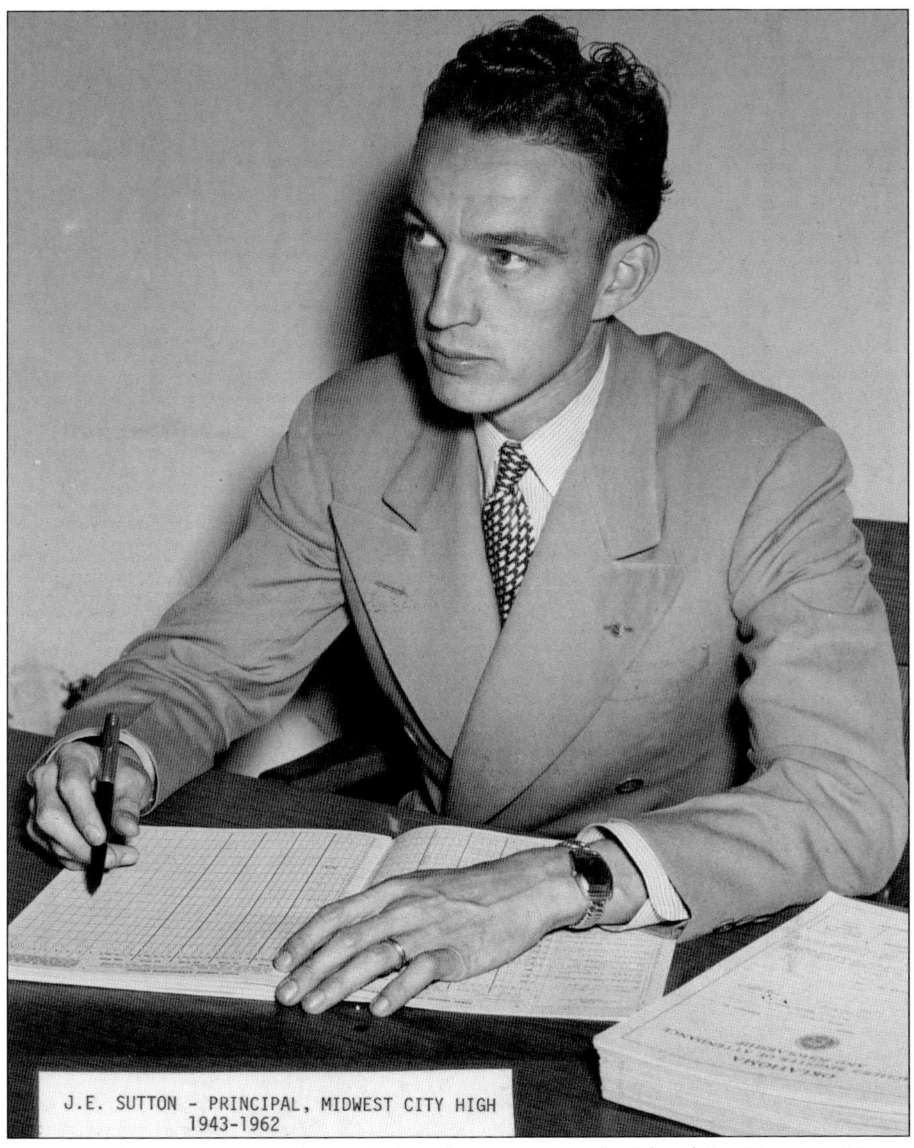

J.E. Sutton was best known as principal of Midwest City High School for 19 years. He was later deputy superintendent of Mid-Del Schools, then elected as Midwest City's only superintendent emeritus in Washington, DC, to advocate for Impact Aid for the school district. Born and raised in Boynton, Oklahoma, he became the superintendent of Schools at Council Hill, Oklahoma, at the age of 24. He served until 1943. In June of that year, he moved to Midwest City with his wife, Irene Lee Powers, and their one-year-old daughter to assist the growing community in the education system and remained there for the rest of his life. Sutton served in numerous leadership roles throughout his life, including the Oklahoma Association of Schools for Impacted Services (OASIS), the Board of Trustees of the Oklahoma Teachers Retirement System, Oklahoma Education Credit Union, Governing Board of the Midwest City Regional Hospital, Midwest City Lions Club, Midwest City Rotary Club, Adult V Department of Midwest City First Baptist Church, and Midwest City Chamber of Commerce. He loved his church and was an ordained deacon. He was later inducted into the Midwest City High School Wall of Fame in 1992. He passed away in 2001. (Courtesy of the Midwest City High School History Center.)

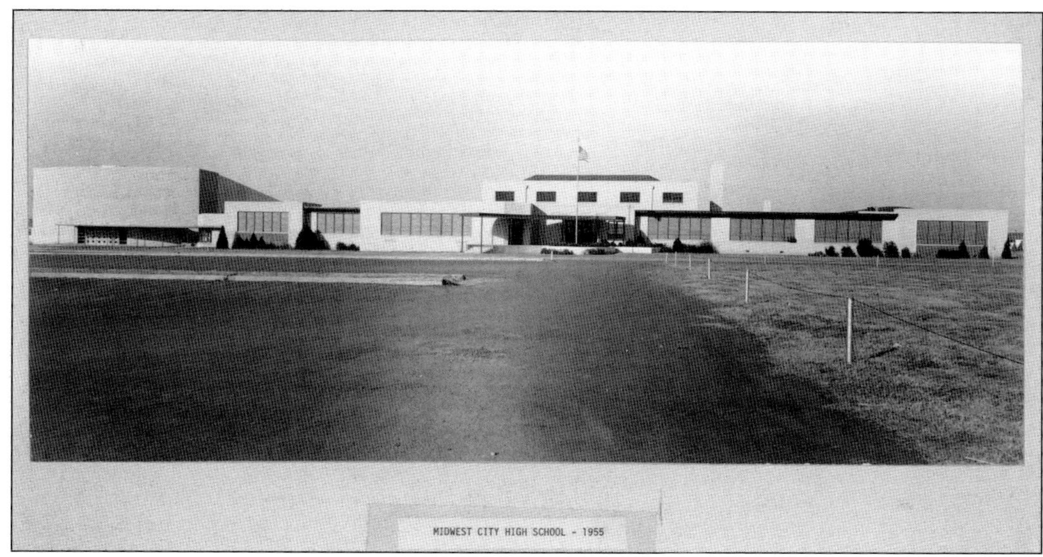

Below, high school students file in for the day at the entrance of the school. Located on Southeast Fifteenth Street between Midwest and Air Depot Boulevards, Midwest City High School was the first high school in the city until Carl Albert High School on Post Road was opened in 1963. The new Midwest City High School hosted grades nine through twelve as the district expanded. (Both, courtesy of Midwest City High School History Center.)

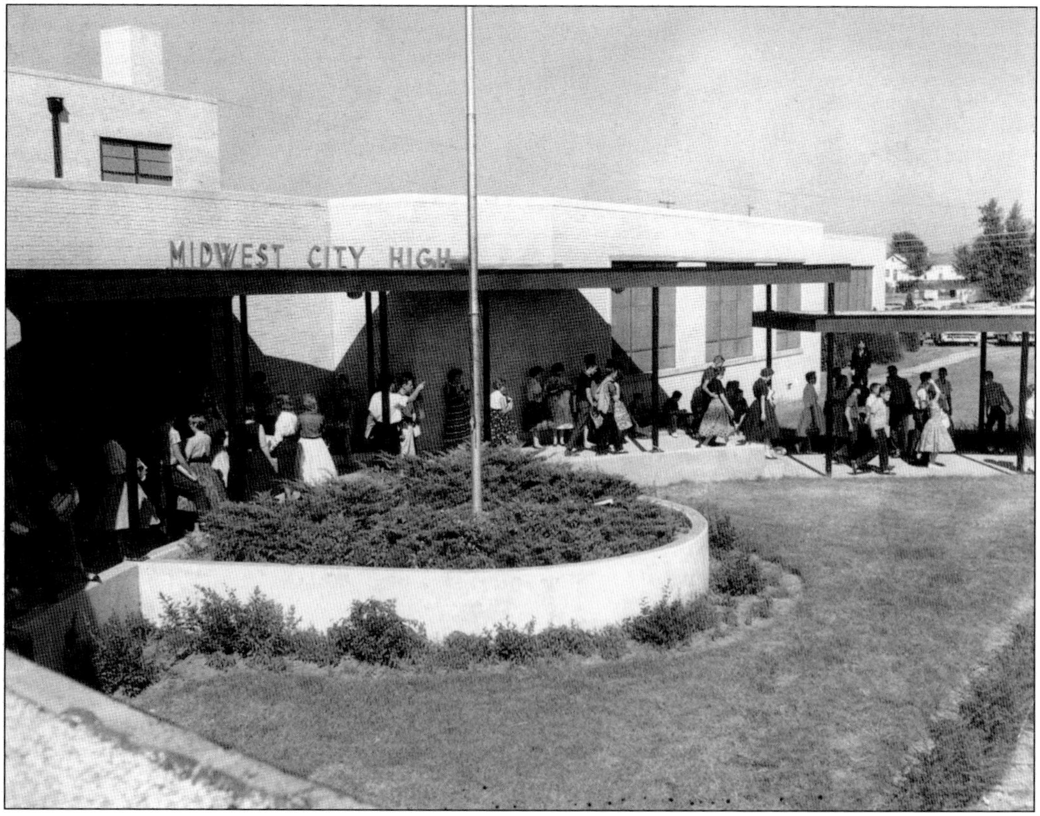

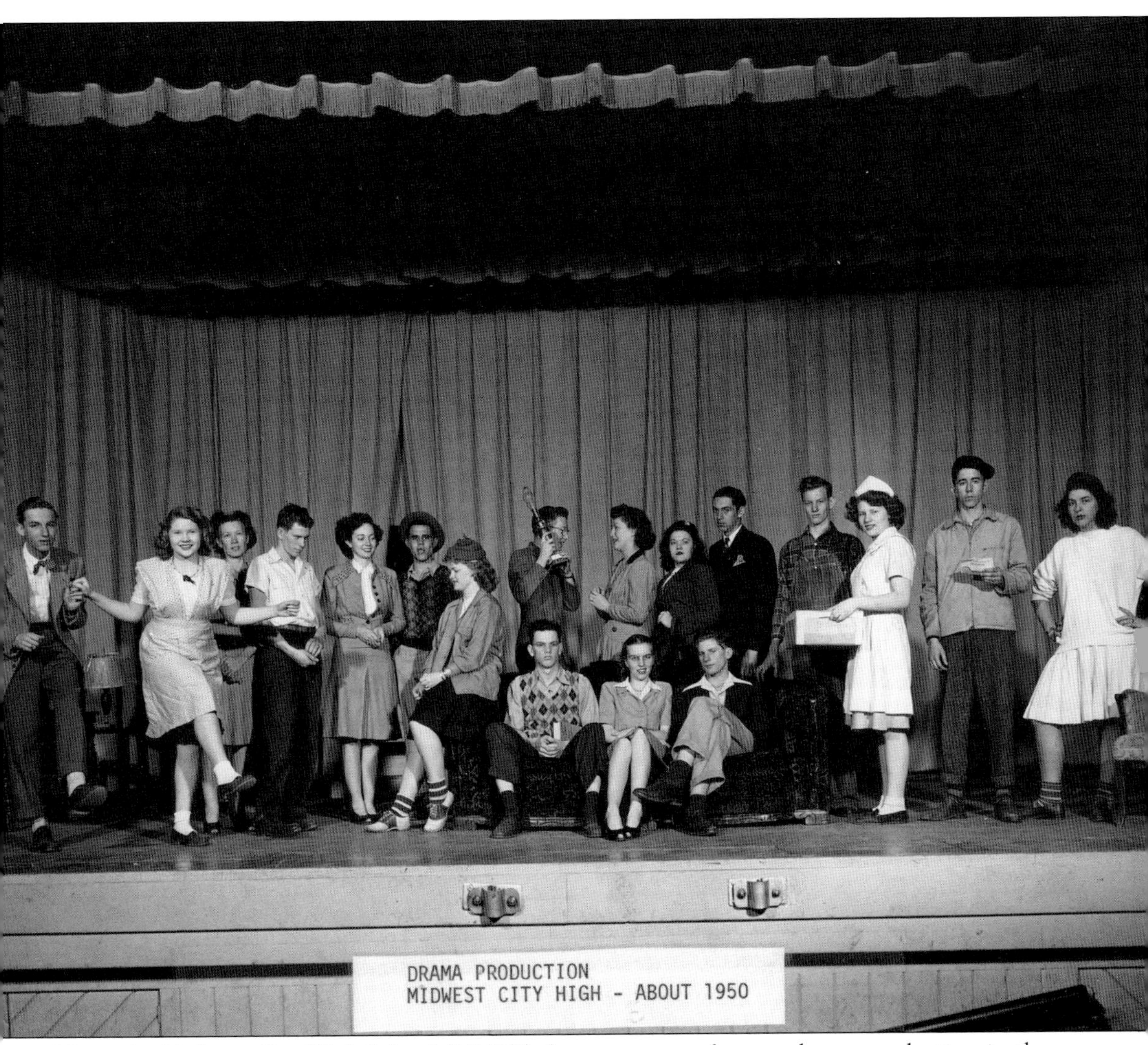

Here, the Midwest City High School (MCHS) drama team performs a drama production in the new Performing Arts Center (PAC) around 1950. The MCHS drama program would continue for many generations, performing classic dramas and musicals and competing in drama competitions. (Both, courtesy of Midwest City High School History Center.)

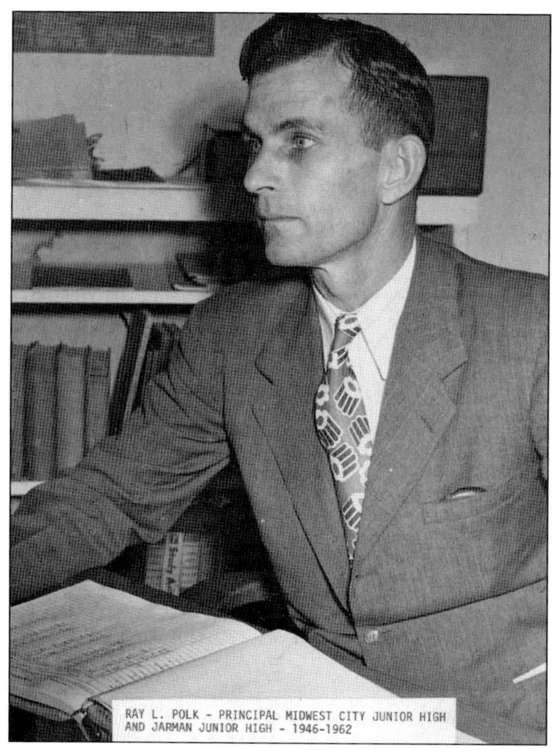
RAY L. POLK - PRINCIPAL MIDWEST CITY JUNIOR HIGH AND JARMAN JUNIOR HIGH - 1946-1962

Ray Polk (left) served as principal of Midwest City High School from 1946 to 1962. He spent 42 years in the education profession in Oklahoma, with 40 of those in public school administration. He served the Mid-Del School District for 27 of those years. During a tribute to him at his retirement from MCHS, it was written, "Ray Polk is a gentleman whose life clearly demonstrates living by the Golden Rule; loyal to students & professional staff; perceptively interested in the welfare of each student, their families & faculty members; open-minded in accepting innovative suggestions which promoted the mission of education; friendly, approachable, easy to talk to, displaying empathy toward the other fellow's problems; possessing a keen sense of humor & tremendous devotion in his responsibilities to his school & profession." Pictured below is Eva Clifford, Midwest City Elementary's first principal, in her office in 1943. (Both, courtesy of Midwest City High School History Center.)

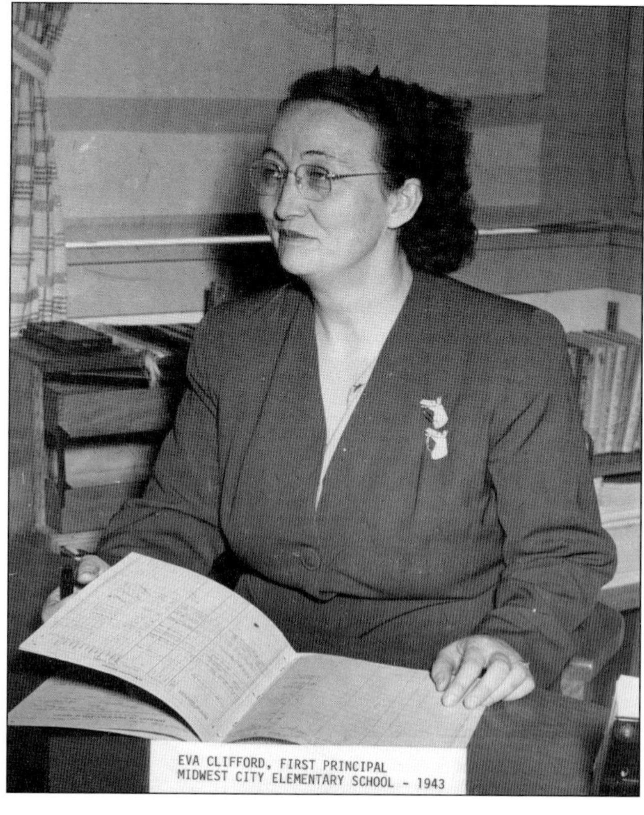
EVA CLIFFORD, FIRST PRINCIPAL MIDWEST CITY ELEMENTARY SCHOOL - 1943

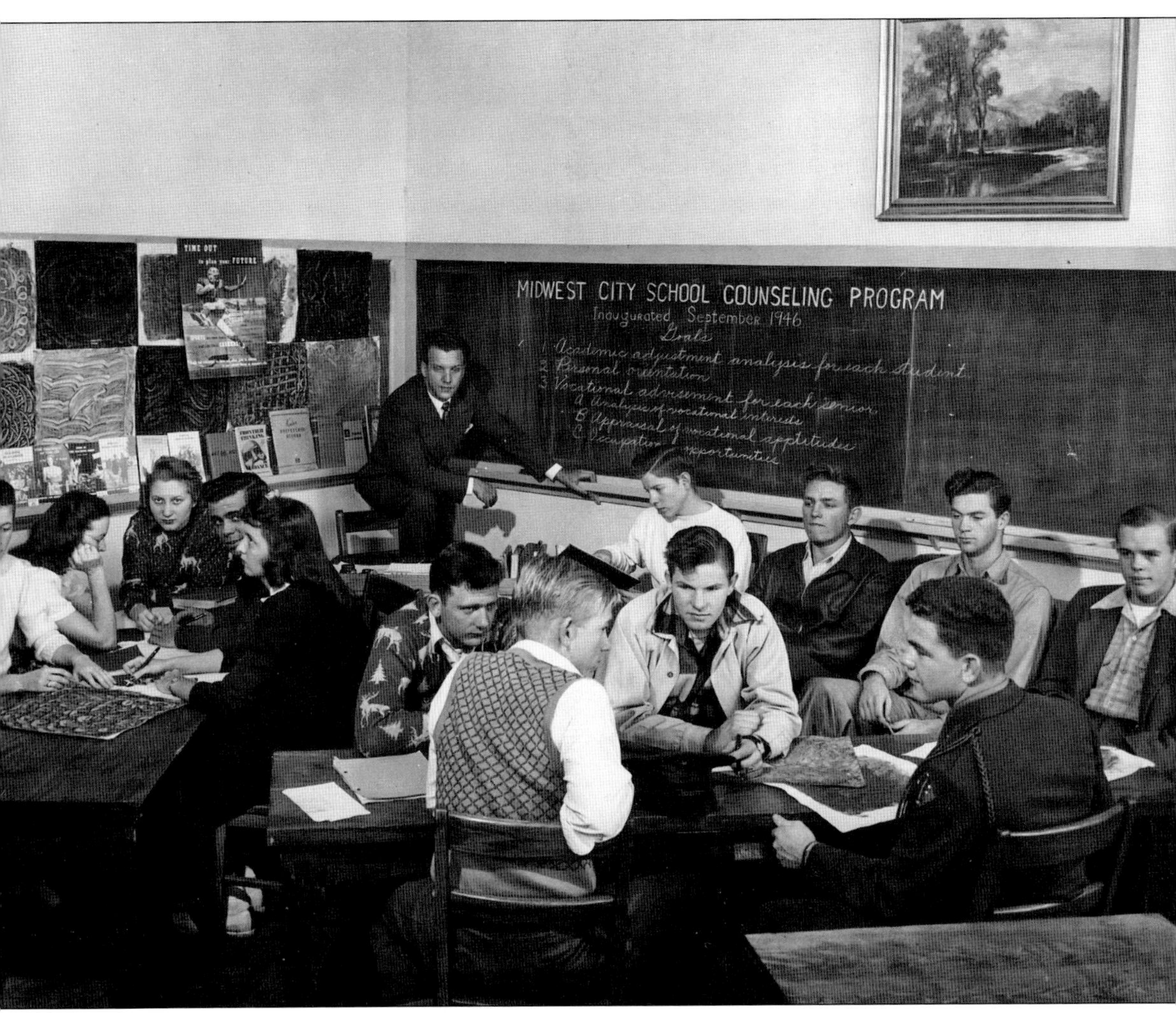

Pictured here are students in Midwest City School's first counseling program. The board reads, "Goals / 1. Academic adjustment analysis for each student / 2. Personal orientation / 3. Vocational advisement for each senior / A. Analysis of vocational interests / B. Appraisal of vocational aptitudes / C. Occupational opportunities." (Courtesy of Midwest City High School History Center.)

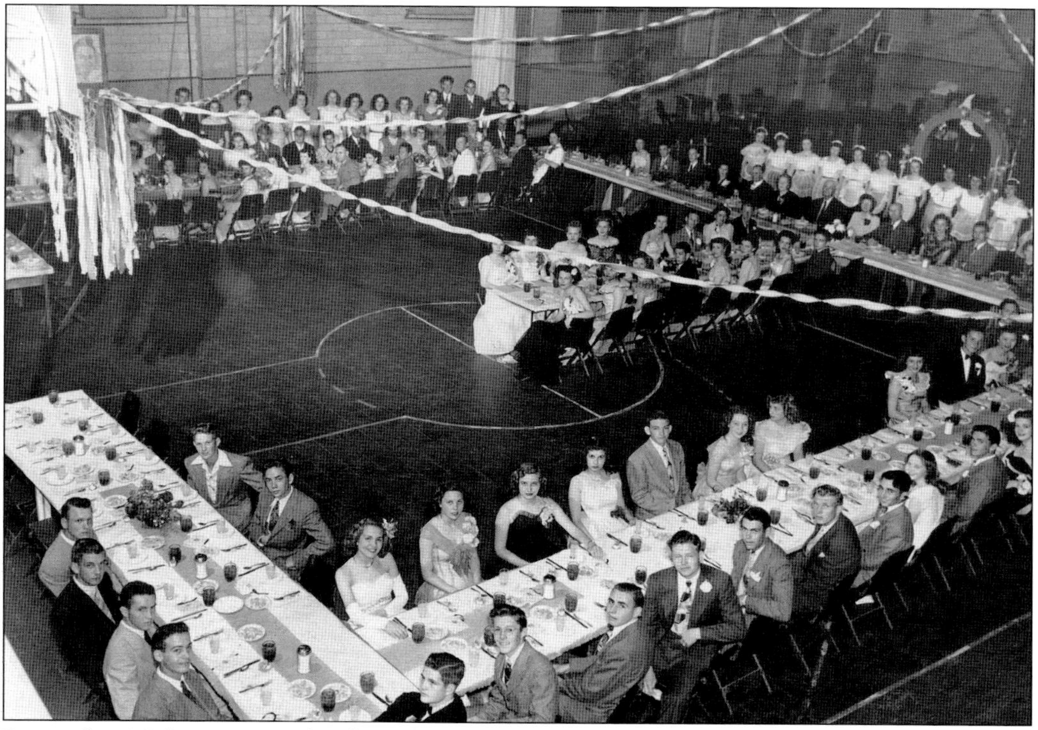

Pictured is Midwest City School's senior prom in 1946 (above) and 1947 (below). These two photographs were taken in the original public school building in Midwest City's Original Mile before it was repurposed for Jarman Junior High School. By 1947, the Midwest City High School junior and senior prom nearly doubled in size (as can be seen below). Held in the school's auditorium on May 9, the theme for 1947 was "Mexican Fiesta," and the women of Wickline Memorial Church prepared the food and even dressed up "Mexican style." The menu consisted of pineapple juice, creamed chicken in patties, Harvard beets, peas and carrots, Waldorf salad, iced tea, and lemon meringue pie. (Both, courtesy of Midwest City High School History Center.)

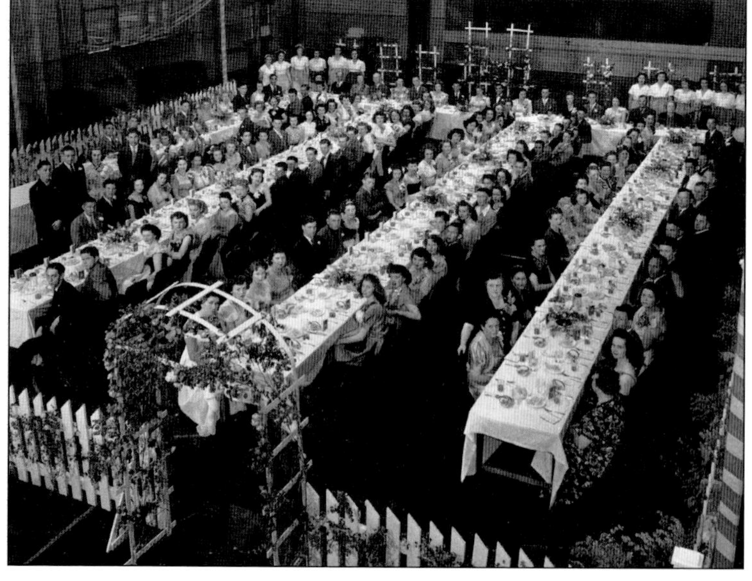

Pictured at right is the first senior class of Midwest City School in 1944 on their senior trip to Turner Falls, Oklahoma. Pictured here are, from left to right, (first row) Velma Bean, Mickey Pappam, Dorothy Harvey, and Bill Price; (second row) Ruth Aylor, Catherine Knox, Ruth Cassios, and Marge Fleck; (third row) Glen Holcomb, Virginia Gifford, Connie Maxey, and an unidentified student. The image below is of two Midwest City School seniors in 1955. (Both, courtesy of Midwest City High School History Center.)

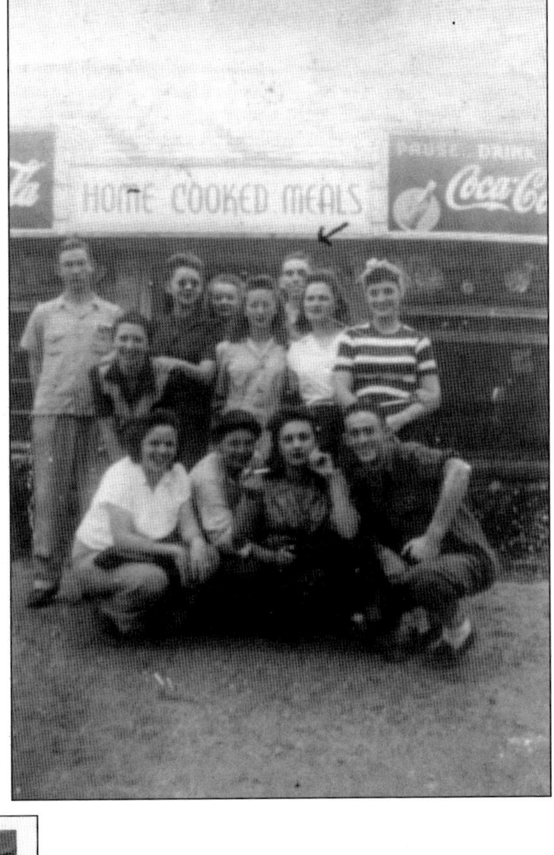

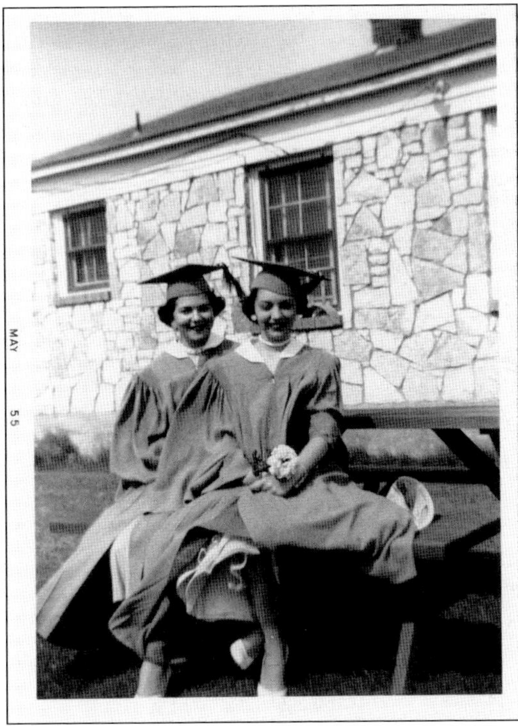

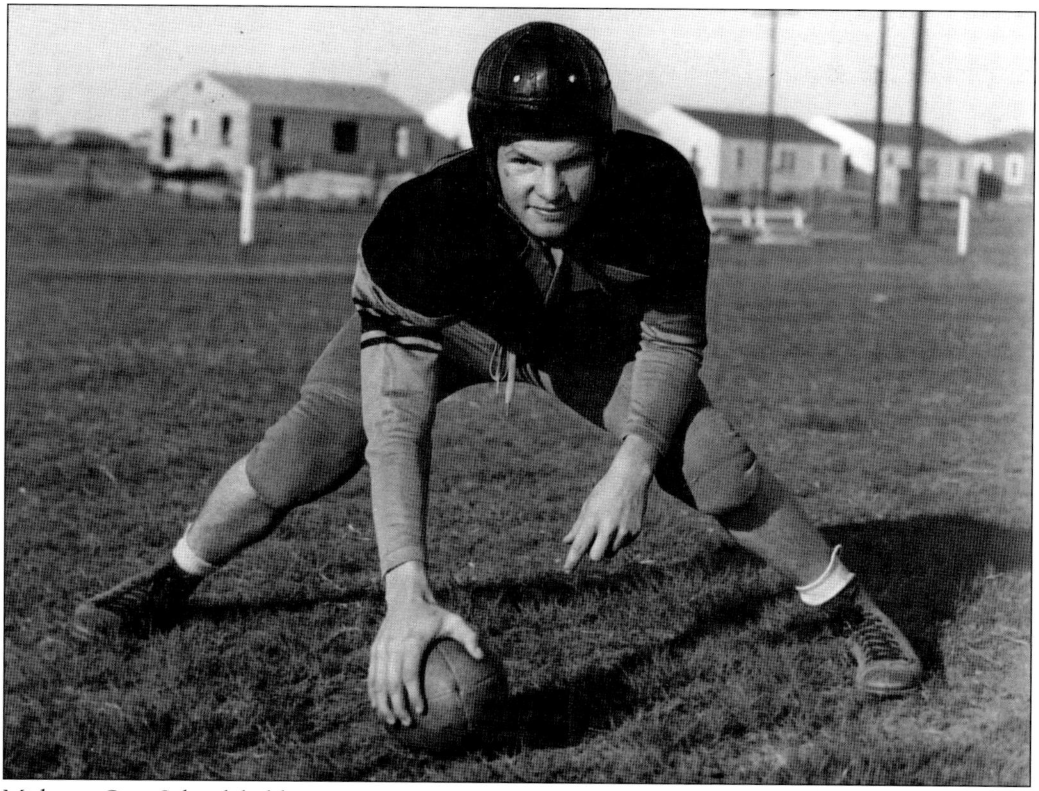

Midwest City School held many sports programs, including football, baseball, and basketball. Pictured above is Robert Allen Fox, Midwest City School class of 1947. He was involved in all three sports during his four years of high school. In the progression of American sports, football players had more padding and head protection than previous generations. Here, Fox is wearing a leather helmet that ties under the chin. Below are the football teams of all Midwest City schools in the late 1950s, showing the growth of the program as the school system became the fourth largest in the state of Oklahoma. (Both, courtesy of the Midwest City High School History Center.)

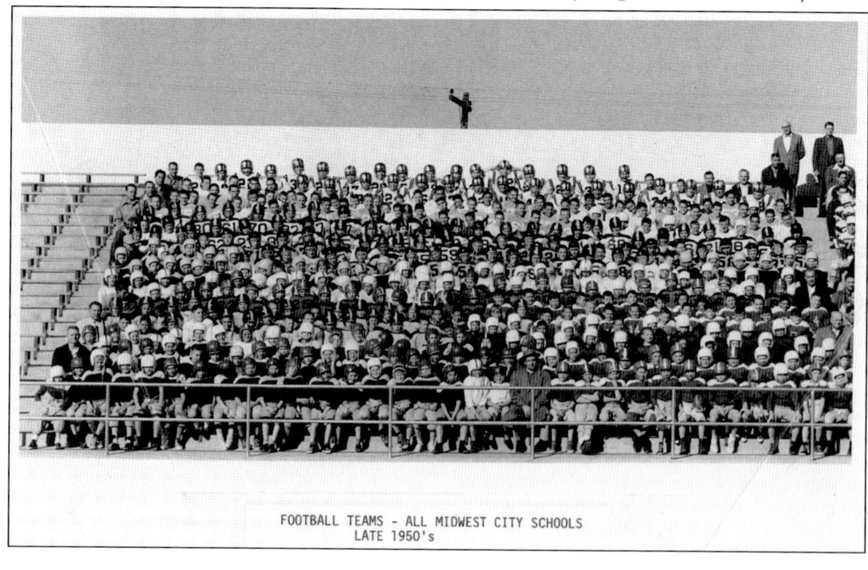

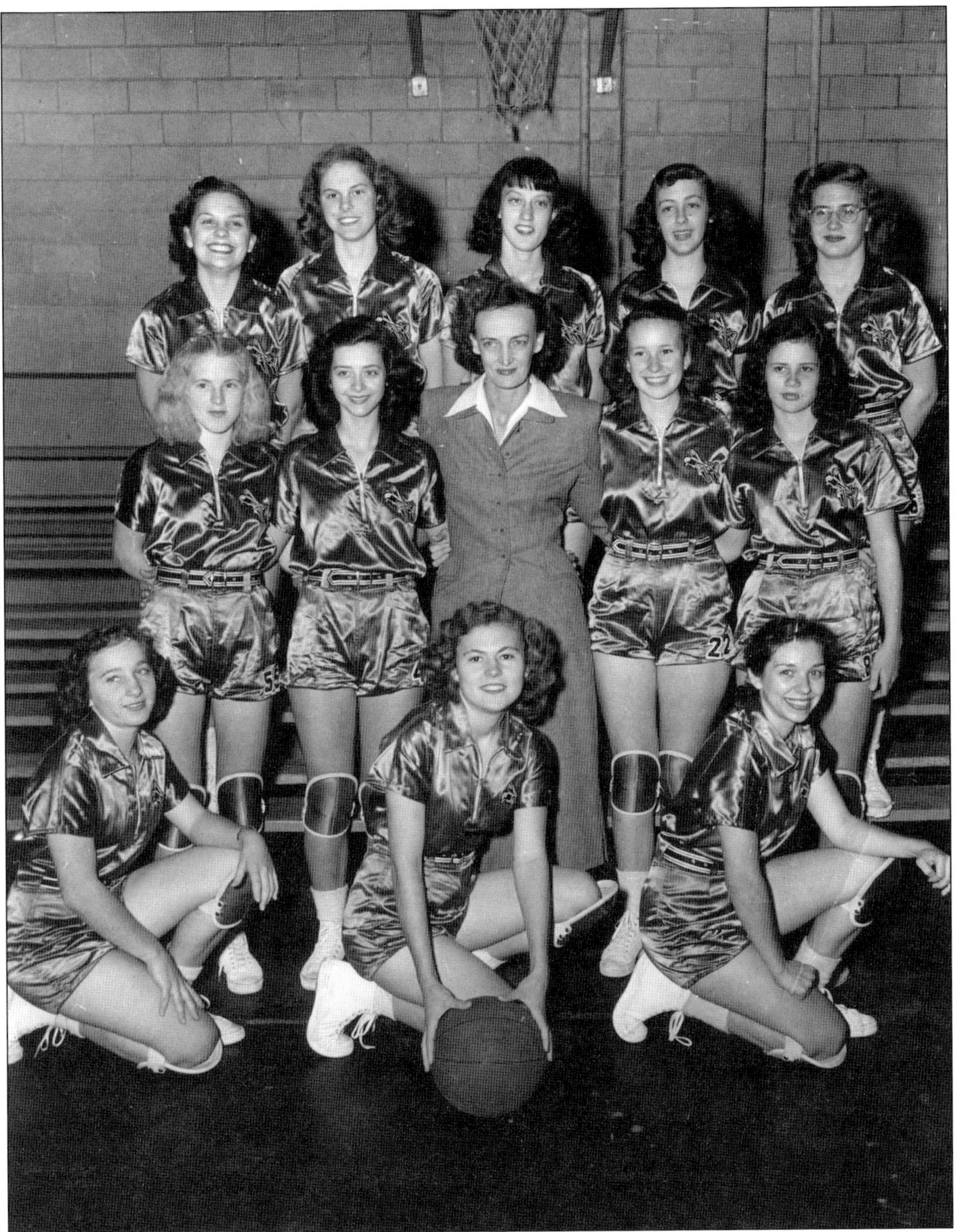

Pictured here is Midwest City High School girls' basketball coach and her team. Coach Delena Melton began coaching in 1946 and went on to win a championship in 1952. It was the first district championship in athletics by any Midwest City High School team. Midwest City High School later discontinued the girls' basketball program. (Courtesy of the Midwest City High School History Center.)

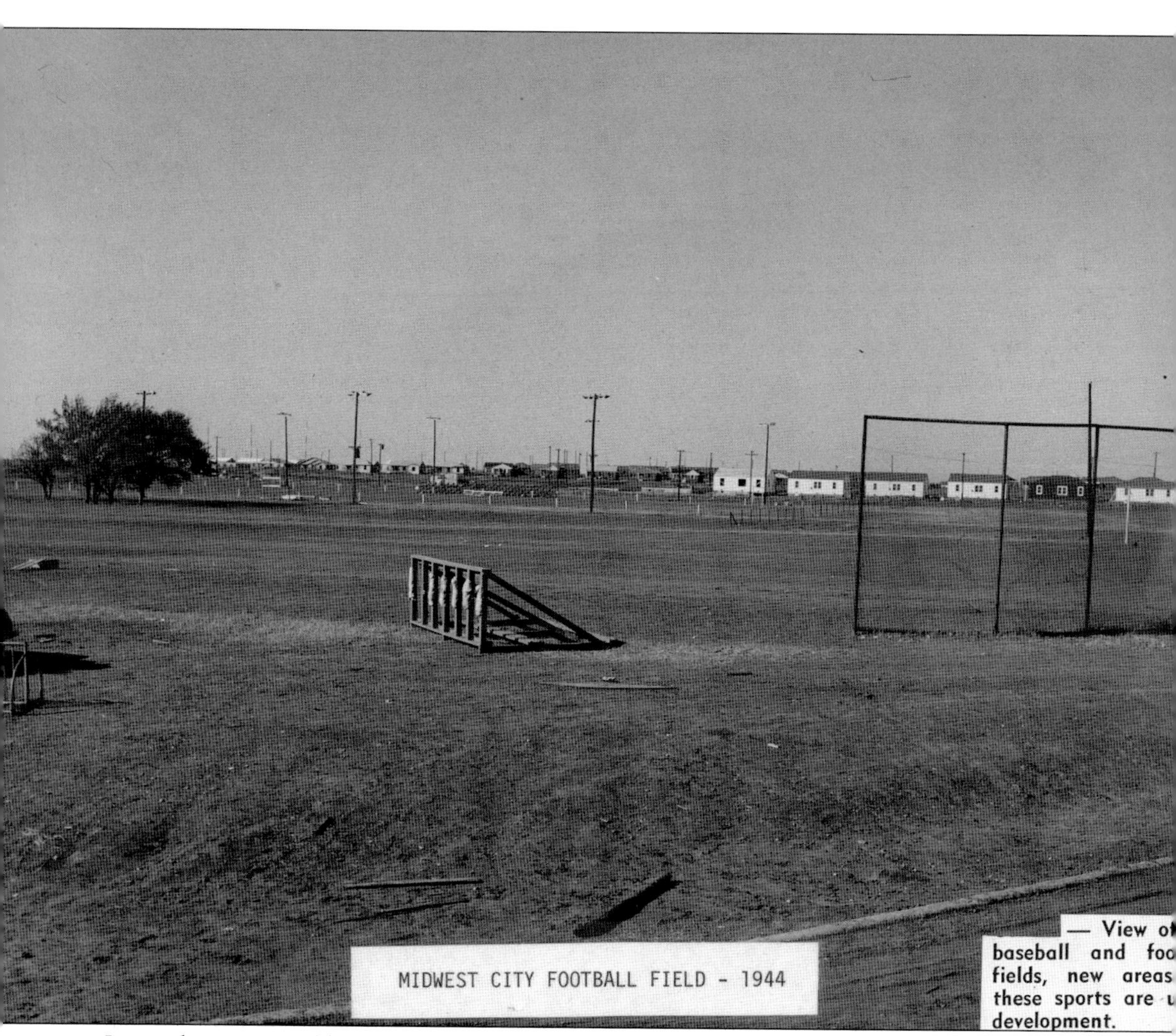

Located on East Lockheed Drive, this is Midwest City Football Field in 1944, later known as Rose Field after Oscar Rose. Before a stadium was built with locker rooms, seating, and a press box, students for football and baseball practiced in this open field. (Courtesy of the Midwest City High School History Center.)

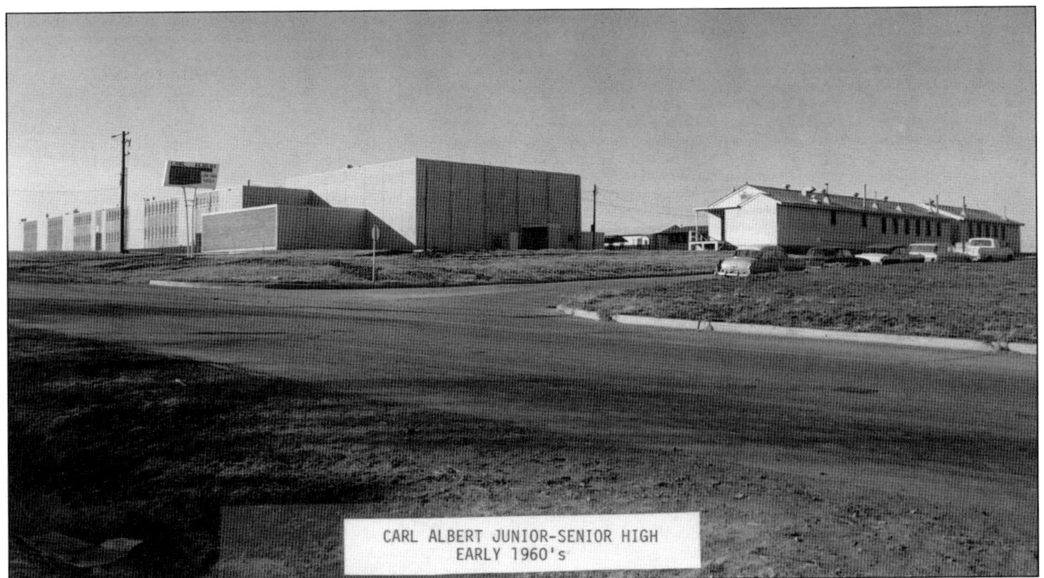

Due to the growth of population in Midwest City, Carl Albert Junior-Senior High School was built and dedicated in 1964. Though there was controversy over why Carl Albert was established, ultimately, it was concurred that its founding was due to population increase and the need for more space. Carl Albert established its own school culture, traditions, and history as it competed in local sports and arts programs and became very competitive academically. (Above, courtesy of Midwest City High School History Center; below, courtesy of the Oklahoma Historical Society.)

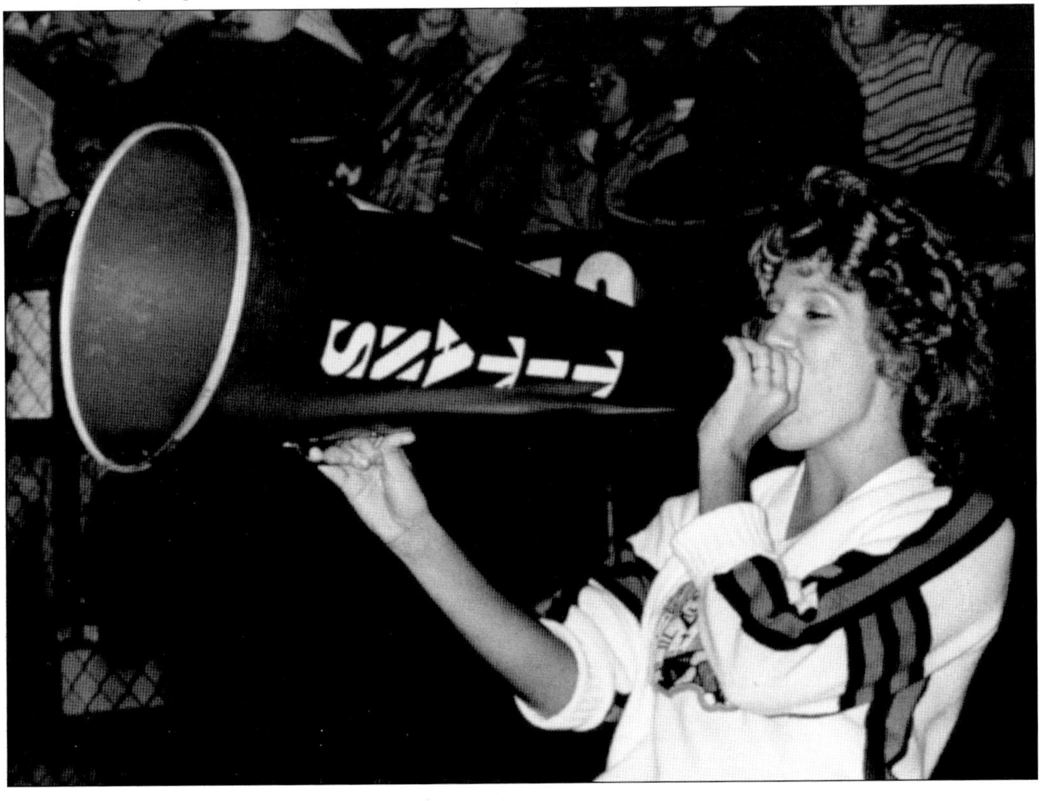

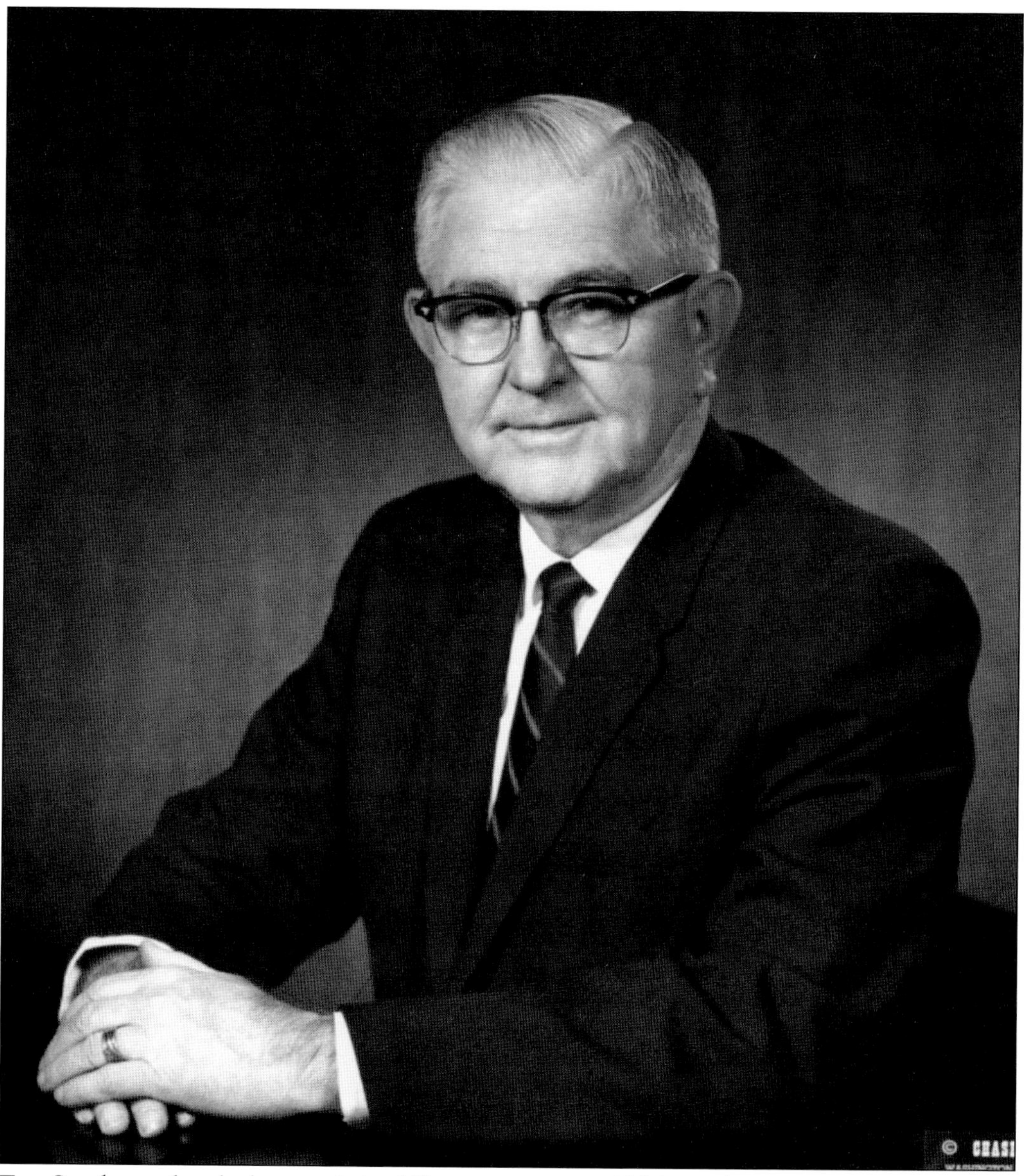

Tom Steed served as the longest-sitting US congressman in Oklahoma history. Steed assisted Oscar V. Rose in gaining funding for Rose State Junior College to create the Education Center during his time on the education committee. In partnership with Robert S. Kerr, Steed sponsored a bill creating Lake Thunderbird, giving access to water for Norman, Midwest City, and Del City. He protected the interests of Tinker Air Force Base as an advocate. He also helped create the nation's vast interstate system. (Courtesy of the Rose State College Foundation.)

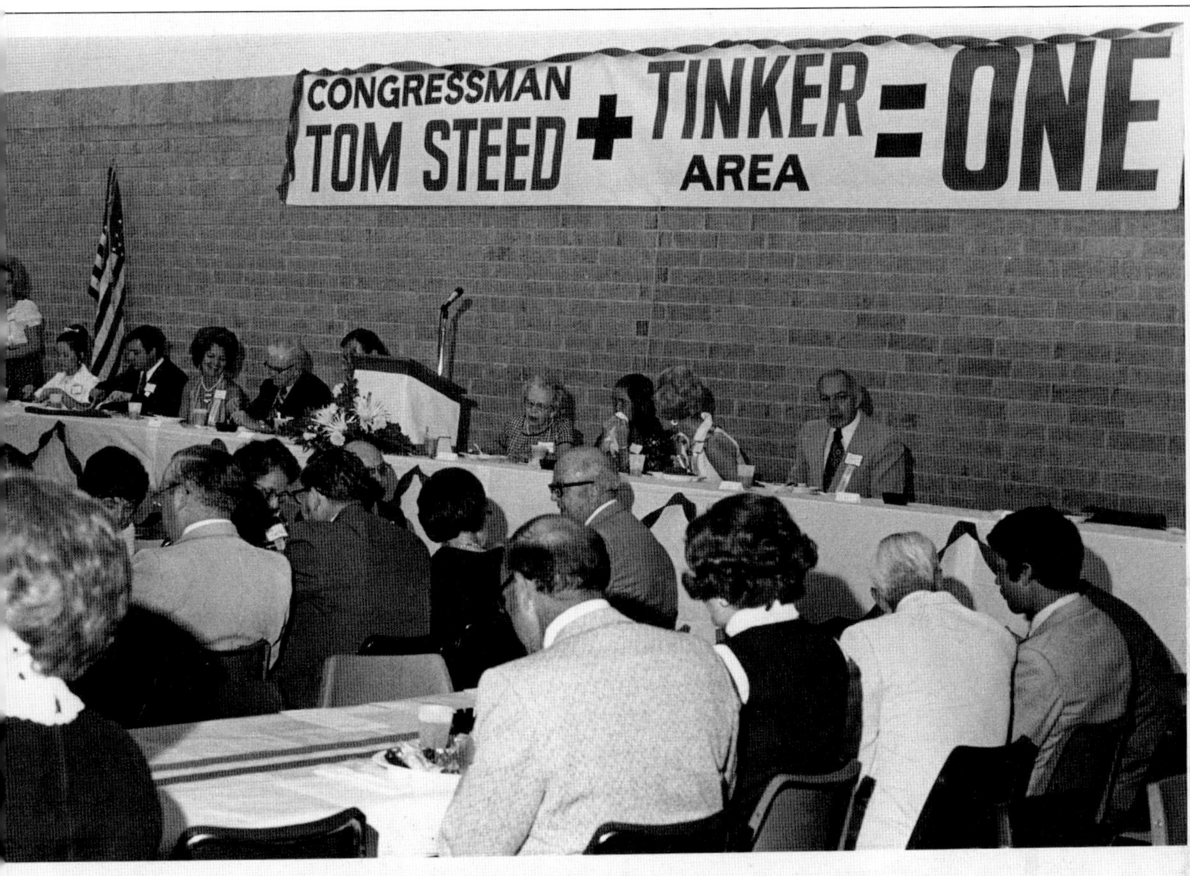

During World War II veteran Tom Steed's run for Congress, Midwest City and Tinker Air Force Base stood by him, hosting dinners and campaign fundraisers. Many Midwest Citians recognize his name today as the inspiration for Steed Elementary. He was elected in 1949 as a Democrat and continued to lead as a congressman until 1980. One contribution he made to Midwest City was helping secure funding for portions of Rose State College. (Courtesy of Midwest City High School History Center.)

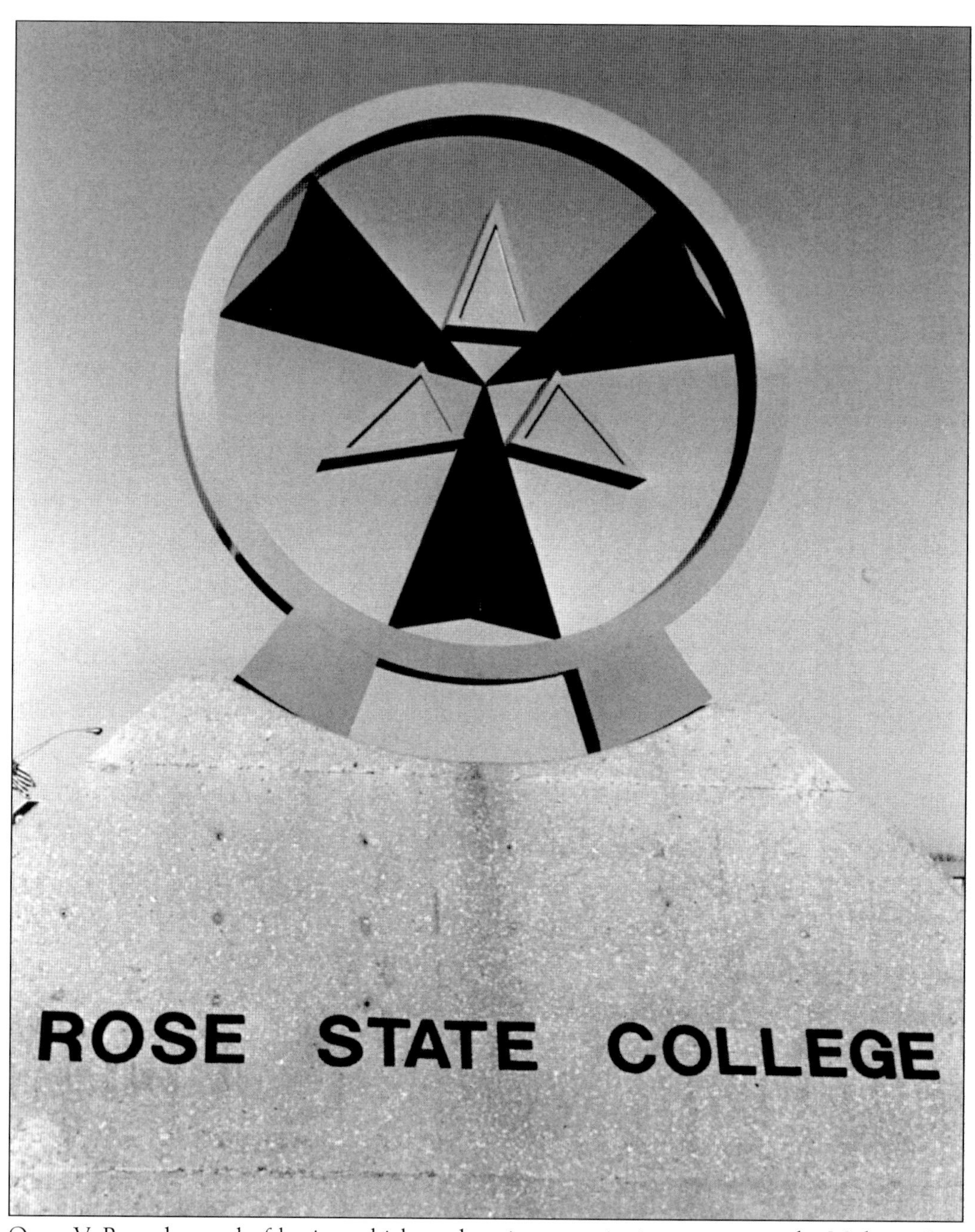

Oscar V. Rose dreamed of having a higher education organization present in the Midwest City area. Through much planning, networking, and advocating for funds in Washington, DC, that desire came to pass in 1970 when his namesake, Rose State Junior College (later Oscar Rose Junior College), was born. Now named Rose State College, this higher education institution began with one structure and a handful of students but grew to welcome over 270,000 students and construct 22 buildings on its campus within its first 50 years. It has become a pipeline to Tinker Air Force Base, the Mid-Del School System, and other employers in the area as it trains the professional workforce. (Courtesy of the Oklahoma Historical Society.)

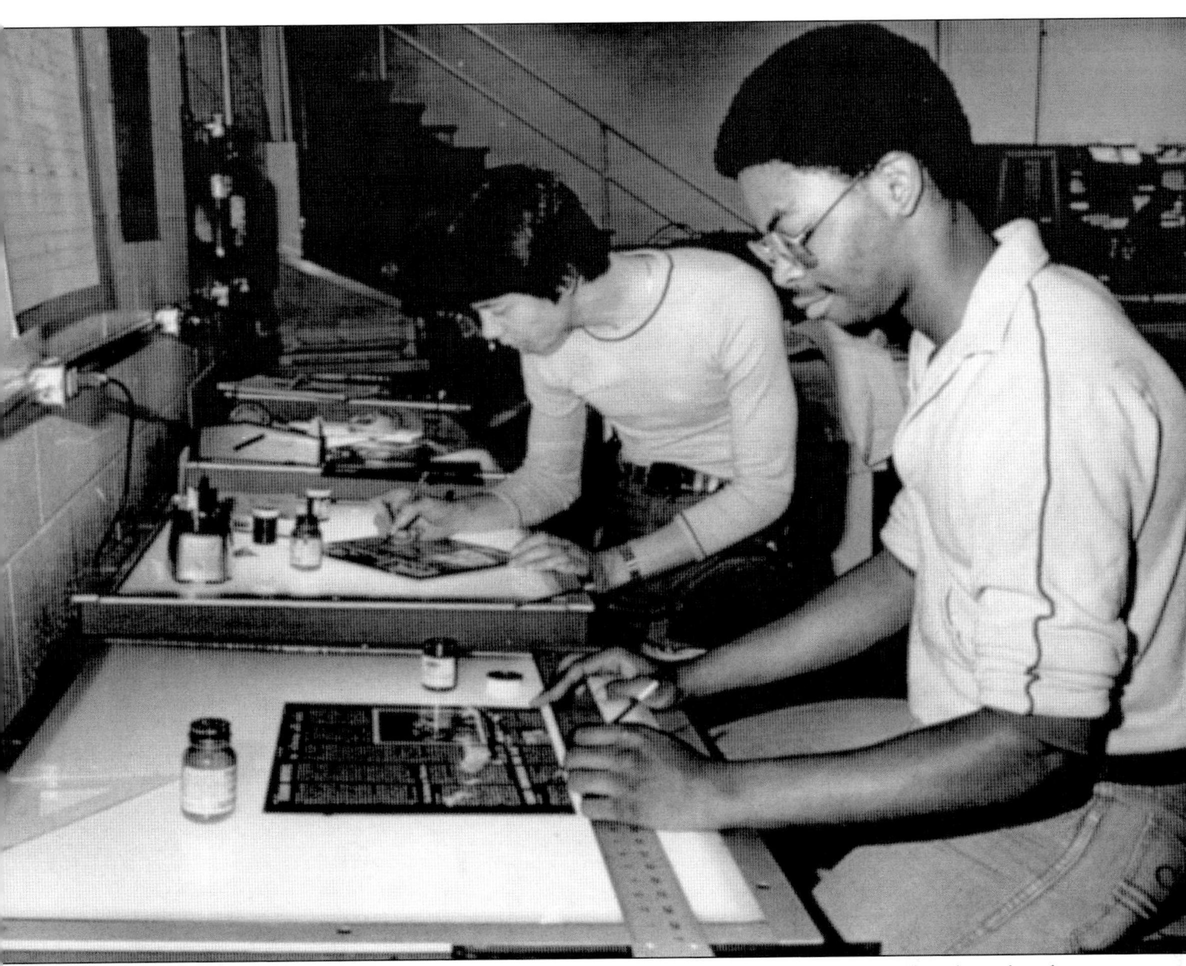

Pictured here are students at the Mid-Del Votech, later to be called the Mid-Del Technology Center. The Mid-Del Technology Center was built in 1965 and offered nine classes during the 1965–1966 school year. The courses available were auto body, aircraft engines, electronics service and communications, printing, upholstery, air-conditioning and refrigeration, and three classes of auto mechanics with 315 students. By the 2020s, the institution had grown to include three campuses providing full-time career training to adults and high school students, short-term special interest courses to the community, and technical aircraft training for military and civilian personnel. (Courtesy of Oklahoma Historical Society.)

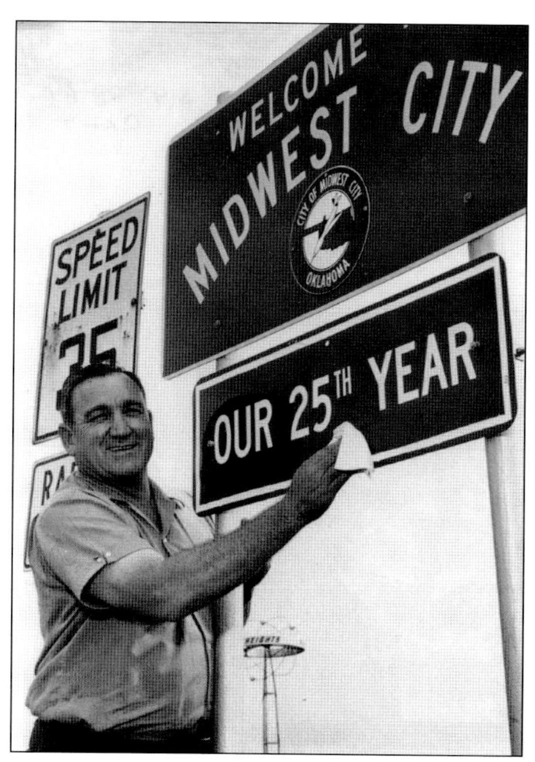

In 25 years, the Model City grew to over 65,000 in population. New houses were being built to accommodate the influx, and the economy was strong. Morale was high, even amongst the social pressures of the Vietnam War and national civil rights movement. (Both, courtesy of the Rose State College Foundation.)

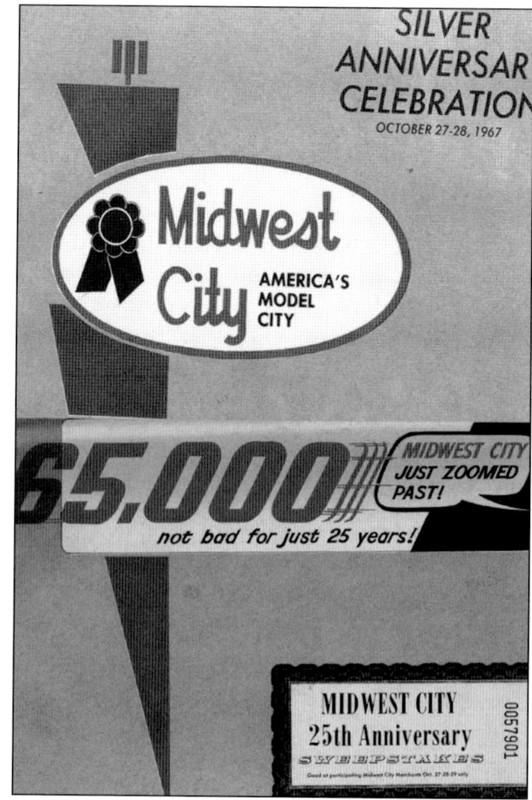

Seven

Ponies, Betrayal, Loss, and a Comeback

As Midwest City continued to grow and thrive, Bill Atkinson began his next endeavor—bigger houses, bigger lots, and a unique selling point of a new Shetland pony. Atkinson believed Midwest City needed more innovative "Homes of Distinction." The Ridgecrest Country Estates addition hosted many of the professionals of Midwest City, such as doctors, lawyers, and those who were advancing in their positions and needed a bigger home to support their families and new lifestyles.

In addition to Ridgecrest Country Estates, Midwest City was beginning to realize the cost of being a military-based support city. Plane crashes endangered local neighborhoods, especially in the housing addition located at the northern approach of planes to Tinker's runway. The Glenwood addition had to be shut down and demolished for the protection of the community. It previously had 835 homes and an elementary school, all of which had to be relocated in the early 1970s. The plane crashes (at least three between the years of 1961 and 1969) also put the future of the air base at risk. Bringing a solution to the Glenwood addition helped protect Tinker, including a state question to support a county bond to tear down the addition and relocate the residents. The bond was approved, and Glenwood was cleared away in about five years, lying empty for about a decade before the military began to use the land for training.

Around the same period, founder Bill Atkinson ran for governor in 1958 and in 1962, losing both elections. Many Midwest City residents supported and kept track of his election and brought more eyes to the growth of Model City. As Scarlett Bowmen wrote about the election, "Atkinson built a city but lost a state." Atkinson attributed most of his campaign loss to media attacks from a disgruntled E.K. Gaylord through the *Oklahoman* newspaper platform. In response, Atkinson used his past experience in media to open up the *Oklahoma Journal*, promising that readers would be privy to "both sides" of the story that may otherwise not be accessible from other news outlets. The *Oklahoma Journal* became very successful, employing almost 250 people at one time in its history and serving Oklahoma from 1964 to 1980.

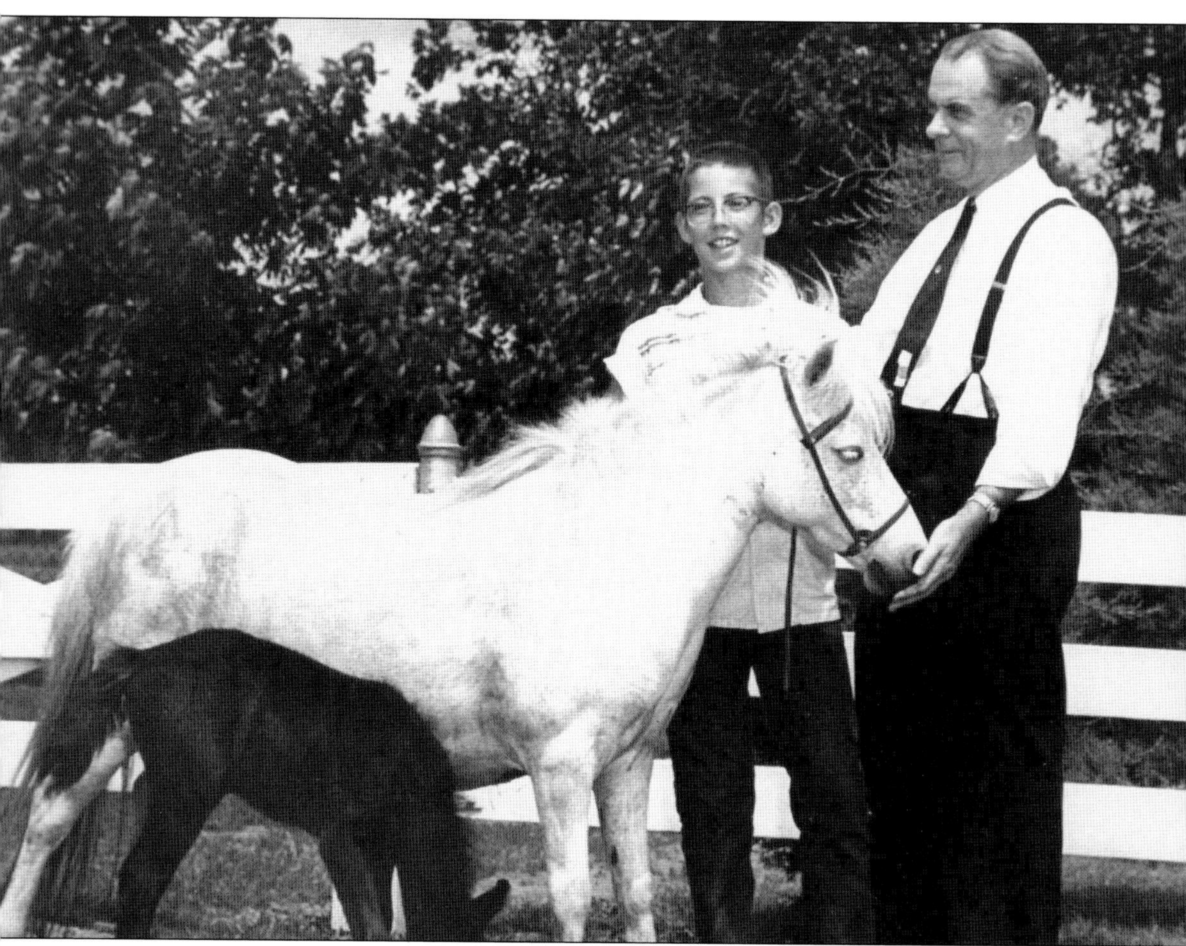

In the 1950s–1960s, W.P. "Bill" Atkinson fought against a slump in house sales, which gave him national recognition through a creative marketing technique—giving away a new Shetland pony with every new home. The Ridgecrest Country Estates addition was located in the square mile of East Reno Avenue, Midwest Boulevard, Air Depot Boulevard, and Southeast Tenth Street. Homes were sold for about $22,000 on average with a free pony. The photograph is of Atkinson and his Pony Riders Club on Morningside Drive. (Courtesy of the Rose State College Foundation.)

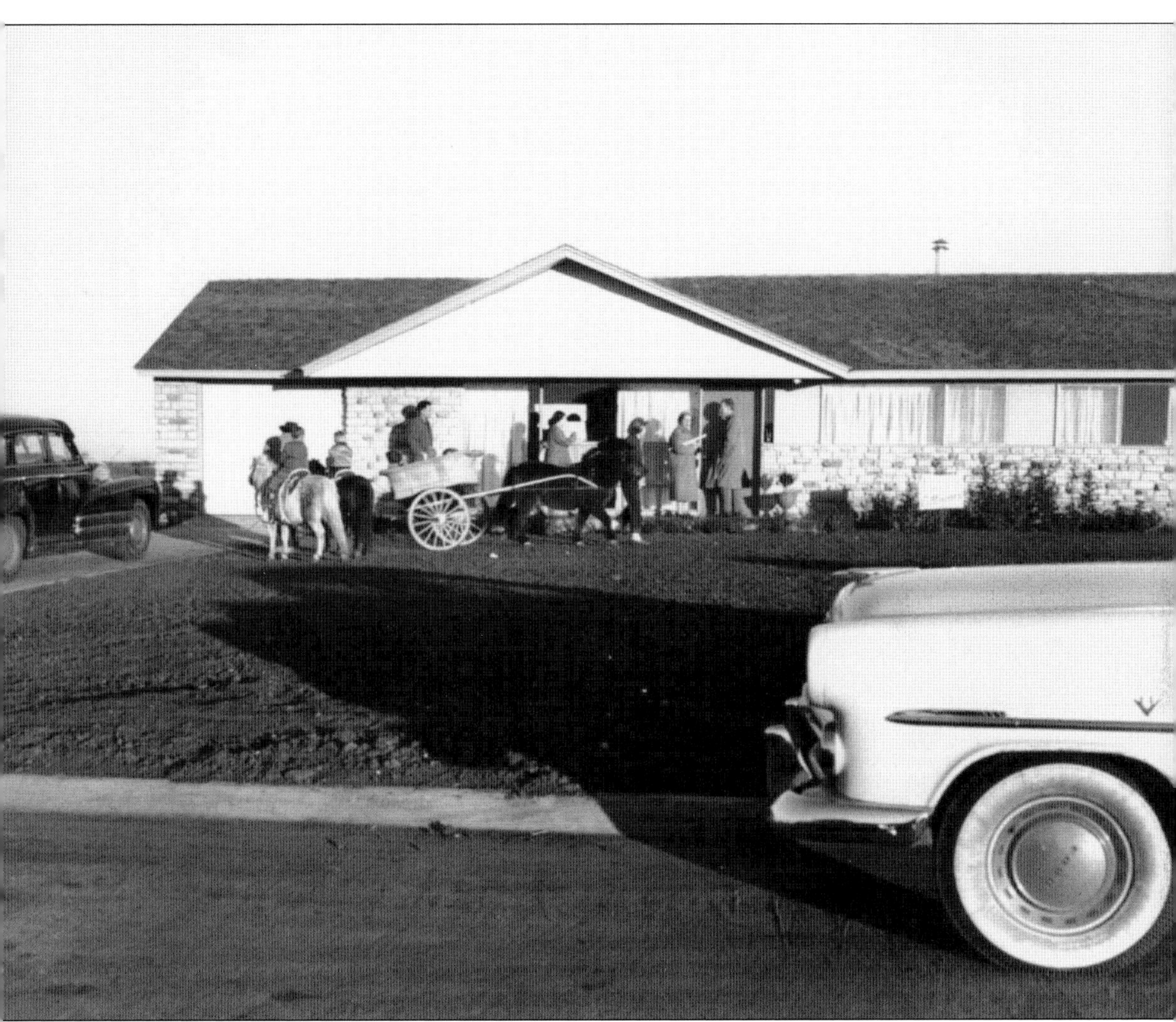

Bill Atkinson's granddaughter Cindy Mikeman recalled that her grandfather would greet a potential family interested in purchasing a home and immediately take the wife to the kitchen to show her modern appliances and the lazy Susan cabinet feature. He would then guide the children to the backyard, where a bucket of oats would be waiting. It was said that Atkinson would pick up the bucket, shake it, and a Shetland pony would approach. Atkinson's clever approach won over the wife and children of the family, and the husband could only say yes to buying the house. Families had a stable in the backyard to protect the pony from the elements. Readers can see this early Ridgecrest home with ponies in the front. Located on the bottom right are the iconic white-walled tires popular in the 1950s. This photograph is from the 1960s. (Courtesy of the Rose State College Foundation.)

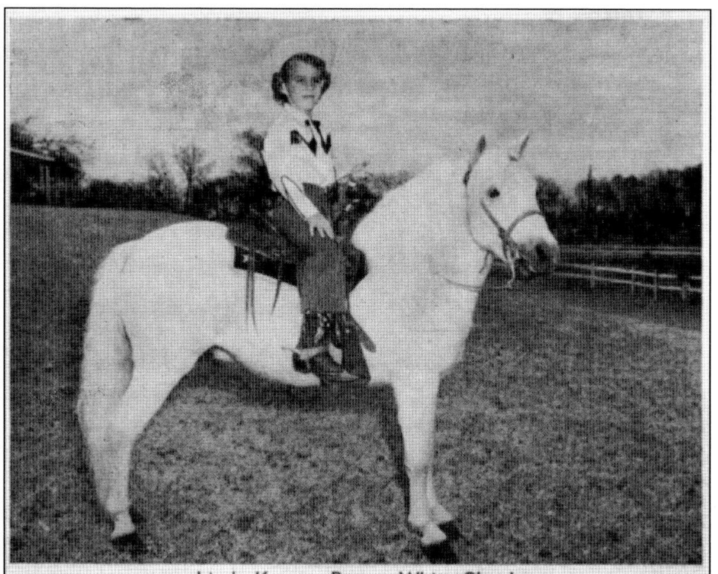

Linda Kerr on Romeo White Cloud

This is

Your Invitation

to visit the

Atkinson Pony Farm

Northeast 10th and Midwest Blvd. (Due North of Midwest City)

Open House — Every Sunday 2 to 6 P.M.

FREE PONY RIDES

For families that did not want the ponies that came with their new home, Atkinson offered to keep them or host them at his red and white stables at his pony farm on his property. Every Sunday afternoon, he would host a pony riding event where Midwest City children and their families could come and ride the ponies. Atkinson also created a Midwest City Country Club for Boys and Girls. (Both, courtesy of Rose State College Foundation.)

1. Boys and girls between the ages of 1 to 12 inclusive who live in the city limits of Midwest City, are eligible for membership.
2. Ages 1 to 8 inclusive must be accompanied by parents.
3. The Club House, located on the Bill Atkinson Pony Farm, will be open to members on Sundays from 2 p.m. to 9 p.m.
4. Club dues are on the basis of $5.00 for one year's season of 10 months, payable in advance. All money from dues will be disbursed in the interest of the club by a board of directors selected from parents of club members.
5. All members agree to abide by rules and regulations which may be adopted by the board of directors.

MIDWEST CITY'S COUNTRY CLUB

for BOYS and GIRLS

This is to Certify
that________________

Address________________
Is a member of Midwest City's Country Club, W. P. (Bill) Atkinson's Pony Farm, 10th and Midwest Blvd., Midwest City, Oklahoma.

I agree to the rules on reverse side

____
Signature of Registered Member

Issued By________________

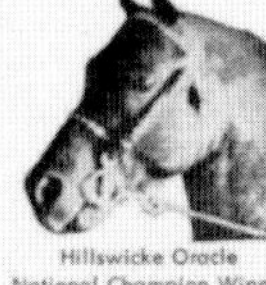

Hillswicke Oracle
National Champion Winner

EXPIRES DECEMBER 31, 1952

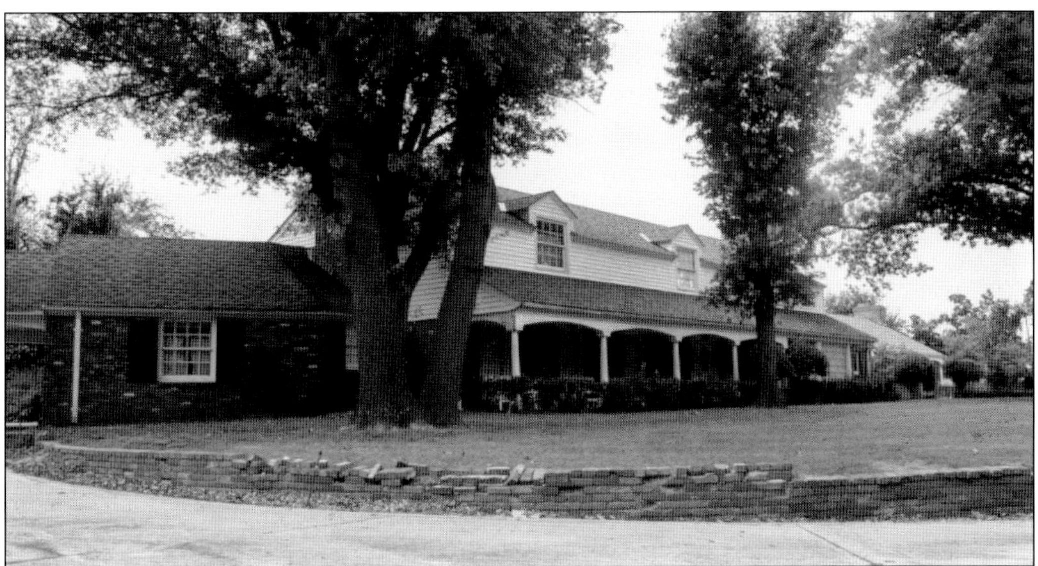

Atkinson always had a heart's desire to become the governor of Oklahoma. In high hopes he would win the election and need to have a space to host important delegates, Atkinson built a beautiful estate that was featured in magazines. Optimist that he was, he ran for governor as a Democrat in 1958. Losing that election was a hard loss, one that Atkinson felt was not warranted and that he attributed to his adversaries in Oklahoma City. He ran again in 1962 and lost to the first Republican governor in Oklahoma history, Henry Bellmon. Researchers remark that Atkinson may have had a chance to win the 1962 election if it were not for his public views on raising taxes. (Both, courtesy of Rose State College Foundation.)

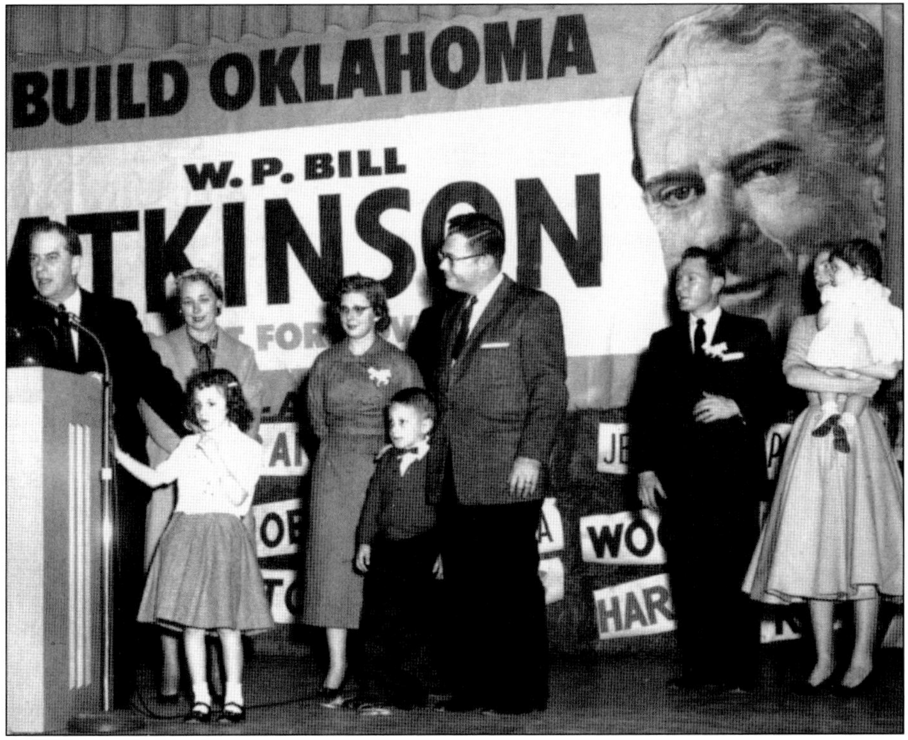

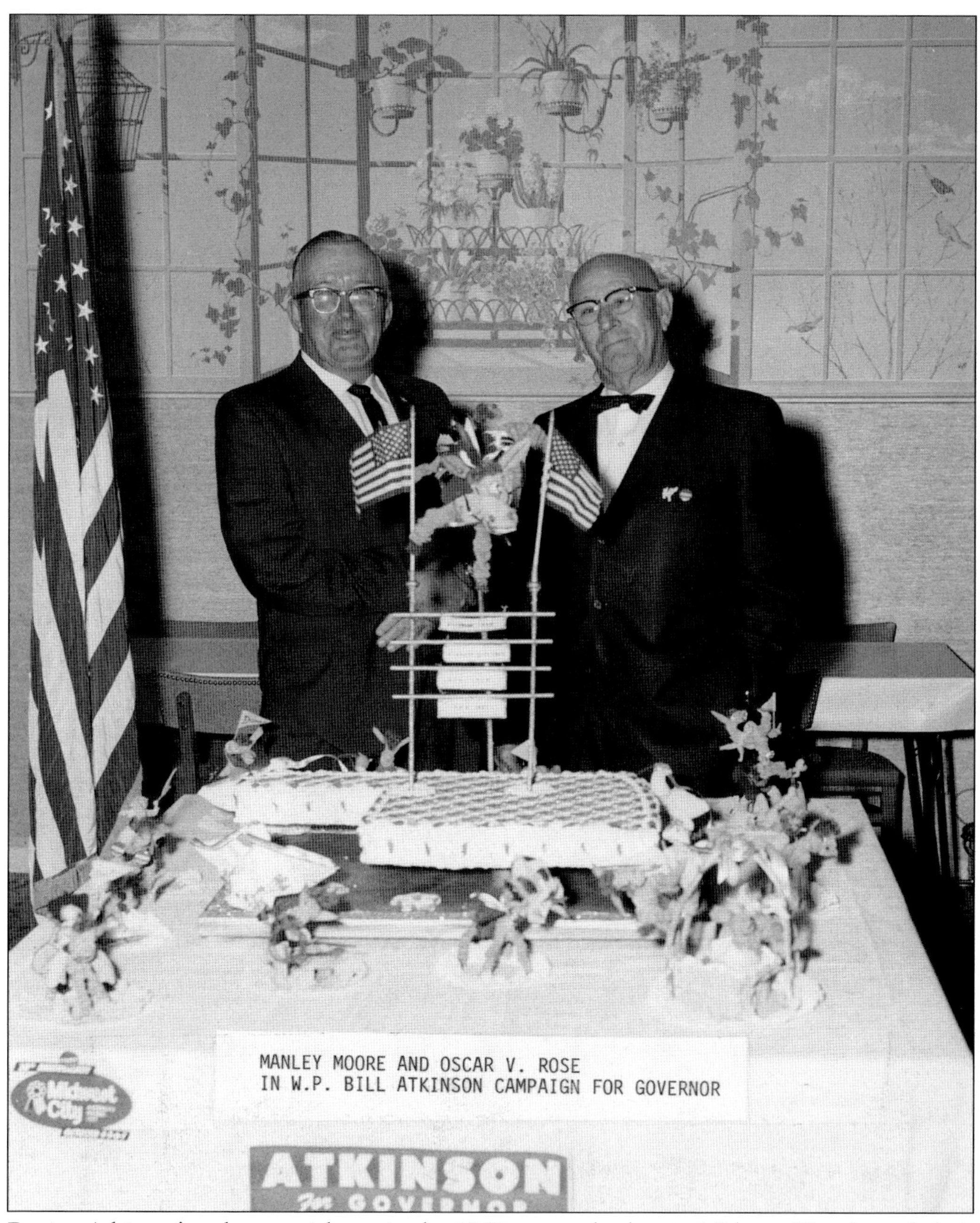

During Atkinson's gubernatorial run in the 1960s, many leaders in Midwest City showed their support at campaign parties. Pictured here is one of the original home builders of Midwest City, Manley Moore (left), and superintendent of Midwest City Schools, Oscar V. Rose (right). Atkinson ran twice for governor and was defeated both times. (Courtesy of Midwest City High School History Center.)

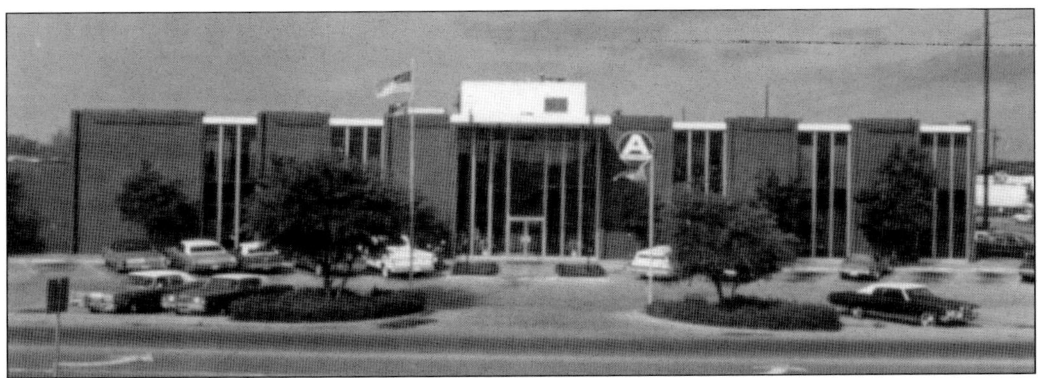

Before the *Oklahoma Journal* was founded, Midwest City was home to other local community papers such as the *Midwest City News*. The *Midwest City News* published the first issue of its weekly paper on August 24, 1944. Harry Eskew was the publisher and editor of the paper, which had a paid circulation of 3,200; his wife, Elizabeth, was the advertising manager. This paper later became the *Midwest City Leader and Midwest City News* and was in publication from 1946 to 1964. According to the Library of Congress, in 1964, Atkinson purchased the paper and its subscribers and named it the *Oklahoma Journal* to tell the "other side" of the news after bitterly losing two gubernatorial elections in a row. He transformed the once local paper to a statewide media platform. Atkinson's ambition motivated him to build a newspaper empire, which was in circulation from 1964 to 1980. (Above, courtesy of Midwest City High School History Center; below, courtesy of Rose State College Foundation.)

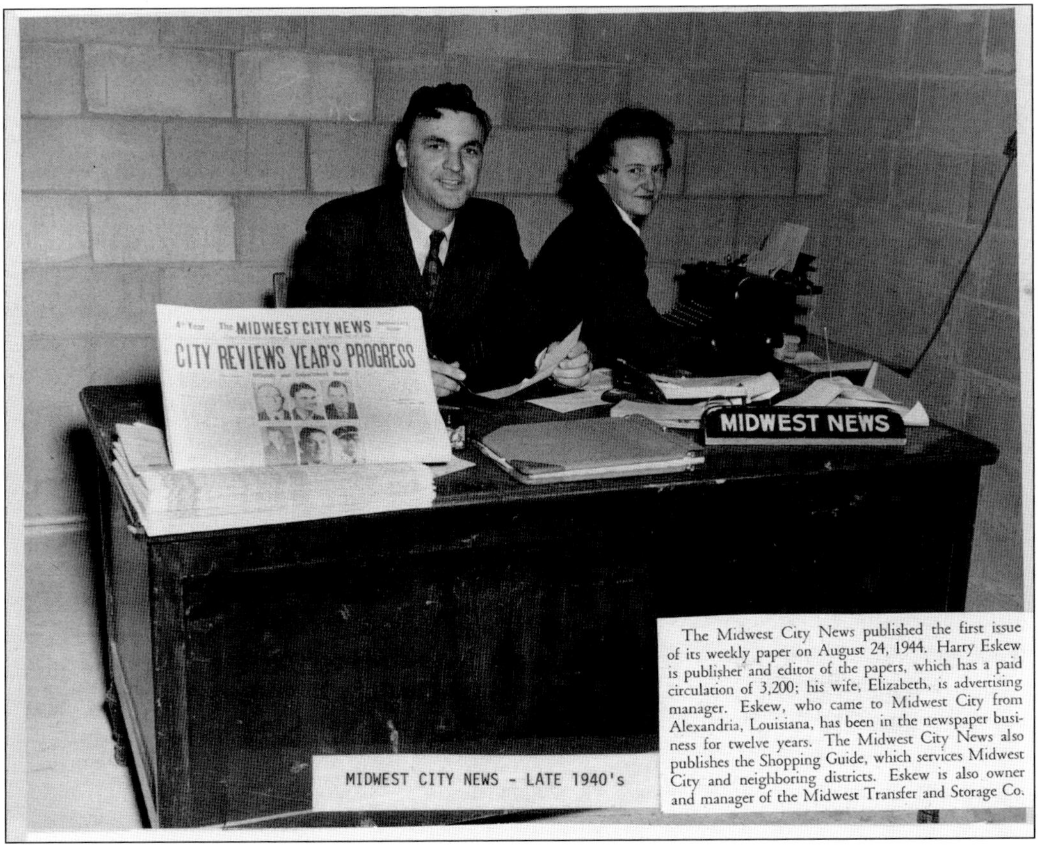

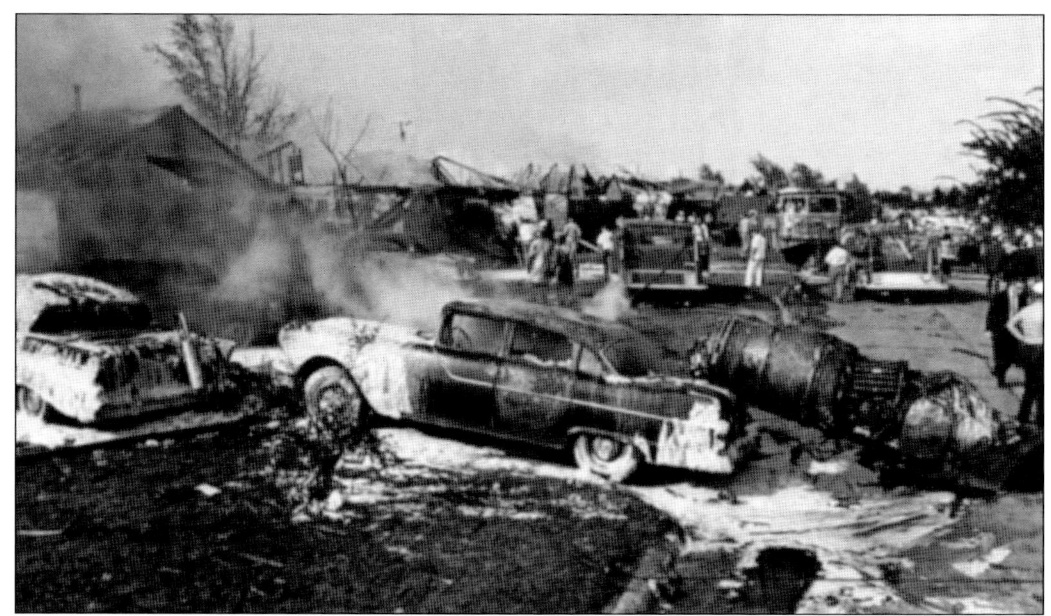

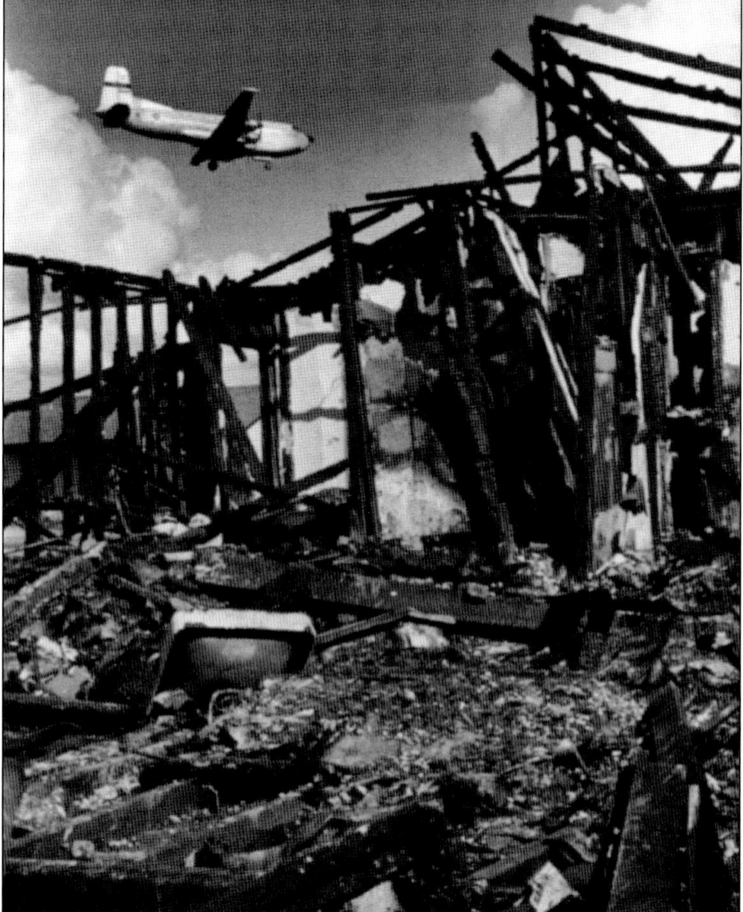

Harrowing scenes are shown in 1961 as fire crews and community members attempt to extinguish the fiery flames sourced from a plane crash in a local neighborhood, claiming two young children's lives. Plane crashes were one of the risks of living in an air-support township that would later require local government intervention to protect lives. Multiple plane crashes occurred throughout the history of Midwest City. The Glenwood addition was demolished over a five-year span due to crashes—a hard moment in many Midwest Citians' memories. (Both, courtesy of Oklahoma History Center.)

By 1967, over 500,000 American soldiers were present in Southeast Asia. In Oklahoma, more than 24,000 men were mandatory drafted into the conflict over the years, raising much protest in the younger generations who questioned the purpose of the war. Many young men, such as Midwest City resident and 1966 graduate of Midwest City High School James "Jim" Dale Guffey, sacrificed their lives for the people of the United States. Guffey volunteered to serve in the US Army and was killed on March 3, 1968. Those who did return from the war returned home and met criticism and rejection for serving in the war instead of being celebrated for their courage and sacrifice. It would be decades before their memory and experience overseas were validated and honored. Midwest City High School History Center opened the Midwest City High School Vietnam War Memorial and Bomber Plaza in front of Midwest City High School on Veterans Day in 2018 in honor of these individuals who paid the highest price for their country and acknowledged them as a city. The photograph below is a message from Guffey to his father saying, "Thank you for the upbringing that you gave me, Dad. Your son, Jim," a little over a year before he died. (Both, courtesy of the Guffey family.)

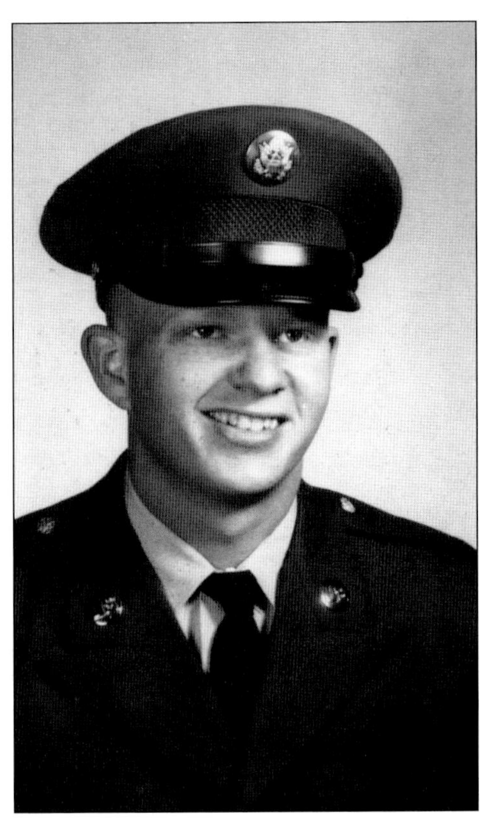

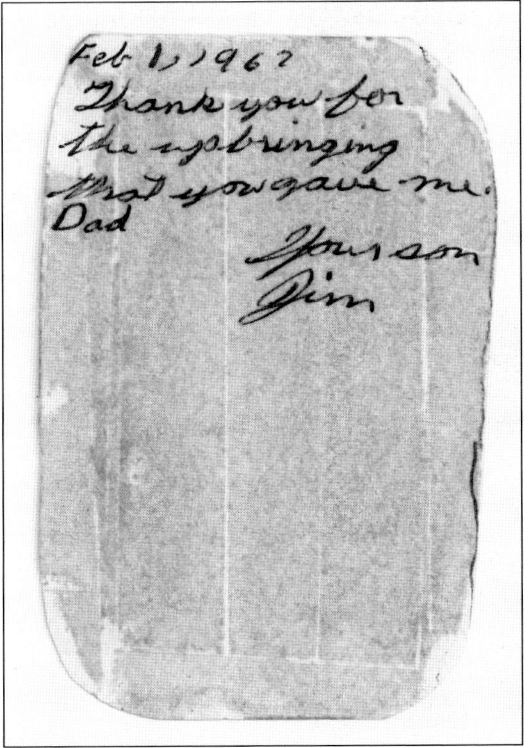

Feb 1, 1967
Thank you for
the upbringing
that you gave me.
Dad
Your son
Jim

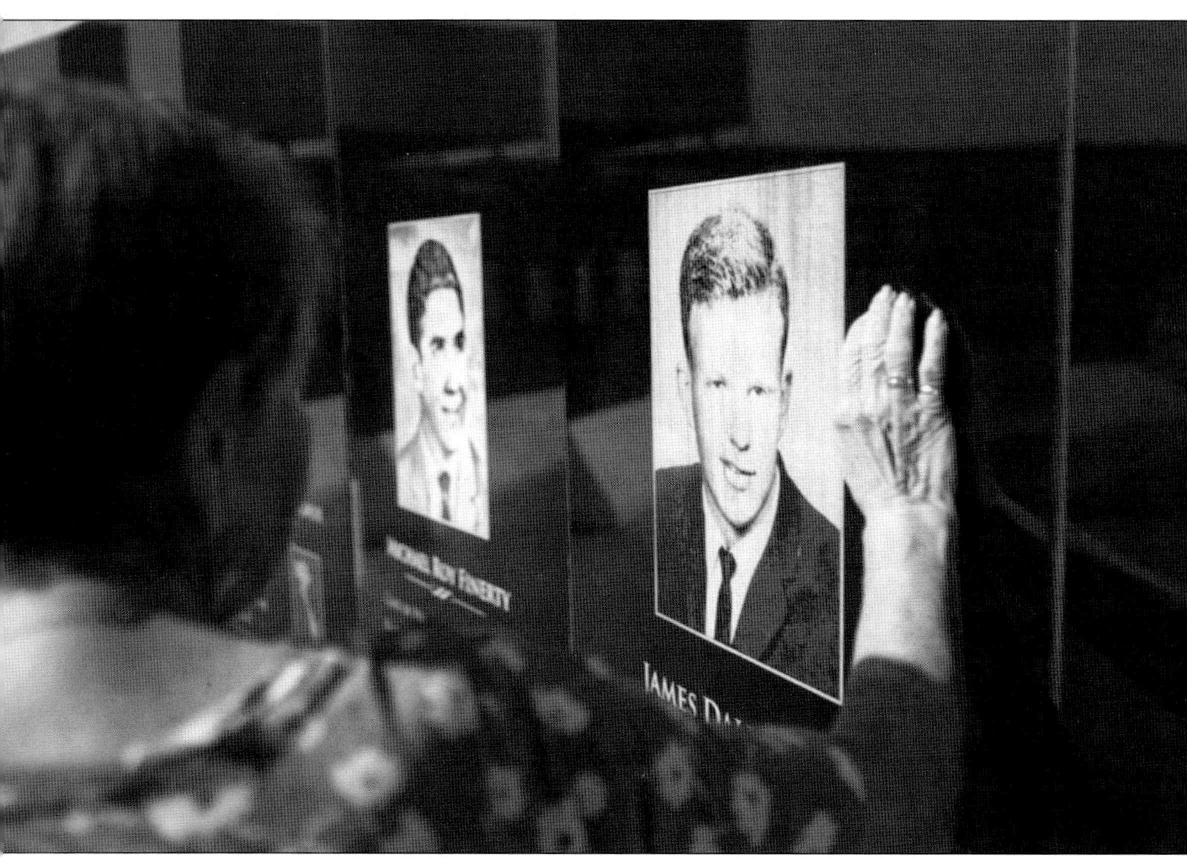

Pictured is the older sister of James Guffey, who died during his service in the Vietnam War. Bob Osmond and Marty Thompson and the board of directors over the history center have ensured that patriots like Guffey will be remembered and honored. The memorial also features a Soldiers Cross and Midwest City High School graduates who passed away in the April 9, 1995, Murrah Federal Building bombing in downtown Oklahoma City. (Courtesy of American Corporate Photography.)

Eight

Honoring Yesterday, Pressing Forward to Tomorrow

In the 1980s, 1990s, and 2010s, Midwest City had to take hardships and make them into gold. Midwest City found itself at a crossroads after many of the founding fathers finished their races and left Midwest City to the next generations. Wars and social and cultural shifts in the United States as well as economic shifts put pressure on the growth. In the 1980s and 1990s, many bases shut down around the United States. As promised, Atkinson laid the foundation of a self-sustaining city, though it never lost its mission to support the air base. Even so, the whole state rallied around Tinker during the Base Realignment and Closure (BRAC) in the 1990s. Tinker was saved and continued its work and even strived to become better than before. A couple of years later, on May 3, 1999, Midwest City and Tinker Air Force Base were hit with a historically strong tornado, the highest recorded on the Richter scale, with winds close to 250 miles an hour on the western side of the base and the city. The city's hotel district and a residential area were hit, and three people lost their lives. Rebuilding from the loss took time, but to honor the memory of that area, a new 60,000-square-foot conference center was built in 2003 called the Reed Center, after beloved Mayor Eddie Reed. The architects who designed the Reed Center intentionally used circular rotundas in the design to bring a testimony of how the city has overcome the horrific tornado and will create new memories in its place.

Midwest City organizations and the City of Midwest City ensured that the past was not forgotten, especially in regard to the founding of the city and the sacrifice of the servicemen and servicewomen who protected the United States' freedom. Many places of memorial lie within the city, such as the Atkinson Heritage Center on the grounds of the founder's home and pony barn, the Midwest City High School History Center, and many structures within this chapter, to never forget the roots of the city. Midwest City is the land of the free because of the brave. As it is the City of Tomorrow, it also ensures that visitors and residents take inspiration and give honor to those who went before. Around Midwest City, special memorials and landmarks have been placed as visual cues for residents and tourists to pay their respects, gain education, and keep values close to home.

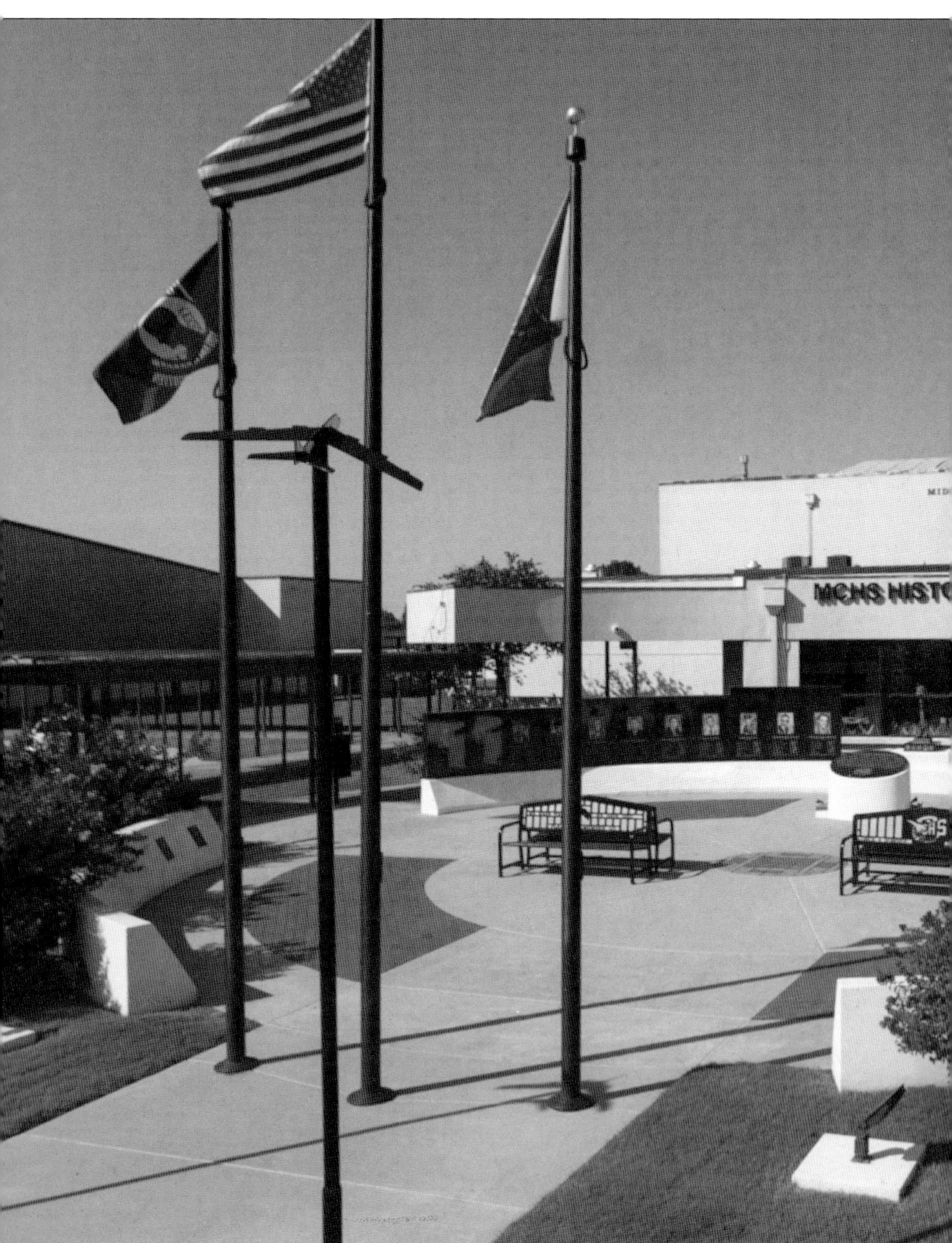

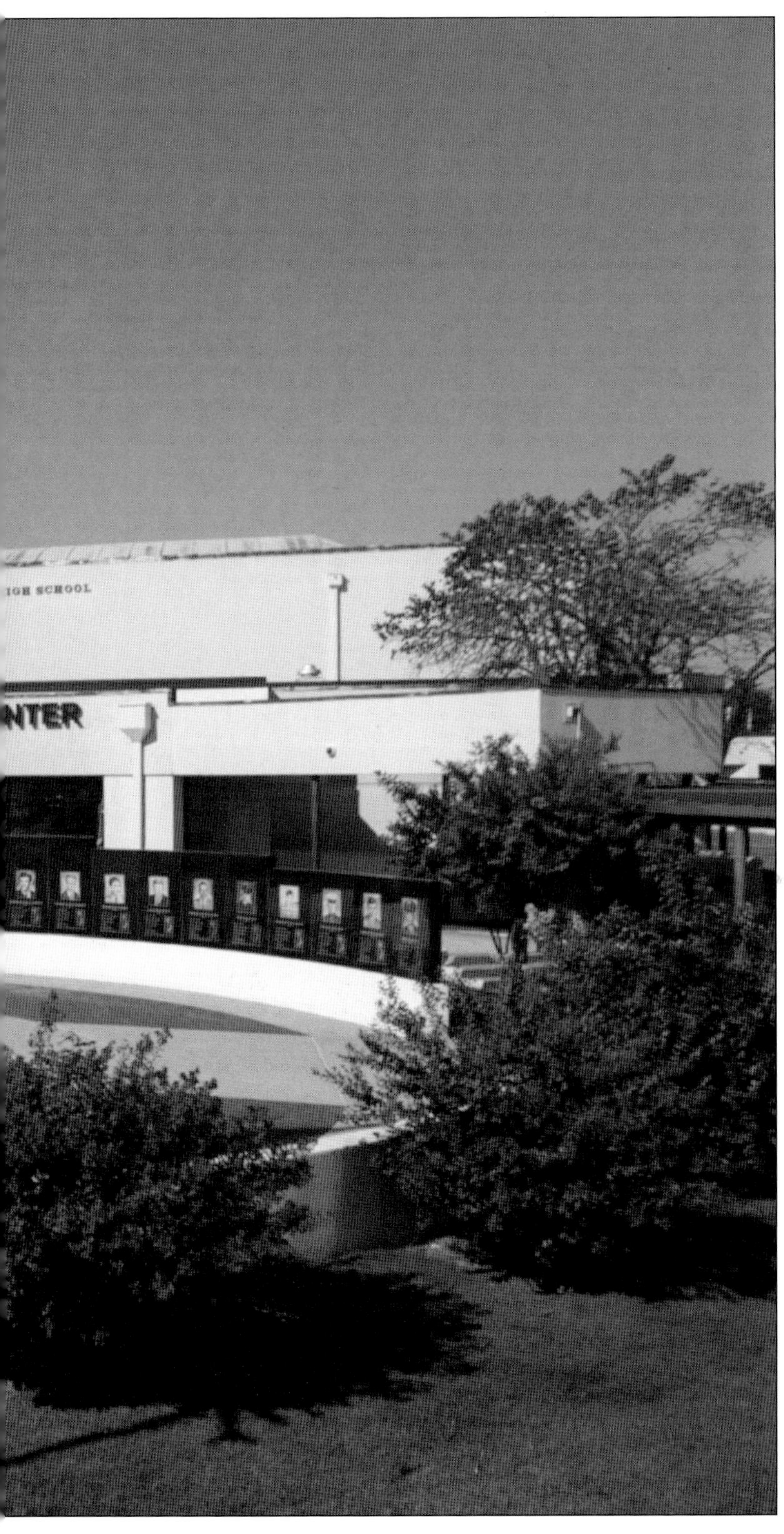

Local residents who spent their lives serving in Midwest City have given back. The Midwest City High School History Center was opened in the original Midwest City High School entrance in September 2001, led by Rick Bachman, Robert H. Croak, David N. Fox, Jennie Lee Maynord, Paul W. Nicholson, J.E. Sutton, and Damon D. Wingfield. The first charitable cash contribution of $100 came from J.E. Sutton, former principal and superintendent of Mid-Del Schools. Local retired police officer Bob Osmond and retired university librarian Marty Thompson reopened the history center to welcome former graduates of the school and the community to learn more about the school system and the city. In 2018, after years of planning, designing, and fundraising, the Midwest City Vietnam Memorial and Bomber Plaza was built in front of the former entrance of Midwest City High School. (Courtesy of American Corporate Photography.)

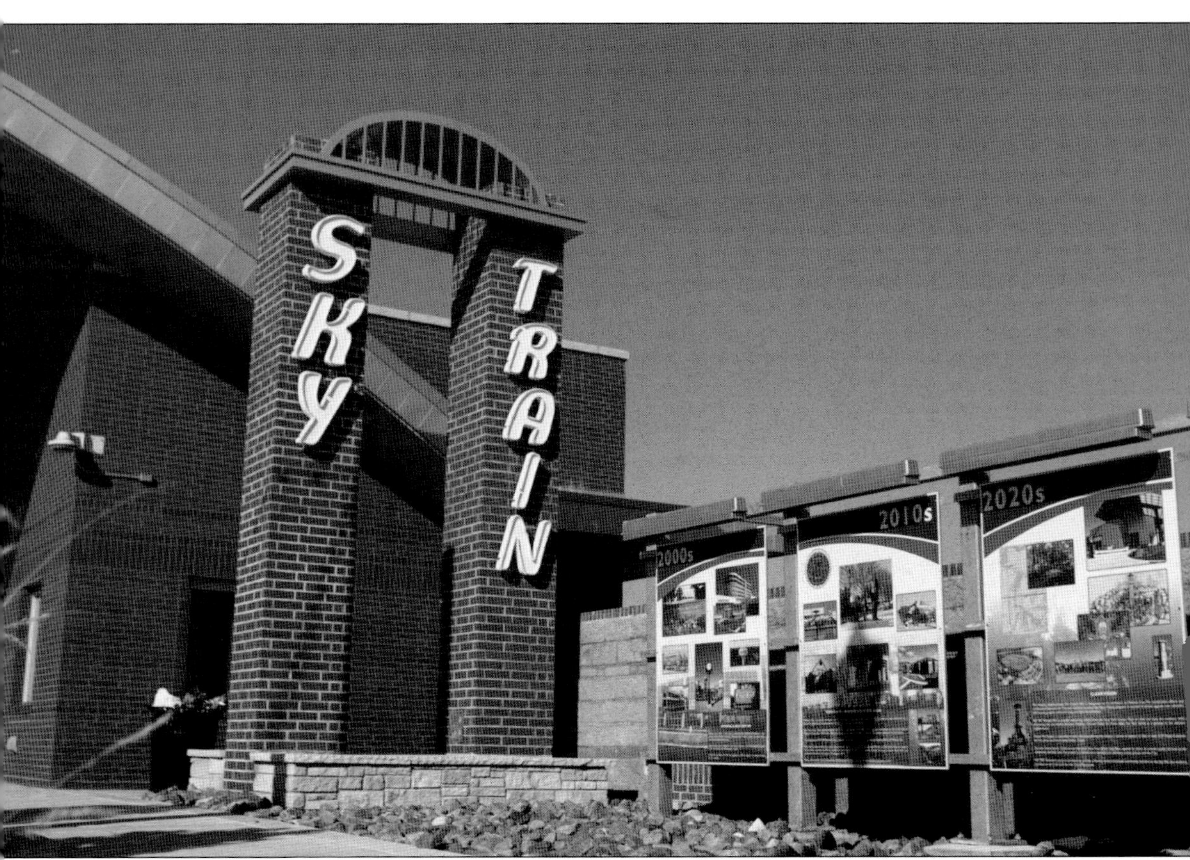

Installed in the 2020s, the area behind what was once the downtown shopping center in the Original Mile has been developed with new shopping areas and a history walk where visitors can learn a brief history, decade by decade, of Midwest City. Pictured here are the repurposed letters from the original Skytrain theater mentioned in chapter three. The city has ensured there are open panels next to the 2020s presentation board for many more decades to come in Midwest City. To the left of the Skytrain sign, a structure has been built to mimic an airplane hangar that cars can park under while visiting the history path. (Courtesy of American Corporate Photography.)

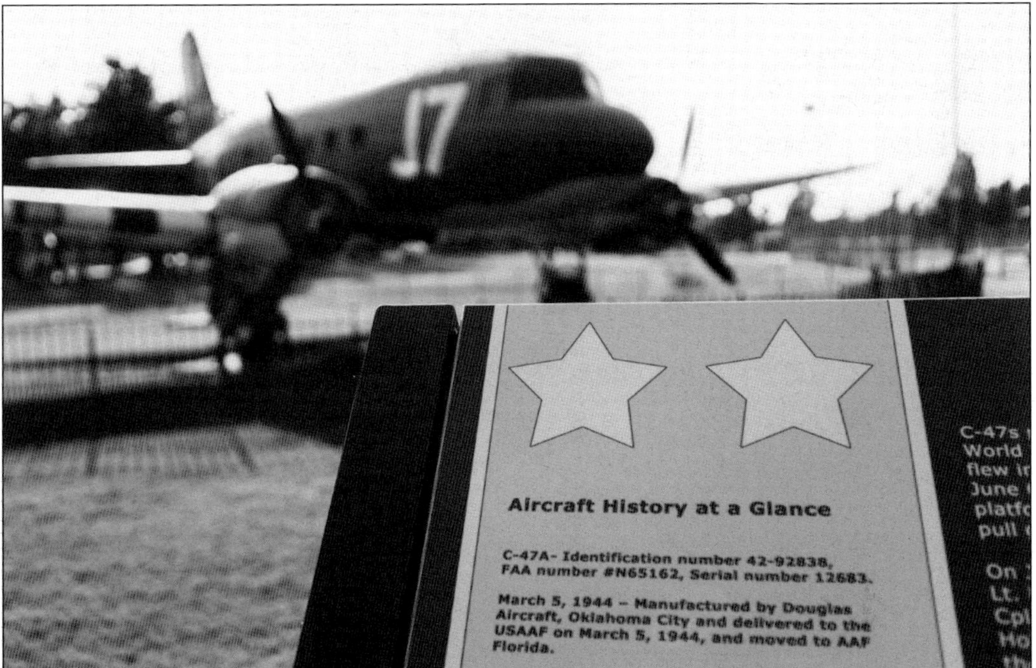

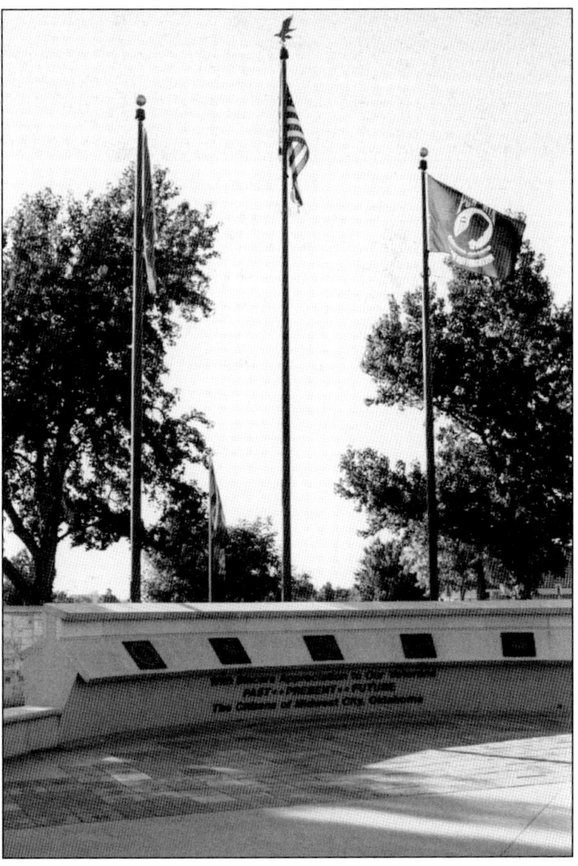

Located in another Midwest City park, the Veterans Memorial lies in Joe B. Barnes Regional Park and includes an original refurbished C-47 "Gooney Bird" from World War II. This plane was built at the Douglas Aircraft Company plant and was flown on D-Day. Located off Douglas Drive between East Reno Avenue and Southeast Fifteenth Street, the memorial features each branch of the military and a brief history of World War II and Midwest City's involvement and support of Tinker. The plane was previously on show at the Oklahoma State Fair Grounds for over 30 years prior. It also features three flagpoles and pavers inscribed in memory of the veterans. Installed in 2013, this site is not a place of sorrow but a place of reflection and gratitude, remembering that Midwest City and all cities in the United States would not exist if it were not for the nation's military servicemen and servicewomen. (Both, courtesy of American Corporate Photography.)

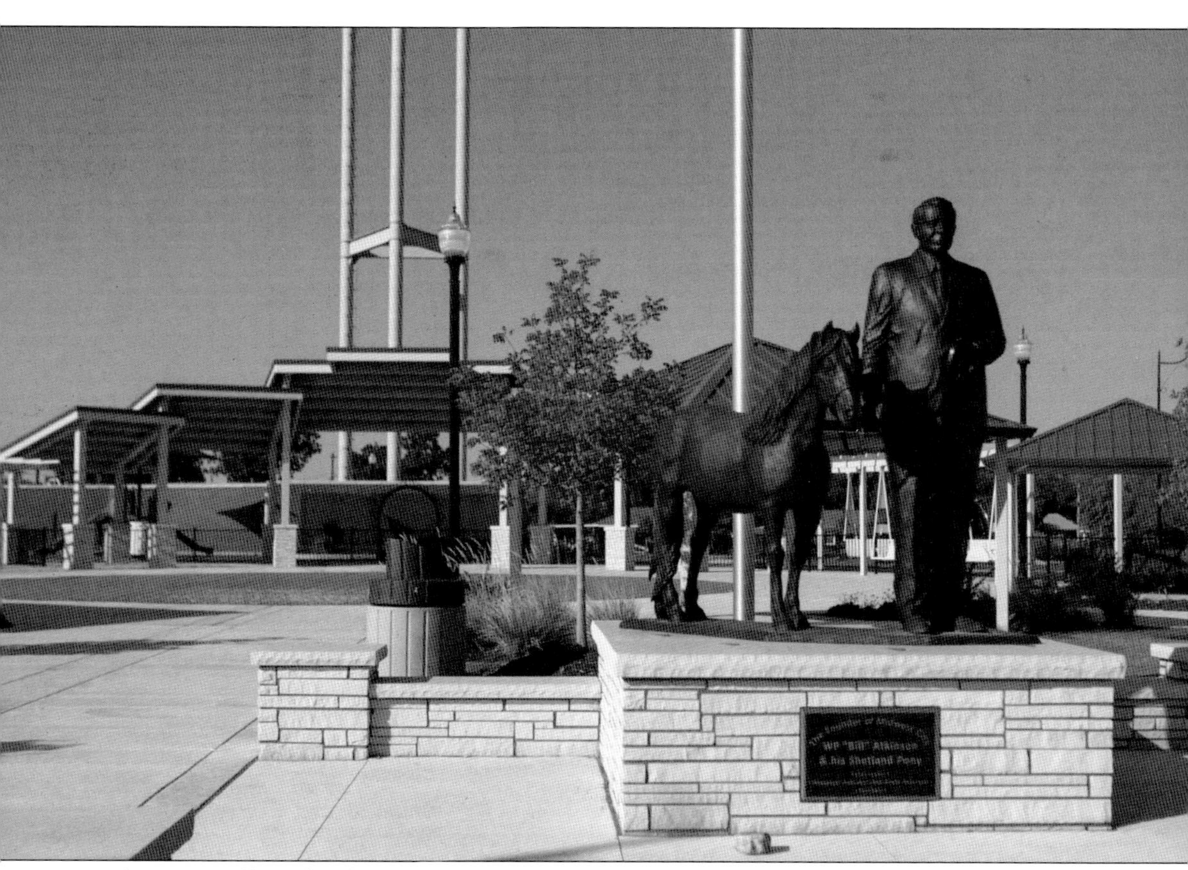

If visitors walk under the hanger and to the other side, they will find an inviting park in honor of Midwest City's founder, W.P. "Bill" Atkinson. The city placed Atkinson's statue with his Shetland pony on the park grounds as the park sits on the original municipal grounds for the City of Midwest City in the Original Mile. This space now cultivates community with local events and continues the legacy of the parks and recreation department for the next generation. The park was opened in 2023 as a testament to the man behind the vision that sparked a multigenerational legacy. (Courtesy of American Corporate Photography.)

BIBLIOGRAPHY

Bowman, Scarlett. "W.P. Atkinson: The Man Who Built a City, Lost a State, and Challenged a King" (thesis, *University of Central Oklahoma*, 2015). https://hdl.handle.net/11244/325246

Crowder, James L. "Faces From the Past, Tinker Air Force Base." May 1993.

——. "Tinker Air Force Base." *The Encyclopedia of Oklahoma History and Culture*, January 15, 2010. https://www.okhistory.org/publications/enc/entry?entry=TI004

Fugate, Tally D. "Midwest City Douglas Aircraft Company Plant." *The Encyclopedia of Oklahoma History and Culture*, January 15, 2010. https://www.okhistory.org/publications/enc/entry?entry=MI010

Hedglen, Thomas L. "Midwest City." *The Encyclopedia of Oklahoma History and Culture*, March 24, 2024. https://www.okhistory.org/publications/enc/entry?entry=MI009

"FOX 25—Sunday PM—Ronnie Kaye and W.P. Bill Atkinson —Part 1." 1993, posted July 25, 2010. https://www.youtube.com/watch?v=aO0Zt5WLx2k

"FOX 25—Sunday PM—Ronnie Kaye and W.P. Bill Atkinson—Part 2." 1993, posted July 25, 2010. https://www.youtube.com/watch?v=aO0Zt5WLx2k

Johnson, Larry. "The Spanish Influenza Pandemic in Oklahoma City, Oklahoma City," Metropolitan Library System. https://www.metrolibrary.org/archives/essay/2019/07/spanish-influenza-pandemic-oklahoma-city

Lee, Susan. "William P. 'Bill' Atkinson: The Father of Midwest City, Oklahoma." The *Oklahoma Chronicles*, 1999.

Meacham & Associates. *Final Report: Reconnaissance Level Architectural/Historical Survey of the Original Mile.* Midwest City, OK: August 31, 1992.

Mullins, William H. "Okie Migrations." *The Encyclopedia of Oklahoma History and Culture*, January 15, 2010. https://www.okhistory.org/publications/enc/entry?entry=OK008

Mikeman, Cindy. "Interview with Malana Bracht, Midwest City, Building Generations." 2023.

Hedglen, Thomas L. "Midwest City," *The Encyclopedia of Oklahoma History and Culture*, March 25, 2024. https://www.okhistory.org/publications/enc/entry?entry=MI009

McAlester, Virginia S., and Lee McAlester. *A Field Guide to American Houses.* New York: Knopf Publishing, 1984.

Sutton, J.E. "New Student Orientation Oral Presentation." Mid-Del Public Schools, Midwest City, OK: August 21, 1971.

Please note: Arcadia Publishing only allows 15 bibliography sources but more can be requested by emailing author.malanabracht@gmail.com.

Consistent with our mission to preserve history on a local level, this book was printed in South Carolina on American-made paper and manufactured entirely in the United States. Products carrying the accredited Forest Stewardship Council (FSC) label are printed on 100 percent FSC-certified paper.

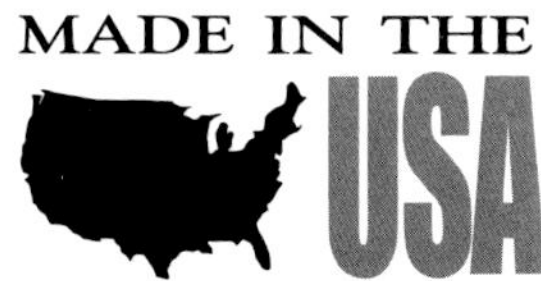